FabJob
Become a Wine Store Owner

MITCHELL WARREN

FABJOB® GUIDE TO BECOME A WINE STORE OWNER
by Mitchell Warren

ISBN: 978-1-897286-56-2

Library and Archives Canada Cataloguing in Publication

Warren, Mitchell, 1977-
FabJob guide to become a wine store owner / Mitchell Warren.

Accompanied by a CD.
ISBN 978-1-897286-56-2

1. Selling--Wine. 2. Wine industry. 3. New business enterprises.
I. FabJob II. Title. III. Title: Become a wine store owner.

HD9370.5.W37 2009   381'.4564122   C2009-905874-X

Important Disclaimer: Although every effort has been made to ensure this guide is free from errors, this publication is sold with the understanding that the authors, editors, and publisher are not responsible for the results of any action taken on the basis of information in this work, nor for any errors or omissions. The publishers, and the authors and editors, expressly disclaim all and any liability to any person, whether a purchaser of this publication or not, in respect of anything and of the consequences of anything done or omitted to be done by any such person in reliance, whether whole or partial, upon the whole or any part of the contents of this publication. If expert advice is required, services of a competent professional person should be sought.

About the Websites Mentioned in this Guide: Although we aim to provide the information you need within the guide, we have also included a number of websites because readers have told us they appreciate knowing about sources of additional information. (**TIP:** Don't include a period at the end of a web address when you type it into your browser.) Due to the constant development of the Internet, websites can change. Any websites mentioned in this guide are included for the convenience of readers only. We are not responsible for the content of any sites except FabJob.com.

FabJob Inc.
19 Horizon View Court
Calgary, Alberta, Canada T3Z 3M5

FabJob Inc.
4616 25th Avenue NE, #224
Seattle, Washington, USA 98105

To order books in bulk, phone 403-949-2039
To arrange a media interview, phone 403-949-4980

www.FabJob.com
THE DREAM CAREER EXPERTS

Contents

About the Authors

Author **Mitchell Warren** is a professional freelance writer currently living in the Dallas-Fort Worth area in Texas. A wine connoisseur who has interviewed wine business owners and experts, Mitchell is also contributing author of the *FabJob Guide to Become a Winery Owner, FabJob Guide to Become an Art Gallery Owner*, and *FabJob Guide to Become a Bar Owner*.

 Contributing author **Brenna Pearce** is senior editor at FabJob, an award-winning publishing company named "the #1 place to get published online" by *Writer's Digest*. She has contributed to dozens of career and business guides, and is the author of the *FabJob Guide to Become a Winery Owner* and the *FabJob Guide to Become a Bar Owner*.

Acknowledgments

For the *FabJob Guide to Become a Wine Store Owner* the authors interviewed wine store owners from across the country.

- *Donnie Austin*
  Owner of House Wine, in the Worthington area of Columbus, Ohio. House Wine is a wine store and wine bar that caters to the needs of novices and aficionados alike.
  www.housewine.biz

- *Michael Cawdrey*
  Manager of Fremont Wine Warehouse, a company that specializes in wines for under $25.
  www.fremontwines.com

- *Kimberly Eakin*
  Certified Specialist of Wine and president of Wine Gourmet, in Roanoke, Virginia, a wine store that also offers wine classes taught by its on-staff wine specialists.
  www.winegourmet.biz

- *Vern Foster and Alice Mae*
  Owners of Shopper's Cache located at 19223 Old Glenn Highway in Chugiak, Alaska, specializing in wine, beer and spirits.

- *Christina Martin*
  Owner of Martin Ulisse Imports located in Corpus Christi, Texas, an importer and wholesale distributor specializing bringing the finest Italian wines imported from smaller, undiscovered wineries to American wine lovers.
  www.martinulisse.com

- *Kyle McHugh*
  Owner of Drinks Over Dearborn, a specialty beer, wine and spirits boutique on Dearborn Street in Chicago, Illinois.
  www.drinksoverdearborn.com

- *Ben Wallace*
  Owner of CellaRaiders, a retail store selling an eclectic variety of wine online and a buyer of vintage wine collections.
  www.cellaraiders.com

1. Introduction

Wine is fun. Wine is not only an industry and a favorite adjunct to dining, it is a remarkable hobby. People enjoy so much wine—from collecting vintage bottles to advocating personal tasting methods—that many proudly profess themselves "wine connoisseurs."

A genuine wine lover is capable of not only recommending a good wine, but can also explain to you in detail just what is wrong with this glass of Merlot and the pros and cons of "full-bodied with oaky character" as compared to "medium-dry".

Imagine how much fun it is to develop a taste for wine and a curiosity for the wine-making process and then visualize this enjoyable hobby as your new full-time dream career. While becoming a wine store owner takes great effort, just as anything else worthwhile in life, it can be accomplished by anyone willing to put forth the effort. This guide is the starting point to your exciting new career as a wine retailer.

1.1 A Growth Industry

Wine appeals to a variety of drinkers, each with his or her own preferred tastes; therefore, it is always an in-demand product. Connoisseurs believe that wine has a more refined taste than beer or spirits because of the complexity and personality of each type of wine and therefore has an appeal that a six-pack of beer or a bottle of cheap vodka never will. Interest in wine continues to grow among consumers.

According to estimates from Gomberg, Fredrikson & Associates, a consulting firm specializing in wine industry trends, wine sales in the United States have increased from $11 billion in 1991 to $30 billion in 2008, nearly tripling. In 2008, U.S. consumers drank 753 million gallons of wine from both domestic and foreign sources, an increase in consumption of 62% over that same period.

Two factors especially account for the growth trend in the wine industry's business since 1991: the growth in numbers and marketing of quality domestic wines, and its positive, even healthful, image. In 1992, a study by Harvard researchers suggested that drinking a moderate amount of red wine every day can reduce the risk of coronary heart disease and cancer because of the antioxidant properties of flavinoids present in the wine.

New opportunities have also arisen in recent years for wine store owners to expand their markets. In 2002, favorable Supreme Court rulings such as support of direct-to-consumer sales, helped to create increased online commerce. Wine retailers can now sell their products from their own websites (with certain restrictions), resulting in an increase in online wine sales. This means that you're not limited by the old brick-and-mortar retail business model, anymore.

In addition, the United States is the world's second-largest consumer of wine, exceeded only by France. This trend continues even through tough economic times. According to a February, 2009, article in the Miami Herald, despite a recession, people are drinking as much wine as ever, although they are opting for cheaper bottles of wine. It's probably a safe bet that the market for less expensive wines will be the fastest growing retail sector in the coming years.

1.2 Owning a Wine Store

It is very possible as you get ready to start your new career as a wine store owner that you already know and appreciate fine wines. However, explaining the art of tasting wine and how to become a true wine connoisseur would call for a much larger book and plenty of personal research. Therefore, if you're absolutely clueless about wine you may need to do some additional research on how to taste and appreciate it before you think about recommending choices for your customers.

Most wine store owners start their own businesses because:

- They have a passion for wine

- They have identified their specific product and market

- They possess the physical and mental stamina to take on all responsibilities

- They enjoy their independence and have a tenacious attitude

- They enjoy interacting with other people

Owning a wine store means knowing your product, as well as having respect for the business aspects of the operation and respect for your customers. You will need to know all the details of running a successful retail business, how to market your store, and be able to work with a variety of people including staff, suppliers, and customers. Your customers will expect you to know more about wine than they do and you should have numerous professional contacts to guide you.

1.2.1 Products

As a wine store owner, the primary product you sell will be wine, but there are also other products you can offer to your customers. Many wine store owners also sell liquor and beer in addition to wine, creating additional revenue streams. Other wine stores concentrate on wines of a certain price point; stores selling the best wines under $25, for example, are common. At the other end of the scale, some wine stores sell collectable or high-priced vintages, along with their regular offerings.

Wine vs. Liquor & Beer

You can find a list in section 5.2.1 of this guide of some of the most popular wines available for you to sell. In addition to wine, you might choose to sell liquor and beer.

Overall, the beer industry by volume and by revenues outsells the wine industry, so it's a good choice for adding as a revenue stream. Keep in mind that there is a lot of competition in the beer market and it is readily available. Pricing competitively might be an issue if you choose to add beer to your inventory.

Liquor is another good addition as a supplementary revenue stream, and there is a huge variety of different kinds of liquors to choose from. You'll find that scotch drinkers, for example, know quite as much about the characteristics of a good scotch as wine drinkers do about their wines. Liqueurs and brandies are also possible additions to your inventory.

Liquor generally has a much higher alcohol content than wine and beer, so it is licensed separately. You will find that adding liquor to your inventory will increase your start-up costs for that reason.

Other Products You Can Offer:

Wine-related products:

- Air-lock devices
- Corkscrews
- Carafes
- Wine racks
- Wine and champagne glasses
- Wine ice buckets
- Wine tags
- Etc.

Bar supplies and equipment

- Bottle openers
- Glassware for beer and liquor/mixed drinks
- Ice buckets and tongs
- Mixers
- Muddlers
- Pouring spouts
- Shakers
- Strainers
- Etc.

Gift items

- Books
- Chocolates
- Coffees
- Gift baskets
- Gourmet cheeses
- Etc.

1.2.2   Services

In addition to the products you sell, there are a great number of services you can offer to your clients. Some of these may make you additional money, but others you might choose to offer for free as an adjunct to your regular customer service policies.

One service that often goes together with a wine store is a wine bar. Wine bars are a place for your customers to try the wines that you sell, often along with a good meal or with appetizers. And if they like the wines they've tried, they can purchase them right next door in your wine store.

Of course, adding a wine bar to your business goes a bit beyond most other services you can offer. For example, your entire business plan will need to be written with this in mind. It will also entail additional start-up costs and increased capital needs. However, it also adds to your potential income and lets you offer additional services such as catering or hosting private events.

Here are a few other services you can offer to your customers:

- Custom gift boxes or baskets

- Online purchasing

- Wine classes

- Wine club

- Wine tastings

- Etc.

In the list above, the wine club deserves special attention. A wine club can take a couple of different forms. One is a marketing device, the other is a business revenue stream or a business in itself.

Many wine stores offer an in-store wine club to their customers. This is essentially a wine appreciation group similar to a book club. Members get together in your store once or a few times a month to taste new wines and discuss their likes and dislikes. You can charge a member-ship fee, which might include discounts on wine you sell through the club, or you can choose to "donate" a bottle or two for each meeting in the hopes that your wine club members will decide to take a few bottles home with them.

The other form of wine club is an online business. Essentially, this is an online or "virtual" wine store. Many use the form of a "wine of the month club", in which members pay membership dues and receive wines each month either chosen by club member consensus or request, or chosen by a wine expert from the business. We'll discuss this type of club as a business niche option in section 3.1.

1.3   Benefits of Being a Wine Store Owner

If you've been looking for a career that offers personal rewards, freedom, and financial independence, then this is the one for you. If bringing pleasure to others, personal freedom, or earning an excellent income appeal to you, then you've found the right business. Being a wine store owner offers these benefits and more.

Bringing Pleasure to People

As a wine store owner you'll bring pleasure to countless numbers of people now and into the future. People often buy wines to serve at dinner parties, weddings, and other major occasions. The wines you sell will become an important part of the celebrations of hundreds, if not thousands, of people.

Your wine store can also be a place that people talk about and recommend to their friends and family. Your excellent customer service and knowledge of wine will help others learn more about wines from around the world. Budding connoisseurs will seek you out to further their knowledge and enjoyment of wine.

Freedom

Another benefit of owning a wine store is the feeling of freedom that comes with being the master of your own destiny when you run your own business. Owning your own business will give you freedom in numerous ways.

For example, you'll have the ability to manage your business as you see fit and not under the yoke of someone else's supervision. You can come and go as you please, although in the beginning your new business will likely need your close care and attention.

Owning your own wine store also allows you to channel your own creativity and vision into your business, which is a wonderful personal outlet for many people. You'll have the freedom to indulge your imagination when it comes to creating an exciting new wine store concept for your market or dreaming up exciting promotions and events.

Be Your Own Boss

Many of the wine store owners we interviewed expressed being their own boss as one of the most rewarding aspect of their careers. If you're coming into this industry from a full-time day job, think of the independence you will have by being your own boss. No more nine-to-five, and you can come and go as you please.

Many day jobs are unappealing, not only because they involve working to grow someone else's business, but because that work can be monotonous and repetitive and involve little in the way of excitement and challenges. Owning your own business has its risks, but it also offers potential rewards commensurate with the effort you put into it. The decisions, creativity and flexibility required of you as a business owner can be challenging, but to those well-suited for such challenges, therein lies the thrill.

Lucrative Income

Another important reward is the lucrative income that is possible in this industry. Wine stores range from small neighborhood stores to huge, warehouse-type businesses or even multiple locations. While many wine stores start off small, and it often takes time to break even and then start making a profit, growing the business carefully over time can be very financially rewarding.

While operating a wine store requires a lot of work, the potential financial rewards (in addition to the personal rewards) can be significant indeed. As a successful wine store owner, you can earn from tens of thousands of dollars in annual profits to a hundred thousand dollars or more.

1.4 Inside This Guide

The *FabJob Guide to Become a Wine Store Owner* will teach you the fundamentals of starting your own wine retail business. This book provides you with insider tips, knowledge, and advice from successful professionals in this field. You will find everything you need to prepare you for an exciting career as a wine store owner.

Chapter 2 ("Developing Your Skills and Knowledge") explains how to learn the skills you will need as a wine store owner. We'll introduce you to the basic skills and knowledge you will need and then cover ways to learn more about these topics. You will also discover how to learn from other wine store owners and other ways to get experience in wine retailing. You'll also find resources for learning more on your own.

Chapter 3 ("Starting Your Wine Store") will help you decide what kind of store you should open. This chapter discusses different specialty niches for wine stores, and will help you decide whether to buy an existing store, operate a franchise, or open a new wine store. It also explains what you need to get started, including your business plan, start-up financing, wine store name, alcohol and other licenses you'll need, and other important matters like taxes.

Chapter 4 ("Setting Up Your Wine Store") offers the information you need to actually set up your new business. It gives advice on possible locations for your store, store design, as well as supplies and equipment you'll need and where to buy it all.

Chapter 5 ("Running Your Business") takes you into the day-to-day challenge of running your wine store once it's open. It explains store operations in detail. It also covers pricing your products, managing your inventory and more. This chapter also covers financial management and hiring and working with staff.

Chapter 6 ("Getting and Keeping Customers") will show you how to market your wine store to get new customers and ways to keep them coming back. We'll look at ways you can make people more aware of your wine store and offer some ideas about ways to get free publicity, and look at some customer service issues.

When you have finished reading this guide you will know what steps you will need to take to prepare for your fabulous career as a wine store owner and you will know where to go to find further information and resources to help you get up and running.

2. Getting Ready

When you own and operate a business, you must learn to market what sells; a concept that is easy to understand, but often difficult to put into practice. For one thing, a wine store owner must put aside his or her personal preferences in wine and put more focus on popular market trends. Additionally, the market changes often so the trends of wine making and wine demand require regular study. This chapter explains how you can learn more about the industry in order to better serve your customers and provide the kind of wines they want.

2.1 Skills and Knowledge You Will Need

2.1.1 Knowledge of Wine

> *"Make sure you know the product you're selling. If you can't inform your customers or your customers know more about the product than you, it's difficult for them to trust you. Operating a wine store effectively can only be done by creating relationships with your customer."*

> — Donnie Austin, owner
> House Wine

A knowledge of at least some very basic wine fundamentals is an important component of success as a wine store owner. Chances are you will frequently need to explain the basics of wine to first time wine buyers or buyers who know wine only by name and not necessarily by process.

Types of Wine

Here are the basic types of wine that wine store owners sell:

White Wines

White wines are made from grapes that are light-colored. There are many different skins including grapes that are green, greenish-yellow, and even pinkish yellow. White wines are made from these grapes and produce wines in colors of gold, yellow or completely clear like water.

Red Wines

Red wines are made from grapes that have dark red or bluish skins. These grapes are crushed and will result in wine that is red, ruby or even reddish purple.

Blush Wines

What truly determines a red or white wine is not the color of the grapes but the wine-making process. Grape juice is colorless and can become either white or red wine, but only when the juice comes into contact with red grape skins does it become red wine. During fermentation the juice absorbs the color of the red grape skins and also the strong substance called tannin. How long the juice is exposed to the skin will determine if the wine will be categorized as red or blush. Blush or rose wine has a pinker shade.

Other Aspects of Wine

Various production factors determine the category, taste and quality of wine. These include the type of container used (oak, stainless steel), the maturing process (how long a grape juice is stored), the amount of alcohol or other substances added later (carbon dioxide, sulfites), and bottle aging.

These are just a few of the basic process variations that can drastically change the flavor and appearance of a wine. Add to that growing conditions in various regions of the world, methods of growing grapes, and advanced winery practices, and you have a tremendous selection of good wine to choose from. The old adage is true: you will never drink two bottles of wine that taste exactly alike.

Running a wine store might be difficult at first, but can be learned quickly if you are organized and dedicated. This business is more about your effectiveness as a retailer than about your knowledge of wines.

Wine Descriptions

If you had to describe each unique aroma and taste in one word what would you say? It's a tough job to describe every unique taste, but many descriptive terms have come into common usage. Here is a small list of common wine taste descriptions you will encounter:

- Sweet (the candy-like flavor, first tasted on the front of the tongue)
- Dry (the opposite of sweet, a complete lack of sweetness)
- Medium-dry (not overly sweet but not totally dry)
- Brut (used in Champagne as a substitute for "dry")
- Doux & Sec (used in Champagne as a substitute for sweet or fairly sweet)
- Fruity (not sweet, but an evident taste of fruit)
- Crisp (high acidity)
- Fat (very little acidity)
- Bitter (high amount of tannin)
- Firm (medium amount of tannin)
- Soft (no particularly noticeable amount of tannin)
- Full-bodied (a heavy-tasting wine that seems weighty and fuller than average)
- Light-bodied (a wine that seems small in comparison to full-bodied)

- Medium-bodied (an intermediate wine)

- Oaky (tastes like oak)

Wine descriptions could include not only characterization of strong, preferred flavors but also the absence of other flavors. Therefore, you might read a description like a "full-bodied, sweet wine with no oaky character" or a "dry wine with no sweetness." Along with these common terms there are also families of wine flavors from fruity wines (citrus flavors) to earthy wines (leaves), spicy wines (cinnamon) to herbal wines (mint), and so on.

You will also encounter unique variants of wine descriptions either by wine manufacturers or customers who create their own interesting descriptions. These other descriptions may be understandable and creative ("round" or "royal") or even confusing ("brooding" or "dense"). Then of course you have wine critics who get very imaginative with their wine descriptions ("cough syrup"). With time and practice a person who studies wine regularly will be able to identify even the most abstract customer request.

Food Pairings

Often, your customers will have questions related to pairing wines with food. This is an extremely important area of knowledge to develop. You'll frequently be asked questions from customers planning a dinner party or other function as to what wine you think would go best with this or that cheese or a particular entrée. What dessert wine is best to serve on this or that occasion? You'll need to know. (We'll look at where you can hone this skill later on in this chapter.)

Wine Production Terms to Know

Here are some additional wine terms from the *FabJob Guide to Become a Winery Owner*, focusing on how wine is produced, that you should know and your customers often will ask about:

Appellation: A wine's appellation refers to the geographic and climatic area where a vineyard is located that grows the grapes that go into the wine. It is somewhat related to terroir (see below).

Enology:	Enology (or *oenology,* from the Greek word for wine, *oinos*) is the science of wine production. A person who practices enology is an enologist. Enology seeks to improve ways to produce wine commercially, and includes aspects of grape growing, fermentation, chemistry, etc.
Terroir:	Terroir is a French term that refers to all the minute characteristics of the growing area and conditions like soil, climate, microclimate, etc., that contribute to a grape's distinctive flavor and by extension the wine's unique flavor.
Varietal:	A varietal is a wine made from a particular variety of grape. Regulations specify the percentage content of a varietal for labeling purposes, usually 75% or more.
Vintage:	This term refers to the particular wine produced by a particular winery from one particular season. Vintage can refer to both the grapes and the wine produced from it.
Vintner:	Generally, the term "vintner" applies to wine grape producers, winery proprietors, and wine merchants. In this guide, we will use the term vintner to include both vineyard owners and winery owners. Although a vineyard owner cultivates and grows the grapes that go into the production of wine, a vineyard owner may or may not own winemaking facilities.
Viticulturalist:	A viticulturalist (also called a viniculturalist) is a person who grows grape vines to produce market-quality grapes. The term viticulture is also applied to the science of growing grapes.
Viticulture Area:	A VA is a special area that is formally recognized as a prime grape growing area. Think of it as a geographic pedigree for wine.
Vitis Vinifera:	This is the species of grape vine that most vineyard owners grow in order to produce commercial grade grapes for wine production. Hybrids, grafts, and clones are commonly used to produce disease resistant varieties as well as varieties that are hardier in cold climates.

Being Recognized As an Authority

"Wine is one of the few products that has not become homogenized. Wine reflects the soil, weather and conditions its grapes were grown in. Wine is a result of a winemaker's techniques and handling methods. Wine changes from vineyard site to vineyard site and year to year. The best wine shops keep up with the changes and employ interactive staff members to relate wine's unique story to its customers."

— Kimberly Eakin, Certified Specialist of Wine
and president of Wine Gourmet

Establishing yourself as an authority on wine is important. You must be a mentor to the new drinker, an equal to the experienced wine connoisseur, and an elementary schoolteacher to the uninitiated. Because your business will specialize in wine, expect more than a few customers to ask your opinion about a good wine to purchase.

You must always be likable of course, but a little bit of wine snobbery is a good thing if you are going to establish yourself as a wine store owner. Your customers and contacts will have no problem with your knowledge. In fact, your knowledge will draw customers to you. "People are starting to turn away from the huge warehouse stores," says Kyle McHugh, owner of Drinks Over Dearborn. "While prices are nearly impossible to match, customers like to talk to someone who really knows the products being sold, and they're willing to pay another few dollars for a true expert who can help them make mistakes by blindly choosing wine from a bin at a huge store with no help."

Rather than recommending your personal favorites, as a professional your job is to try to determine the tastes of each individual customer who needs help in their selections. Asking pointed questions as to what kind of wine he or she likes will help both of you. You are actually directing customers to what they already prefer, even though they are unsure themselves. As a result, your customer will walk away satisfied with a purchase that fits their tastes.

In addition to paying close attention to what customers say they're looking for, you must also compare that information with common market trends. After selling to a variety of customers you will start to notice patterns of tastes and popular brands of wine being repeated by name or by well-known characteristics. After working with wines for a period of time, determining your customers' needs and recommending wine based on that information will become second nature. You will be selling your clientele exactly what they want to buy.

2.1.2   Interpersonal Skills

As a wine store owner you must learn to adapt to the conversational style of individual customers. You cannot come across as too overbearing or too opinionated, because, after all, your customers will expect good customer service, not lectures about wine.

A friendly but cordial style is the best to use when approaching customers. You are expert enough to know what you're talking about with respect to wine, and respectful enough to be courteous of your customers' needs. This might involve drawing out your customers who feel intimidated by wine selection with pointed questions such as what kind of wine they like or telling them more about brands they haven't tried before.

Conversing with a wine connoisseur is even more fun, as he or she will be more than willing to show off their own accumulated wine knowledge and tasting tips. You might even learn something new from them. You need to be open and willing to learn from your customers, too. That way, they will know that you respect them and appreciate their business.

Listening

While listening seems like an easy skill to master, most of us experience challenges in at least one of the following areas involved in listening: paying attention, understanding, and remembering. You can become a better listener by focusing fully on someone when they are speaking.

Here are some ways to do that:

- Don't interrupt the other person. Hear them out.

- Keep listening to the other person, even if you think you know what they will say next. If you make assumptions, you may miss the point they're making.

- Ask questions in order to clarify what the other person has said. Take notes if necessary.

- Don't be distracted by outside interference. Loud noises, the other person mispronouncing a word, or even an uncomfortable room temperature can break your concentration and distract you from the conversation.

- Give feedback to the other person. Nod occasionally; say things like "I see," and smile, if appropriate. Let them know you're listening.

- Use paraphrasing. In other words, repeat back in your own words your understanding of what the other person has said. It can help alleviate misunderstandings later on.

Verbal Skills

Clear communication is essential because you will need to explain your store's sales or return policy, and you will need to describe to customers your current inventory. When making sales, customers can become frustrated if they find it difficult to understand what you're saying. To improve your verbal communication skills, ask friends or a vocal coach for feedback on any areas that could be improved, such as: use of slang, proper grammar, or altering your tone of voice to eliminate any harshness.

Reading Non-Verbal Messages

In addition to hearing what people say, a skilled business owner also notices non-verbal communication (tone of voice, facial expression, body language, etc.). These signals can give you valuable clues about what the other person is thinking.

For example, did a customer fold their arms when you made a particular suggestion? If so, they may be communicating that they disagree, even if they don't actually say so. Although body language can't tell you precisely what someone is thinking, it can give you clues so you can ask follow-up questions, even as basic as "How do you feel about that?" If you want to improve this skill, you can find some excellent advice in the book *Reading People*, by Jo-Ellan Dimitrius and Wendy Patrick Mazzarella.

2.1.3   Business Skills

If you are well prepared for being a wine store owner, the better the chances are that your venture will be a success. It's crucial to know where your business stands financially at all times. While you don't have to learn it all, staying on top of your accounting will help you avoid finding yourself in the awful position of being out of cash to pay your bills or replenish your inventory.

Running a successful wine store requires an overlap of a variety of business skills. Aside from a knowledge and expertise about the particular products you sell (and training employees to be knowledgeable as well), you will need to know about:

- Business planning

- Financial management

- Merchandising

- Operations management

- Inventory management

- Hiring and supervising employees

- Marketing and sales

The more you can keep your expenses down while building a solid customer base to build sales volume, while at the same time turning over inventory frequently, the more successful your wine store will be. For some of these tasks, you can hire employees or contractors to help you, such as a bookkeeper or someone who can handle the marketing and promotion for your business. Keep in mind, though, that the fewer people you need to hire to help you manage your business, the lower your overall costs of running the business. Developing business skills takes time, so be thorough, and don't be in such a rush that you neglect to fill in any gaps in your knowledge or skills.

Experience you have in other retail environments can be helpful, and there are a number of ways you can develop your skills and knowledge in all of these areas. In this chapter, you'll find specific ideas to help you increase your experience and knowledge of running a wine store.

You'll also find detailed advice throughout the remaining sections of this guide.

You will probably find reading the entire guide before you launch your business helpful, but you can quickly identify particular areas you may want to focus on by reviewing the table of contents. For example, section 5.5 provides advice on financial management, covering everything from budgeting to bookkeeping to building wealth, and section 3.5 gives you advice about start-up financial planning. Both these sections provide website links to online resources to help you find further help in these areas.

One tool for helping you to focus on what business skills are involved in being a wine store owner is business planning. Section 3.4 looks in detail at how to develop a business plan to get your business up and running by outlining and clarifying what products you will offer, deciding how you will finance your business, creating a market plan, etc. In addition to addressing these important business issues, a business plan will also help you to understand some of the other basic "hard" skills required of a business owner, such as marketing and accounting skills.

Other Business Skills

In addition to the business skills listed above, you will need to deal with a good amount of paperwork. This includes handling important business and legal issues pertaining to your business such as collecting and paying sales taxes, obtaining proper licenses to operate your business, and maintaining adequate insurance for your business.

We'll discuss some of these issues in greater detail later on, but it's important to note that you will want to educate yourself on these issues and develop these skills if you do not already have them before you open your business.

Research Skills

Having good research skills is another important asset. You will need to use these skills from the moment you begin, for developing your business plan (including the population demographics of any areas you are considering), searching for the right location for your business, finding vendors and suppliers, learning about new trends and products, and other purposes.

Computer Skills

You will also need to know how to operate computers and software and use the Internet, as these are key for tracking sales data, inventory, and other important information. Computer skills can be learned, and many local school districts, community and other colleges offer continuing education or extension courses on how to operate a PC or Mac, as well as how to use several major software programs and making use of the Internet for research and marketing.

Resources for Developing Business Skills

The following resources can help you develop your business skills:

SBA

The Small Business Administration (SBA) is a leading U.S. government resource for information about licensing, taxes, and starting a small business. You can find a range of resources including information on financing your new business, business plans and much more at **www. sba.gov**.

SCORE

The Service Corps of Retired Executives (SCORE) is an organization of U.S. volunteers who donate their time and expertise to new business owners. You can find information on taxes, tips for starting your business, or even find a mentor who will coach you and help you maximize your chances of succeeding as a new business owner. Visit them at **www.score.org**.

Canada Business Service Centers

This Canadian government website offers information on legislation, taxes, incorporation, and other issues of interest to Canadian business owners or those who do business in Canada. For more information and a list of services they offer visit their website at **www.canadabusiness.ca**.

2.2 Learning by Doing

There are two aspects of being a wine store owner that you will need to develop (as you've probably realized by now): a good working knowledge of wines, and retail experience. There are numerous ways you can develop one or the other, or both at the same time. In this section, we'll look at some different ways that you can get the knowledge and experience you'll need. You may even get paid while you're doing it!

2.2.1   Work in a Wine Store

Working in a wine store for a time can be a valuable way to learn much-needed skills for running your own store one day. Not only will you learn how to deal with customers, you will more than likely learn how to use the systems used by many wine stores (covered in Chapter 5 of this guide). This includes learning about inventory control systems, purchasing, sales techniques, staff procedures, etc.

Working in a wine store (or in a liquor store) even if only on a part-time or volunteer basis, is probably the best way to prepare yourself for opening your own wine store. Working for a time in a wine store will give you valuable insight into pricing merchandise, what sells (and, equally important, what doesn't), how to deal with customers, how to arrange merchandise to its best advantage so that it looks attractive to buyers, and exactly what it takes to keep a wine store running smoothly on a day-to-day basis. As time goes by you will also find out where the owner obtains most of the inventory. This information will help when you're ready to open your own store.

Visiting the wine store you'd like to work in as a customer, and purchasing there frequently, before applying for a job will help you to get to know the owner (and the store) a little. Remember, it will help if the owner recognizes you because you have been there before. Never phone or write a letter; face to face works much better.

Here are some suggestions for introducing yourself and what you can do for a prospective employer:

- Explain that you are interested in learning about running a wine store.

- Tell them if you've had any previous experience (whether it's selling wine or working in retail or something else related to the job).

- Think of some extra service you could offer, such as helping to design a website or writing a newsletter.

- If no job is available and you really love the store, and want to work there, volunteer to work for free. It could pay in the long run.

Finally, when applying for a job in a wine store ensure that your demeanor, personality and dress reflect the qualities that you would be looking for in an employee. These characteristics are outlined in more detail in section 5.6.2, "Recruiting Staff".

> TIP: Remember that, even if you can't find a job at your favorite store, almost any retail or wine related experience is valuable so you could apply to stores that sell wine kits, or a local micro-winery if you can't find a job at a wine store.

Vocation Vacations

As another option, consider turning to VocationVacations, a company that can set you up with an opportunity to test-drive a job you are interested in. For a fee, you get to experience the career hands-on as you work one-on-one with a mentor for two days. Vocation Vacations currently offers Wine Retailer (cost is $849-$949), where you'll work at a wine store in Boulder, Colorado, under the tutelage of a master sommelier and store co-owner. Vocation Vacations also offers related vacations in wine making with various opportunities to work in vineyards and wineries (who also retail) across the country. Prices for these vacations range from $549 to as high as $2,000.

You can learn more about these vacations at **www.vocationvacations. com** (click on the "Dream Jobs" link and then the "Dream Job Vacations" link and look for the job titles mentioned above).

2.2.2   Work at a Winery or Vineyard

Knowing the wine production process is an important factor in becoming an expert on wines. Your more knowledgeable customers might want to discuss this in-depth when it comes to certain wines. One good way to learn more about wine and how it is produced is to work at a winery. Working for a time in either a vineyard or winery will give you first-hand experience with aspects of vineyard management, crushing grapes, winemaking, bottling and labeling, and so on. You'll learn a lot in a very short period of time.

Internships

Vineyards and wineries are increasingly offering internships to people interested in learning more about the industry. Internships are often unpaid, although many wine industry internships do offer a small hourly wage (around $10-$12). A recent survey of the website, **www.winejobs. com**, included internships for grape maturity samplers, harvest cellar interns, and general internships that included a wide range of duties throughout the vineyard and winery.

Another website that lists wine industry jobs, with occasional internships as well as seasonal jobs, is Crazy About Wine at **www.crazyaboutwine. com/jobs**. You can also find a list of wine job boards at **www.wineinstitute. org/resources/external-links/wine-jobs**. You can check sites like Monster.com or Yahoo! HotJobs (**http://hotjobs.yahoo.com**) for general listings under the search term "winery".

Offer to Work for Free

Another way to find work in the wine industry, if you can't find a paying job, is to simply offer to work for free. Many wineries will be only too happy to accommodate you, especially if you are enthusiastic and willing to learn. Wineries most often need extra labor during the harvest, crush, and bottling periods. These are the best times to find an opening, and you should contact the winery well in advance of these times.

To find a winery in your area, you can visit the Appellation America website where you'll find a clickable map of the U.S. and Canada, at **http://wine.appellationamerica.com/wine-region-index.aspx** (click on your state or province, choose an appellation, then look for the "What wineries are based here?" link). You can also try the Wine America website, **www.wineamerica.org/sac/stateassoc.cfm**, where they list state wine associations with links to each. The state associations have lists of member wineries and links to their websites.

2.2.3   Volunteering For Charity Events

Another good way to learn more about wine is to volunteer, either at charity events or at a wine store or at a winery or vineyard. Volunteering doesn't pay anything, but you will be helping your community and getting to know a few people if you help out at a charity event. You may also find that some wine stores, vineyards or wineries that might not be willing to hire you are more than willing to take you on if you simply volunteer to help them out.

Imagine being able to learn more about your favorite subject, get valuable experience, and make a difference in your community at the same time. You can do all of these things by volunteering to work at charity functions that include wine.

One frequently seen charity event is a wine tasting. As we'll explain later in section 6.1.7, wine tastings often include participants sampling wines from around the world, wines of different vintages, different wines of the same vintage, and multiple different varieties of wines. The concentration of wines often seen at charity wine tastings will give you exposure to a great variety of wines that you may not have encountered before. Often, these events will include wines from nearby wineries, too, giving you a chance to learn more about local wineries and what they offer.

While opportunities will vary from one community to another, here are some other possibilities for charity events that might include wine service:

- Charity art shows

- Charity wine auctions

- Culinary charity events (which often feature wine and food pairings)

A good place to start your search for charity events like those mentioned above is a volunteering aggregator site such as Volunteering in America, **www.volunteeringinamerica.gov** (choose your area of interest and state from the drop-down menus under "Find a Volunteer Opportunity"), or Volunteer Canada at **www.volunteer.ca**.

These sites have directory listings of volunteer centers across the country. Once you find a volunteer center near you, look in the "food service" or "events" sections to see what opportunities the center offers. Some volunteer centers even have listings under the three headings above.

2.3 Be Your Own "Mystery Shopper"

You have probably heard of mystery shopping, where companies hire people to go into their various retail outlets and pose as shoppers. This is an excellent way for management to get feedback about what their retailers are doing wrong — and right. In order to take a first-hand look at how other people are running their wine stores, you can become your own "mystery shopper" using these tips. You will find this information particularly helpful as you put together your business plan (see section 3.4) and marketing plans (section 6.1).

To begin, take a look in your local Yellow Pages under categories such as wine retailers, spirits retailers, or wine stores. Take time to visit several stores that interest you. Take a friend, and have fun, but remember that your main purpose is research.

As you go to a number of stores and record your observations, a couple of things will begin to happen. First, you will begin to know what stores are in your area and which, if any, will be competition for you. Second, you will get a chance to see stores in action. There is no substitute for seeing first hand how wine stores really run and operate.

Take a small notebook and pen so you can discretely take notes. After you have been to each wine store, use a Store Impressions Form like the one on the pages that follow to record your observations.

> **TIP:**   As you assess local wine stores, remember that what you see there should simply serve as ideas. There are no hard and fast rules about what features or services your own wine store needs to include.

In addition to observing anonymously, getting a wine store owner's permission to let you observe them in action is also a wonderful way to learn. If you have a friend or a business contact who will let you spend a day seeing how they operate their business, it will be an excellent learning experience. In the next section you'll find advice on how to contact wine store owners.

Store Impressions Form

The Storefront

1. Is the store easy to spot from the street? ❑ Y ❑ N

2. Is it easy to park? ❑ Y ❑ N

3. Is there plenty of free parking or street parking? ❑ Y ❑ N

4. Is it an area with foot traffic? ❑ Y ❑ N

5. How is the area?

6. What kinds of people do you see on the street?

Entering the Store

1. What do you notice about the atmosphere?

2. What do you like about the way the store looks?

3. What do you notice about the physical layout of the store?

4. Does the store seem inviting or uninviting? Why?

5. Is the store clean? ❑ Y ❑ N

6. Do you think you could get to a section you were looking for without assistance? ❑ Y ❑ N

The Staff

1. Are you greeted?   ❏ Y   ❏ N

2. Does the staff seem:

   Approachable?   ❏ Y   ❏ N   Grumpy?   ❏ Y   ❏ N
   Pleasant?   ❏ Y   ❏ N   Pushy?   ❏ Y   ❏ N
   Bored?   ❏ Y   ❏ N

3. When you ask a question, how do they respond?

4. Are they knowledgeable?   ❏ Y   ❏ N

5. Are you able to get your questions   ❏ Y   ❏ N
   answered to your satisfaction?

6. Does the staff make you feel comfortable   ❏ Y   ❏ N
   about asking a question?

Using the Store

1. Can you browse easily?   ❏ Y   ❏ N

2. Are you comfortable?   ❏ Y   ❏ N

3. How is the lighting?

4. How are the restrooms?

Merchandising

1. How is the merchandise arranged?

2. What is the quality of the merchandise?

3. What are the floor displays?

4. Is the merchandise priced according to quality? ❑ Y ❑ N

Buying

1. Is the cash area organized? ❑ Y ❑ N
2. Is it easy to get served? ❑ Y ❑ N
3. Does the staff member speak pleasantly to you? ❑ Y ❑ N
4. Do you buy? ❑ Y ❑ N

   Why or why not?

Leaving

1. What are your impressions when you leave?

2. Does a staff member notice you are leaving? ❑ Y ❑ N
3. Does anyone thank you? ❑ Y ❑ N
4. Does anyone say goodbye to you? ❑ Y ❑ N
5. Do you feel positive about your experience? ❑ Y ❑ N

Overall Impressions of the Store

1. What did you like most about the store?

2. What did you like the least?

3. What did you notice about the store's logo, bags or other printed material?

4. Will you go back to the store in the future?   ❑ Y ❑ N
5. Will you recommend the store to anyone?   ❑ Y ❑ N

Other Notes

Use this space to record any other notes you may have:

2.4 Learn From Other Business Owners

2.4.1 Talk to Wine Store Owners

After speaking with dozens of business owners, we recommend approaching wine store owners via e-mail, through an organization of store owners, or by driving to a non-competing store and asking their advice. The wine store owners we spoke with were eager to offer advice and point out many additional resources.

If you can get a wine store owner to talk to you, you can learn an amazing amount of insider information from someone who could be doing just what you want to do. Keep in mind, however, that while some may be quite willing to talk, others may be too busy. But if you ask nicely for information many people are very glad to share it.

TIP: You will probably have a hard time if you approach a wine store owner who could be considered your direct competition. There is a difference between sharing knowledge and giving away trade secrets. Make sure that the experts you try to contact are not your direct competition.

So, how do you contact wine store owners? Try the following:

- Identify first what it is you are trying to accomplish
- Make a list of questions you want to ask
- Identify who you think you should talk to
- Make a list of contacts
- Take the steps to make contact (email, telephone, in person)

For example, let's assume you went to a great wine store in a neighboring town. First (after you have made your list of questions), find out the phone number and the owner's name. Then call and ask to speak to the owner. Here is a sample phone script:

"Hi, I am Wanda Winestore. I was in your store while I was on vacation and I really enjoyed it. Could you tell me who the owner is? *(After you are connected to the owner, Ima Infogiver, you proceed.)*

"Hi, Ima Infogiver? My name is Wanda Winestore and I am considering opening a wine store in another part of the state. I was on vacation and had a chance to stop in your store, and I loved it. *(Now, ask permission to ask   an old sales trick.)* I was wondering if you would be willing to let me ask you a couple questions about how you do things. I could use some expert advice."

TIP: It never hurts to tell experts you think they are experts. Most people like being recognized for their accomplishments.

Make an appointment to call back the store owner at their convenience. Then take some time and decide on a couple of questions you really want answers to. Ask only these questions. Also, offer to correspond with your contact using email if the expert prefers this. Always thank the expert for their time and make sure they know you appreciate the information. If you build this relationship slowly you can ask for more help and advice, and perhaps you can even find a mentor.

Remember to:

- Ask permission to ask questions
- Be sensitive to the expert's time

- Decide ahead of time what you will ask

- Don't overwhelm your expert with too many questions

- Build the relationship slowly and ask for more time at a later date

As you do research on the Internet, you will undoubtedly begin to notice wine store websites that interest you. All of these sites have contact information you can use to directly ask for help and advice.

Remember to adhere to the same advice in email that you would use on the phone. Be courteous, brief, and grateful. Don't worry if you have to send out a number of letters before you have a response. Wine store owners are busy people. If you are polite and persistent, some wine store owners will be willing to talk to you.

Job Shadowing

Job shadowing involves spending a day, a week, or some other limited period of time observing someone work. It allows you to learn more about a career, ask questions, and actually see what a job entails on a daily basis. Most job shadowing is arranged through personal connections, although you might be able to arrange a job shadow by calling wine stores that interest you.

2.4.2 Join an Association

Wine Retail Associations

To learn more about the beverage service industry, consider joining your state's beverage licensees association. These associations are open to retailers, bar owners, and restaurants. Joining your state association allows you to network and take advantage of membership benefits.

Most state associations offer benefits like a conference where you can meet other wine store owners and attend workshops to learn more about the business, as well as discounts on insurance, an industry newsletter or magazine, and insider information to help you better run your store. A good place to find your state association is the American Beverage Licensees Association at **http://ablusa.org/affiliate.asp**.

You can also learn more about wine and the wine industry at the following association websites. While you may not be eligible to join all of them, they have lots of resources to help you learn more about the wine industry.

Wine Related Associations

- *American Society for Enology & Viticulture*
  www.asev.org

- *American Wine Society*
  (An association that promotes the love of wine to anyone who is interested.)
  www.americanwinesociety.org

- *Canadian Vintners Association*
  (Members include wineries and vineyards across Canada.)
  www.canadianvintners.com/

- *Wine America*
  (An association for wineries across the United States.)
  www.wineamerica.org

- *Wine and Spirits Wholesalers of America*
  (Represents the wholesale sector of the wine industry.)
  www.wswa.org

- *Wine Institute*
  (An association for winery owners in California.)
  www.wineinstitute.org

Retailer Associations

You may also want to consider joining a national or regional retailer association. These can help you learn specific aspects about the retail environment, as well as being good sources for information about government resources and regulations that might affect you (such as taxation, for example). Following are some national retail associations for you to consider. Most have regional affiliates.

- *North American Retail Dealers Association*
  www.narda.com

- *National Small Business Association*
  www.nsba.biz

- *National Federation of Independent Business*
  www.nfib.com

- *Canadian Federation of Independent Business*
  www.cfib.ca

Once you're an established wine store owner, it's a good idea to join a national or state association because membership gives customers confidence to see the association's logo displayed in your place of business.

You can also join a number of excellent organizations designed for business owners to learn and network in an organized setting, such as your local Chamber of Commerce. Chambers usually have an annual fee and are set up to aid the local businessperson with a variety of business-related issues. Members attend local meetings and can also take part in events designed to help them be more successful.

To find out how to contact your local chamber, visit the national websites. For the U.S. Chamber of Commerce visit **www.uschamber.com/chambers/directory/default.htm**. For the Canadian Chamber of Commerce Directory visit **www.chamber.ca/index.php/en/links/C57/**.

2.5 Educational Programs

Nobody can become a wine connoisseur overnight, nor can you as an ambitious rising wine store owner learn perfect "wine speak" in a short period of time. Furthering your education in the science and art of wine tasting will help you develop added expertise, something that can only help your business.

If you're competing against local grocery stores and liquor stores, then chances are the staff hired by the owner doesn't know much more about wine than how to punch wine prices into the cash register. This is where extensive wine knowledge can make the difference. Wine is not just stock to a wine store owner entrepreneur—it's a hobby and a life-style. You can afford to be that much more helpful to your customers.

You may want to take some business courses, too. These will help you to develop skills mentioned in section 2.1.2. Business skills and knowl-edge are as important as a knowledge of wine, since you will need these to help you to understand how to run your business. If you already have some experience running a business, then you may want to brush up or further your knowledge in some areas.

2.5.1 Business Courses

Earning a degree, diploma, or certificate in business can be helpful in running your own business. However, a formal business education is not necessary to run a wine store. There are many successful business owners who are self-taught and have never studied business. Others have taken a course here and there but do not possess a degree. How-ever, the skills you learn in business classes can come in handy. Depend-ing on which of your skills you would like to develop, consider taking courses on topics such as:

- Advertising

- Basic Accounting

- Business Communications

- Business Management

- Entrepreneurship

- Marketing

- Merchandising

- Retailing

Your local college or university may offer courses in these and other business subjects. Through the continuing education department you may be able to take a single course on a Saturday or over several eve-nings. If you can't find a listing for the continuing education depart-ment in your local phone book, call the college's main switchboard and ask for the continuing education department. They will be able to tell you about upcoming courses.

If you are not interested in attending courses at a school, or you don't have the time, another option that can easily fit into your schedule is distance learning. Traditionally these were called correspondence courses and the lessons were mailed back and forth between student and instructor. Today, with the help of the Internet, there are many on-line courses available. Again, check your local community college, university, or business school to see if they offer online courses.

If you're already an experienced retailer or have managed a wine store, have the money to start your own business, and have put together a comprehensive business plan, then the extra education you're seeking is for self-improvement so that you can better run your business. You might want to consider courses to raise your level of knowledge of business issues like business management or bookkeeping.

To find schools in your area offering continuing education programs try online directories such as **www.petersons.com** or **www.schoolfinder. com**.

Your local Chamber of Commerce may also offer training courses and seminars for new business owners. Many also offer consultations with retired executives and business owners who are well-qualified to offer advice. Visit **www.chamberofcommerce.com** to find a Chamber near you.

2.5.2   Wine Appreciation Courses

You probably already know a great deal about wine if you are considering opening your own wine store. If so, then this will be familiar territory for you, although perhaps you might like to round out your knowledge even further. If you are a relative novice or perhaps know a lot about a particular type of wine, for example you know your reds but aren't as familiar with the whites, rosés, sparkling wines, etc., you might want to learn more about other wines before opening your store.

Your local community college might offer extension or continuing education courses in wine appreciation. Universities with specialty research departments in wine or grape growing frequently offer such courses to the public. Regional or local wine grape growers' associations also offer them, as do some tourist organizations that specialize in wine country tours. You can also look for wine appreciation courses offered online (although these are sometimes fairly limited in scope).

What to Look For

For an introductory course, be sure to look for one in which a broad range of topics is covered. A good course for a novice wine store owner will look at more than one type of wine or varietal. You'll want to learn as much about dessert wines as you do about the Pinot Noirs and the Chardonnays. You'll also want to sample wines from around the country and around the world if possible in order to get a good idea how terroir affects the taste of otherwise similar wines.

Find a course that focuses a bit on the history of each wine, including the grower, the fermentation method, aging methods, how it is marketed, and so on. You want to get out of the course a good appreciation for what went into making the final product and getting it to market.

Wine appreciation courses are also good if you feel you would rather not spend thousands of dollars on a degree program. A course of study like the certificate courses offered by Fine Vintage Ltd. (see below), can give you a solid grounding in your understanding of wine. The beginner's course includes topics like the styles of wine, characteristics of grape varieties, and so on. The intermediate and advanced certificate courses include the study of wines from around the world, viticulture, vinification (how fermentation creates wine from grape juice), labeling regulations, and more.

Another benefit to taking a wine appreciation course is that many of them are directed more toward the retail or restaurant trades. This benefits you as a wine store owner because you will begin to develop an appreciation for how wine gets into those markets. Knowing how wines are marketed at this level will help you to develop your own marketing plan.

Here are a few examples of wine appreciation courses available online:

- *Culinary Institute of America Free Online Course*
  (Although this online introductory course is free, you need to register with a first and last name. They also offer courses for the wine professional on location in the Napa Valley.)
  www.ciaprochef.com/winestudies/online.html

- *Wine Spectator School*
  (Offers courses for the wine professional; look for the "Attention Wine Professionals" link)
  www.winespectatorschool.com/wineschool/

- *University of California, Davis Online Wine Courses*
  (Scroll down to the "Winemaking" section and click on the "Viticulture and Enology" link.)
  http://extension.ucdavis.edu/unit/online_learning

Here are some examples of the kinds of wine courses you might attend where you live:

- *Culinary Institute of America's Professional Wine Studies*
  Cost: Prices range from $150 to $995 depending on the course.
  Location: Classes are held in the Napa Valley, CA
  Website: **www.ciaprochef.com/winestudies/**

- *Fine Vintage Ltd. Wine Courses*
  Cost: Prices range from $300-$1595 per course depending on which course you take and do not include exam fees.
  Location: Vancouver BC, Seattle WA, Calgary, AB, etc. Check the website for further details.
  Website: **www.finevintageltd.com/wine-courses**

- *Professional Culinary Institute (PCI): Professional Sommelier Course*
  Cost: Contact PCI for details
  Location: Campbell, California
  Website: **www.pciwine.com**

- *Wine and Spirit Education Trust Classes*
  (Classes are offered worldwide. Click on "Where to Study"
  then choose your region.)
  www.wset.co.uk

2.6 Resources for Self-Study

If you don't want to return to school or you simply don't have the time
to take any formal courses, you also have a wide variety of self-study
learning options. These include:

- Books

- Magazines

- Websites

- Conventions and Trade Shows

2.6.1 Books

Amazon.com lists almost 500,000 books on the subject of wine, but of
course you do not have the time to read them all! So here is a selection
of excellent books you may want to start with. Look for them at your
local library, browse through them at a local bookstore, or order them
online.

- *The World Atlas of Wine,*
  by Hugh Johnson and Jancis Robinson

- *The Sotheby's Wine Encyclopedia:*
  The Classic Reference to the Wines of the World,
  by Tom Stevenson

- *The Wine Bible,*
  by Karen McNeil

- *The New Wine Lover's Companion,*
  by Ron Herbst and Sharon Tyler Herbst

- *The Science of Wine: From Vine to Glass,*
  by Jamie Goode

- *Judgment of Paris: California vs. France and the
  Historic 1976 Paris Tasting That Revolutionized Wine,*
  by George M Taber

- *Red, White, and Drunk All Over:
  A Wine-Soaked Journey from Grape to Glass,*
  by Natalie MacLean

2.6.2 Magazines

If you already have the basics down, you can always subscribe to popular wine magazines to keep up with the newest information about market trends in wine.

- *Food and Wine Magazine*
  www.foodandwine.com

- *Vines Magazine (Canada)*
  www.vinesmag.com/sitepages/default.asp

- *Wine & Spirits Daily*
  www.winespiritsdaily.com

- *Wine & Spirits Magazine*
  www.wineandspiritsmagazine.com

- *Wine Business Monthly*
  www.winebusiness.com

- *Wine Enthusiast*
  www.winemag.com

- *Wine Spectator Magazine*
  www.winespectator.com/Wine/Home/

2.6.3   Websites

There are literally thousands of websites related to wine. Here are a few of the better ones to get you started.

General Wine Websites

- *Vinquire*
  (You can search this site by wine varietal or winery and find prices from hundreds of wine retailers.)
  www.vinquire.com

- *Appellation America*
  (The best site on the web for information about North American wines and wineries.)
  http://wine.appellationamerica.com

- *Wine Glossary*
  www.thatsthespirit.com/en/wine/wine_glossary.asp

- *Wine Grape Glossary*
  www.wineloverspage.com/wineguest/wgg.html

Industry Websites

- *The Wine Collector Blog*
  www.vinfolio.com/thewinecollector

- *Ship Compliant Blog*
  www.shipcompliantblog.com

- *The Wine Institute*
  www.wineinstitute.org

- *Wine Business Online*
  www.winebusiness.com

- *Wine America—the National Association of American Wineries*
  www.wineamerica.org

- *Canadian Vintners Association*
  www.canadianvintners.com/index.htm

Forums

Here is a list of some of the busiest wine forums on the web.

- *Wine Spectator Forum*
  http://forums.winespectator.com/6/ubb.x

- *Vinquire Forum*
  www.vinquire.com/forums/

- *Wine Web Forum*
  www.wineweb.com/fusetalk/forum/index.cfm?forumid=1

- *Wine Lovers Discussion Group*
  (Of particular interest are the "Wine Forum" and "Wine Focus" discussions.)
  www.wineloverspage.com/forum/village/index.php

3. Starting Your Wine Store

Starting your own wine business is a thrilling venture. It is a career that creates a sense of accomplishment even while requiring much more personal effort than a regular nine-to-five job. When you are the owner of a company you're the only one with collateral to lose, but many self-motivated entrepreneurs are more than willing to invest in their vision and go the extra mile to make their businesses work.

Now that we've looked at ways to develop your business skills, it's time to look at how to go about actually starting your own store. This chapter of the guide will walk you step-by-step through the process.

Use the checklist below as a guideline to help you complete the steps necessary to get your business going. In fact, you may want to print the checklist and keep it nearby as you go through the rest of this guide so you can add items as you learn more about them.

Getting Started Basics Checklist

❑ Choose your niche.

❑ Prepare your business plan.

❑ Obtain a business license.

❑ Locate several potential locations and weigh pros and cons of each.

❑ Secure financing.

❑ Lease or purchase store space.

❑ Obtain any necessary permits or certificates.

❑ Purchase store fixtures.

❑ Purchase software your store will use for inventory.

❑ Decide what merchandise you will offer for sale, locate suppliers and purchase inventory.

❑ Start advertising your grand opening.

❑ Decide if you need help. Interview and hire additional employees, if necessary.

❑ If you are planning to hire employees, obtain an Employee Identification Number (contact details later in this guide).

❑ Complete your store operations manual and finalize any policies.

❑ Make a plan for your grand opening.

❑ Set up systems for record keeping.

❑ Set up window displays.

❑ Open your business.

Consider Your Market

When planning your niche, you should also consider your local market. Are you competing against grocery stores and liquor stores? Maybe your store is conveniently located in comparison to the others and so your strategy is to stock all sorts of drinks, including wine, beer and ale, liquor and even soda.

But if your store is located nearby a local grocery store or liquor store, then you really have to pull out all of the stops to take away business from a strong, established and all-inclusive store. The better strategy might be to not stock other alcoholic drinks but to focus solely on the wine market—heavily promoting wines that the other stores don't carry.

Studies of wine purchasing trends suggest that supermarket and chain stores are starting to dominate wine sales. One of the largest wine retailers in the United States is, believe it or not, Costco; the same place you buy food, lawn furniture and computers. This would indicate that customers who want wine probably will go to the supermarket and pick it up on the way home as they pick up their meat and vegetables.

Customers who are willing to venture away from the easy pick up want something more intricate like better variety or an exclusive wine from a store with a savvy staff of sales personnel. You need to create a reason for them to want to visit your store. A well chosen niche can mean the difference between success and failure.

3.1 Choosing Your Niche

The first thing to consider for your store is what types of products and services you will offer. This is your "niche" or specialty.

Initially, as you consider what niche to fill with your own store, remember that the simplest approach is to sell something you are familiar with. Look at areas of your life and experience to help you decide. Stick with what is familiar at first, but don't make your store's niche too narrow in your first year. Starting with a wider range of products and services will help you adapt to the needs of your clientele. Over time you will likely find some products and services are more profitable for you, and you can change your offerings as you learn more about what your customers want.

To help you choose your niche you'll need to do some market research to give you an idea of trends in the industry you are entering. You'll need to determine:

- Is there a need in your community for what you plan to sell?

- Can you effectively compete?

The best place to start is by studying other successful stores similar to the one you are planning to open. Don't be afraid to ask other retail store owners for their advice. You may hear that sales of certain types of products are booming, while some products may be losing popularity.

Also find out if any stores similar to yours have opened or closed in the area recently. If you're new to the area, you may have to speak to other business owners and locals to get this information. While your marketing and customer service might be better than the stores that closed, the fact that a similar store has been unsuccessful might indicate that a particular type of retail outlet doesn't do well in your area. If at all possible, try to track down the previous store owner through the local phone book and ask a few questions.

You'll find some additional resources for doing market research in section 3.4 on business planning to help you focus in on your market, but even if you already have an idea of your specialty, this section may help you refine it further.

3.1.1   Wine Boutique

There's a shift for boutique wine shops to carry boutique producers or specializing in a specific region to differentiate their brand from the grocery stores and other smaller competitors.

> — Donnie Austin, owner,
> House Wine

The wine boutique is the classic type of wine store. It can feature wines priced from less than $20 to wines worth hundreds of dollars. Staff are knowledgeable, and often a sommelier is hired as the resident wine expert (or is the owner) in some of the higher end boutiques. It may offer any or all of the products and services mentioned in section 1.2. Generally, a wine boutique does not carry much in the way of beer or liquor, but may offer limited selections of each.

In many ways, a wine boutique is like any other type of boutique. By definition, it is a small store that sells "elite or fashionable items" (Wikipedia). In this case, the elite or fashionable items are wines.

As we've already discussed, the reason people will come into your wine store is that they are looking for products they can't find elsewhere, just as a bride-to-be visits a bridal shop to find a unique dress she can't find anywhere else in town. Your wine boutique will specialize in unique product lines not found at Costco or the local grocery store. You will offer the latest in "fashionable" wines, perhaps building on a trend like the growth in popularity of Pinot Noir after the release of the movie "Sideways".

Another way your wine boutique will differ from grocery and department stores selling wines, is that you will offer special services. These might include having a sommelier on staff to answer even the toughest questions from oenophiles, or hosting a wine club, or special tasting events. (Information on how to host a wine tasting is found in section 6.1.7.)

The information in the rest of this guide will help you to set up this type of wine store, and can be applied to any of the following niches.

3.1.2   Wine Store and Wine Bar

Wine stores with wine bars attached are a frequently seen niche. Obviously these two businesses work well together. The one side of the business caters to tasting and trying new wines by the glass or carafe, while the other sells the same wines by the bottle that the bar's customers are trying by the glass.

Running a wine bar is a business endeavor with its own unique challenges. Wine bar concepts involve creating a special place for wine lovers to come to enjoy wines from around the world and discuss the merits of each with other oenophiles. In addition, most offer entertainment and special events for customers.

Entertainment doesn't need to be fancy. You can create a classy atmosphere by having a live jazz group perform on occasion. You might consider playing piped in classical, jazz, or other non-intrusive music. Of course, wine tastings are popular events and almost every wine store and wine bar features these as often as possible. Often, you can convince a wine agency or vineyard to hold a special promotion in your wine bar. Inviting a wine expert to give a talk is also a great way to get your customers interested in the various wines you sell.

Menus for a wine bar can also be varied. You don't necessarily need a full menu in a wine bar. You can offer appetizers or a tapas bar or sushi; whatever makes sense in your market. But remember that food pairings are a notable feature of the whole wine experience. In order to get people to try more wines, you may need to offer a variety of menu items with which customers can experiment.

3.1.3   Virtual Wine Store or Wine Club

Another way to get started selling wine without going through most of the challenges of opening a brick and mortar retail store is to start by selling wine online.

Virtual wine stores usually go by the name "wine clubs", and are a relatively new business model. They take advantage of the ubiquity of the Internet, as well as somewhat more relaxed wine laws in some jurisdictions the last few years. Wine club businesses include stand-alone businesses (i.e. this is the only way they sell), as well as wine clubs that sell wine from a brick and mortar retail wine store's website.

To start a wine club you will need the following:

- A well-developed website capable of accepting payments, as well as tracking inventory, customer preferences, customer orders and shipping.

- A well thought-out concept and marketing campaign

- Wineries willing to get on board with your idea

- The proper licensing in your jurisdiction (this might include several different licenses related to selling alcohol)

First, you'll need to set up your website so that you can process on-line transactions. This includes the ability to accept major credit cards and, if you choose, PayPal payments. You'll need a shopping cart and you'll have to set up an online catalog of your wines. One company that can help you with setting up your online store is 1 Shopping Cart (**www.1shoppingcart.com**). A basic package costs about $60 a month or you can try it out for one month for $3.95.

Most wine clubs offer a lot of information about the wines they sell and wines in general on their websites. In most cases, you can get the wine information from the agency or winery that is supplying your club. A wine club owner does not actually carry any wine inventory. Instead, the wine is essentially drop shipped from the original producer or wholesaler. Generally, wine clubs sell their wines to each customer in case lots of increments of six (i.e. cases of six, twelve, eighteen, etc. bottles, or multiple cases). Wine is cheaper to ship when shipped in larger quantities (at least for the seller).

You'll also need to set up a shipper, such as FedEx or UPS to ship your wines. Another requirement of the shipper will be to have a person of drinking age at the other end to sign for the order. The recipient will need to be able to prove that they are of legal drinking age. Otherwise, the shipment gets returned to you.

One company that offers help for the wine club business owner is Ship Compliant. They offer software that does all the work for you. The program integrates into other applications on your website and determines whether the shipping address of the purchaser (or where the purchaser is sending the wine if it is a gift) is part of the allowed jurisdictions. You can learn more about this software at **http://shipcompliant.com**.

Many states do not allow interstate trafficking in wines. Therefore, there are some states you will not be able to ship into unless their laws change in future. One requirement you'll find in most jurisdictions that allow the wine club business model is that you list on your website all of the states you do ship to, as well as those that you do not ship to.

To find wineries willing to work with you, you'll need to do a lot of online research. This is where your well-developed marketing plan and business concept comes into play. You'll need to convince wineries that you are serious, that you know the market and the legal issues involved, and that you are providing them with a service that will benefit them. Wine Web offers website start-up services for would-be wine club business owners.

To learn more about the legal issues involved in setting up this type of wine retailing company, visit the Specialty Wine Retailers website at **www.specialtywineretailers.org/members.html**. This organization is dedicated to improving the laws regarding wine and creating a freer market.

3.1.4   Wine Store Within a Store

One business model is the store within a store concept. This is when you locate your wine store on the premises of another, complementary business. One of our experts, Michael Cawdrey, manager of Fremont Wine Warehouse, started his first wine retail business this way, inside his family's grocery store.

Of course, you may not be so lucky as to have a grocery store owned by a family member available. However, the model works well in any grocery store, gourmet food store, wine bar or other complementary business. You may be able to approach an existing business in your area and propose this type of relationship.

Generally, retail businesses that operate on this model pay the store owner a flat fee per square foot rent, sometimes with an additional charge based on sales. In many ways, this is similar to renting a store space in a mall. The advantages to you are that your overhead is lower, since you don't have to pay for utilities, heat, and so on, and you have a steady stream of foot traffic passing your store. The advantage for the store owner is that they get a unique service and product that other similar stores do not have. This makes them more competitive.

You should be aware that you will still need to apply for all the licensing required for a regular wine store operator. This includes a business license, as well as any licenses related to selling alcohol. You may need to get both on- and off-premises licenses, if you plan to offer other services such as wine tastings or other promotional events. There may be complications related to licensing for the store owner, too, so be sure to do your homework and check with your local alcoholic beverage control board before approaching any store owners.

3.2 Options for Starting a Wine Store

Once you have decided on your niche, you'll need to decide whether to buy an existing store, buy a franchise, or open a new store. Deciding which route is right for you is an important decision.

An established store will cost more than starting from scratch, but it also comes with customers, inventory, and reputation, which means it's likely to continue with its pre-established success. A new store typically costs less to start up, and you can tailor it specifically to your own vision. Unlike buying an established store, though, you will need to spend more on advertising, gaining clientele, and making a reputation for your business — and new businesses have a higher risk of failure. Franchises might be another option to consider. We'll explain more about how these work in section 3.2.2.

3.2.1 Buy an Established Store

One way to start is to buy an existing business and make it your own. Buying an existing store can show you a profit on the very first day you're open. You'll still need a business plan, financing, a lawyer and an accountant, but many of the other decisions – like what to call it and where to locate it — will already be made. In addition, you will acquire all or most of the equipment, furniture, supplies, and inventory you will need to get started. You also get clientele and the established business name.

However, you should also look very careful at whatever else you might be acquiring. The business may have outstanding debts and you may have to assume any liabilities that come with the store, such as bills it owes to its suppliers, or repairs or maintenance expenditures that haven't been paid.

If this option for starting your business appeals to you, begin by looking for stores for sale in your area. Do not be afraid to approach local store owners and inquire if they are interested in selling their business, or if they know any store owners considering retirement. And, don't forget to look in your local newspaper, local business publications, and contact the Chamber of Commerce for information on shops that may possibly be for sale.

What to Look for Before You Buy

Purchasing an existing business can be a good way to get into the retail trade immediately, but there are a few cautions. You could be purchasing a failed business with a poor financial history, bad reputation, or even some hidden liabilities as mentioned earlier. You need to perform a due diligence investigation, meaning you need to look at the operations of the business, including revenues, cash flow, assets and liabilities, licensing, and so on, before purchasing.

To protect yourself, before making a deal for any business hire an accountant to go over the company's books. This will help you to determine if the seller is representing the business accurately and honestly. Then, before signing an Agreement of Purchase and Sale, you should enlist the services of a lawyer to review the written agreement.

Following are a few things to look for as you start your search for an existing business to buy.

Why the Business is For Sale

Here are a few of the most common reason why business owners offer their businesses for sale:

- The owner is retiring or has health problems

- The owner is moving on to another store or another business altogether

- The business has failed and the owner wants to get out as quickly as possible

- The owner is afraid of increasing competition

- One key element of their business strategy is faulty, such as the type of inventory offered

- The business is part of a chain and is not doing as well as other stores owned by the same company

- A partnership has fallen apart and the partners are liquidating all or a part of the company's assets

Before purchasing an existing retail business answer the following important questions (with assistance from the seller whenever possible).

- Why is the vendor selling the business?

- What is the sales history of the store?

- What is the average cost to maintain the store?

- What assets or liabilities will come with the purchase?

- Are there any tax, legal or property issues you will have to contend with?

The previous owner may help you with many of these issues or you may have to do your own research, perhaps by consulting local government, realtors or other merchants. Whatever the situation, you should never buy an existing business without knowing all of the details.

You should have complete access to the previous owner's store records, including financial statements. With these you will have information about the customer base and noticeable patterns in the store's business practices. Unwillingness by the previous owner to provide financial statements for your complete inspection might be a tip-off that something isn't right with the business.

Potential buyers often work in the store for a short time before purchasing it. Owners are often willing to train the buyer. If the business owner you are thinking about buying from is unwilling to do this, you should find out why.

Hidden Costs

When you purchase an established business it seems like you're purchasing a turnkey operation with license, location, traffic and inventory all in place and you just have to open the doors. However, there may be hidden expenses that you will have to pay for, such as back taxes, needed repairs or building code violations, so be sure to watch for these. You don't want an angry supplier showing up at your door demanding money for inventory purchased by the previous owner but never paid for. (You've already purchased the inventory from the owner and now you'll have to pay for it a second time.)

In addition to paying for the business, and any miscellaneous expenses, you will also need money to pay for equipment and supplies, and additional inventory. You may also want to start a marketing campaign in order to make people aware of the fact that you're the new owner and let the community know that you're open for business. This is particularly important if you've bought a business that might have been on the decline for whatever reasons.

Finally, if you plan to remodel a store after buying it, perhaps to give it a fresh new image, then that could easily become another significant expense depending on the size of the job and the contractor you hire. Keep all these additional potential costs in mind as you consider buying the existing business.

Creating a Spec Sheet

A spec sheet is a summary of the business and includes the book value (total assets minus total liabilities and goodwill), market value (the book value figure adjusted to reflect the current market value of assets), and the liquidation value (how much the owner could raise if the business was liquidated). Earnings potential should also be considered.

If the value you arrive at is significantly different from what the owner is asking for the business, ask the seller how he or she arrived at the price. You can then make your offer based on your estimate of worth and the owner's asking price. You don't need to accept that the business is actually worth what the owner thinks it is.

The real worth of a business is in its continuing profitability, so examine the financial records closely (especially the profit and loss statements and cash flow statements) to get a good idea of what your revenue would be, as well as your expenses and net income. Try to buy a business for its annual profit. Don't be distracted by the listed price.

One helpful resource is the Due Diligence Checklist at FindLaw.com. The full website address is **http://smallbusiness.findlaw.com/starting-business** (click on "More Topics", then on "Buying an Existing Business" then on "Due Diligence Checklist" under Tools & Resources). This checklist shows you everything that you should check out about any business you're thinking of purchasing in areas like the business's organization and good standing, financial statements, physical assets, real estate, and much more. Be sure to consult this checklist or one like it as you perform your due diligence investigation.

The Canada One Business Tools website has an excellent page at **www. canadaone.com/tools/buy_a_biz/index.html** (scroll down to "Section II: Assessment and Valuation"), that details everything you need to consider when purchasing an existing business. Information includes advice on how to determine asset and earnings value, how to valuate a business and a detailed list of questions to ask when looking at a business you're thinking of purchasing.

Purchase Price

Purchase prices are determined by a number of factors. These include region and neighborhood location, profit and local economy, potential growth, and the owner's own sense of what the company is worth based on reputation or goodwill. BusinessesforSale.com, Business Nation, the Business Resale Network and others offer listings of many types of businesses that, for whatever reason, are being offered for sale. These sites list each business's asking price, and usually state its turnover and profit.

Expect to pay anywhere from around $100,000 to upwards of $500,000 for an existing wine store. This usually will include all contents of the shop and often means taking over an existing lease or rental agreement for the location. Often, the lower priced wine stores you will see for sale will not include inventory, so be sure to check whether or not inventory is included in the asking price.

Many existing stores for sale also operate as liquor stores, and sell spirits and beer as well as wine. You can purchase a liquor store and then gradually phase out the other revenue streams, while keeping and enhancing the wines offered. However, you should keep in mind that you'll need to thoroughly research the location to be sure that it can support a wine-only store.

Starting your own store requires a lot of energy and devotion — whether you build from scratch or buy an existing store. You should plan on waiting two to five years to earn back your purchase price.

Recent listings of wine store businesses for sale on these websites included:

- An established liquor store in a strip mall in Connecticut with $200,000 in annual revenues for $51,000. Inventory valued at $45,000 was not included in the purchase price. The price did include furniture, fixtures and equipment. The owners were selling because they wanted to start a larger store.

- A combination wine and gourmet foods store in a leased location for sale in North Carolina for $75,000. Furniture, fixtures and equipment were included in the asking price, but inventory valued at $15,000 was not included. The owner was willing to train prospective buyers.

- A wine shop with a wine bar and restaurant in Maryland for $480,000. All furniture, fixtures and equipment were included in the asking price, as was inventory. The owner was willing to train. The reason for selling was that the owner wanted to get out of the business to pursue other interests.

You can search for other wine stores for sale at the following websites:

- *BusinessesforSale.com*
  (Includes business for sale in the U.S., Canada, U.K. and other countries)
  www.businessesforsale.com

- *Business Nation*
  www.businessnation.com/Businesses_for_Sale/ Retail/Liquor_Stores/

- *BizQuest*
  www.bizquest.com/buy

- *BizBen (California only)*
  www.bizben.com

Try entering the keywords "wine shop" or "wine store" into each website's search engine or search by industry. All of these sites also have a category of liquor stores for sale under "Food and Beverage" or "Retail".

TIP: Beware of business for sale websites that require a fee or ask for personal information to view their listings. Real Estate agents make their money on sales and not on people browsing.

Financing

Some owners will allow you to finance an existing business if you can come up with a good down payment but are unable to purchase it outright. Many of the owners of the businesses for sale at the websites above are willing to negotiate financing with potential buyers. Be sure you understand the terms of any financing you set up with the seller. See a lawyer before agreeing to anything.

If you are considering borrowing from a lending institution such as a bank then financing an existing, profitable business is much less of a risk than starting a new one. A lending institution will want to see your detailed business plan before agreeing to lend you any money. (See section 3.4 for more on how to write a business plan, and section 3.5 for more about financing your new business venture.)

Making an Offer

When you have done your research, figured out what the business is worth and decided you want to buy the business you may then decide to make an offer, possibly less than the asking price based on your own valuation of the business. Usually the owner then will make a counteroffer. Keep in mind that you may have less leeway to negotiate a better purchase price if the owner will be financing the purchase for you.

You will usually be asked to pay a non-refundable deposit. This is standard and ensures the owner that you are a serious buyer. Be sure to get a deposit receipt and get any purchase agreement in writing after you've arrived at a mutually agreeable price. Also be sure that every important detail about the purchase is mentioned in the contract. Because so much money is at risk, a lawyer should draw up or at least review the contract before either party signs.

Buying an Existing Building

A second option rather than buying an entire business is to buy an existing building in which to set up shop and then move your business into it. The obvious advantage here is that buying an existing building often is less expensive than buying an established business along with the building housing it. Another aspect to consider is that, as already mentioned, if you buy an existing business you inherit both advantages and disadvantages from the previous owner.

One advantage of buying a building is that it most likely has already passed fire and building codes, unlike a new project that will require inspections and approval by municipal authorities before you can occupy it. Be sure to check first with zoning laws to be sure you're safe to operate your business there.

There are disadvantages as well. The building may require heavy infrastructure repairs (such as utilities or plumbing) or you might have to completely remodel the interior. Repair and remodeling costs can be expensive, even into thousands of dollars, so be sure to inspect the building carefully for any structural problems before you buy it.

Do a thorough investigation of the building's interior and exterior. Check the electrical systems, cooling and ventilation systems, bathrooms, walls and ceilings. If possible, interview the previous owner and ask about any potential problems that might create extra costs for you.

You should consider hiring a building inspector to conduct a thorough, professional evaluation of the property. Hiring a professional building inspector, though an added cost to buying a building, could save you from a disastrous purchase (and thousands of dollars in repairs) so consider finding one to look at any property you're thinking about purchasing. To find building inspectors in your area, check the Yellow Pages under "Building Inspection Service."

Dealing with Contractors

By the time you and a contractor agree on a job and sign a contract, he or she should know exactly what needs to be done. At this point you have to let the contractor do the job and not stand in the way with second-guessing questions. If you researched the contractor well and signed a comprehensive contract, then you should have nothing to worry about.

In regard to payment, beware of any contractor who demands money in advance. The best working contractors have credit accounts with suppliers and will not need money up front to buy materials. On large projects a contractor may want to be paid a portion of the money before the completed assignment.

A common payment schedule may be:

- 35% of the total payment is due at the half way point

- 50% more of the total payment is due after the completion

- 15% of the remaining balance is paid 1 month after the completion

Every contractor is different and may prefer a different payment schedule, perhaps with money due at the 30% or 40% mark. Use your own judgment here, but remember that professionals do not demand too much too soon, and are willing to put everything in writing.

In dealing with contractors, it is very important to be clear and firm in your communication. You and the contractor(s) must be clear about total costs, even if you pay in installments. Both parties must clearly understand the quality of materials that are to be used as well as the time frame that is set to finish the work.

You must be careful not to pay contractors too much money too soon. Unfortunately, not all contractors are as honest as you would like them to be, so make sure you only pay for work that has been completed. You owe it yourself and your business to get every agreement you make in writing. Never take anyone just at their word.

Building Codes and Inspections

If you are building a new wine store, you will need a building permit which can be obtained by contacting your local city or county building department. The department will review your blueprints and make sure that your plans are up to date with current building codes of the city and state. If you're not sure of your municipality's building codes, then it may help to hire or consult with an architect to help design your store. An architect will be familiar with the local building codes and can also offer advice on market-friendly designs.

A municipal building inspector will usually come during the construction process whenever an important job is completed, for instance an electrical system. The building inspector will then sign off on the building permit whatever was just inspected. After construction and set-up is complete, upon a final passing inspection, a certificate of occupancy will be issued.

Fire Codes

One important part of building a safe commercial business is meeting fire code requirements. Every locality has strict rules about building a safe property with convenient emergency exits. Failure to include an adequate fire escape may mean that your building will not pass the building code, and will have to be remodeled at your additional expense.

If you are purchasing an existing property you will still need to keep up to date with certain building requirements. For instance, fire extinguishers must be inspected and passed in order for the city to give you a favorable inspection.

3.2.2   Franchising

If you are eager to start your own store, but are concerned about the many facets involved in getting everything set up, you may want to consider franchising.

Franchising is a business model which allows someone (you) to run a local business using an established regional or national company or corporation name, logo, products, services, marketing and business systems. The original company is known as the "franchisor" and the company that is granted the right to run its business the same way as the franchisor is known as the "franchisee."

You have probably bought products and services from many franchises. Burger King, Wendy's and many other fast-food outlets are franchises, as are many others. Recent figures from industry analysts estimate that franchising companies and their franchisees accounted for more than $1 trillion in annual U.S. retail sales from 760,000 franchised small businesses in 75 industries so clearly franchises can be very successful business models to start with.

Pros and Cons of Franchising

Often, people who choose to franchise do so because they want to minimize their risk. By working with an established system, franchisees hope to avoid costly mistakes and make a profit more quickly, especially since the business probably already has name recognition, products and marketing concepts that are popular among the public.

Franchising offers some unique advantages. Buying a ready-made business means you do not have to agonize over the minute details of a business plan, you do not have to create a logo and letterhead, and the organization of your store is already done. Plus, there is less risk with a ready-made business with a proven track record.

Franchises are good for people who want support running their businesses. The franchisee may receive assistance with everything from obtaining supplies to setting up record keeping systems. Many franchisors are continuously working to develop better systems and products and you can take advantage of those developments.

Franchisors typically provide a complete business plan for managing and operating the establishment. The plan provides step-by-step procedures for major aspects of the business and provides a complete matrix for the management decisions confronted by its franchisees.

If you choose to franchise, remember that although you own the store you do not own any of the trademarks or business systems. A franchisee must run their business according to the terms of their agreement with the franchisor. In exchange for the security, training, and marketing power of the franchise trademark, you must be willing to give up some of your independence. If you are a person who likes to make most decisions on your own or to chart the course of your business alone, a franchise may not be right for you.

Since someone else is ultimately "in charge," you may be wondering how having a franchise is different than being an employee. In fact, there are significant differences. You have more freedom than an employee; for example, you might choose your own working hours. And you could ultimately earn a lot more money than an employee.

On the other hand, franchisees must pay thousands of dollars up front for the opportunity to work with the business. In addition, you will be required to cover your own operating costs (including the cost of staffing your store to the levels required by the franchisor), pay a franchise fee and a percentage of total sales.

Costs

Entrepreneur Magazine describes a franchise fee as a one-time charge paid to the franchisor "for the privilege of using the business concept, attending their training program, and learning the entire business." Other start-up costs may include the products and services you will actually need to run the business, such as supplies, store fixtures, computer equipment, advertising, etc.

The fees for operation will vary from franchise to franchise, and may rely heavily on location, but expect the franchise fee to be somewhere between $25,000-$50,000, with additional start-up costs.

There are a variety of factors involved in determining the initial investment. For example, if you are interested in operating a Wine Styles franchise, the average investment will cost anywhere between $150,000 to more than $350,000 depending on the geographic location and the size of the store. Most franchise owners obtain financing for their business by providing approximately 35% of the total capital, and then arrange a business loan from a local bank or investors for the balance of the total investment required. (See section 3.5 for more information on start-up funding.)

In addition to your initial investment, you can expect to pay the franchisor ongoing royalties, generally on a monthly basis. These royalties are usually calculated as a percentage of your gross monthly sales, and typically range from 2 percent to as much as 10 percent; the exact amount will depend on the company you franchise with. This is the corporation's cut for providing you with their business model and good name.

Choosing a Wine Store Franchise

It is important to do your homework on the company you are interested in franchising with — gather all the information you need to make an informed decision. Speak with other people who have invested in the company you are investigating and have an attorney examine the franchisor's contract.

Get some professional opinions on any franchise opportunity you're interested in. Work with an attorney who understands the laws associated with franchising. Also, you may want to work with an accountant to examine your anticipated expenses, your financing needs, and your prospects for achieving your desired level of profitability before you sign any agreement.

Key points to research:

- The type of experience required in the franchised business

- Hours and personal commitment necessary to run the business

- Background of the franchisor or corporation

- Success rate of other franchisees in the same system

- Franchising fees to open the franchise

- Initial total investment required to open the franchise

- Cost of operation to continue the right to operate the business as a franchisee

- Any additional fees, products or services, such as advertising, that you must buy from the franchisor and how they are supplied

For excellent advice on franchising, visit the following websites:

- *Canadian Franchise Association*
  www.cfa.ca

- *Entrepreneur's Franchise Zone*
  www.entrepreneur.com/franchises/index.html

- *Small Business Administration: Buying a Franchise*
  www.sba.gov/smallbusinessplanner/start/buyafranchise/

There are a few companies offering franchise opportunities in the wine retail market. Their specialties are varied so no matter what type of retail franchise you're interested in, you'll probably find one that fits your needs and interests.

Here are a few well known franchises for you to consider. Please note that this list does not represent our endorsement of any of these businesses. They are provided for information purposes only. Only you know which franchise, if any, is right for you.

Wine Styles

Wine Styles has 128 franchisees in the United States. Wine Styles stores offer wine for sale classified according to its own system, a monthly wine club, and sells gifts and accessories, as well as gift baskets. They offer 5 days of training at the company's headquarters and 3 days of on-site training at your location. Ongoing support includes a company newsletter, purchasing cooperatives, Internet support, marketing support including regional and national advertising, etc.

Address:	5100 Copans Rd., #310 Margate, FL 33063
Phone:	954-984-0070
Contact:	**info@winestyles.net** or call 866-424-9463
Website:	**www.winefranchise.net**
Franchise Fee:	$25,000, and royalty fee of 6% on gross sales
Initial Investment:	$229,000-$381,000

Vino 100

Vino 100 offers "100 wines for less than $25". Their target market is wine buyers who want help choosing wines of good quality and at a lower price. They offer franchisees training at their company training facility, on-site training at your location, help with computer systems, etc.

Address:	3 Bala Plaza East, Suite 102 Bala Cynwyd, PA 19004-3481
Phone:	866-846-6425
Contact:	**www.vino100.com/application.fx**

Website:	**www.vino100.com**
Franchise Fee:	$30,000
Initial Investment:	$145,000 to $400,000+

Vintner's Cellar

Vintner's Cellar has approximately 60 locations in the U.S. and Canada. This franchise is a micro-winery where customers make their own wines, as well as a retailer. They also offer a wine club. They offer training for one week at company headquarters and one week's training at your location. Ongoing support includes a company newsletter, Internet support, co-op advertising, etc.

Address:	4020 Somers Dr. Flint, MI 48529
Phone:	810-743-9463
Contact:	**michael.eccles@vintnerscellar.ca**
Website:	**www.vintnerscellar.com**
Franchise Fee:	$45,000, and no royalty fees
Initial Investment:	$120,000 to $191,000

3.2.3   Opening a New Wine Store

Of course, you can always start from scratch and open a brand new store. That way, you can have complete control over every step of the process and make sure that your shop is everything you want it to be. The information in the rest of this chapter will show you how to do just that.

3.3   Choosing a Store Name

If you decide to start up your own store from square one, choosing a name may be one of the most important decisions you make for your new business. You want something catchy that will draw people into the store while clearly indicating it is a wine store.

If you have the financial resources, you could hire a naming professional to help you choose the right name for your company. Known as name consultants or naming firms, these organizations are experts at creating names, and can help you with trademark laws.

> **TIP:** Business names don't have to be trademarked, but having them trademarked prevents anyone else from using the same name. Trademark laws are complicated, so if you think you want your company name trademarked it's a good idea to consult a lawyer with expertise in that area.

Most people starting up a new retail store, however, don't have the money necessary to hire professional name consultants. The cost of these services can start at a few thousand dollars. Instead, to come up with a name yourself, consider your niche and what types of customers you are trying to reach. You might even hold a brainstorming session and enlist family and friends for suggestions. If somebody comes up with a really good one, you'll probably know it right away.

Here are name samples from the wine store owners we surveyed.

- D'Vine Wines

- House Wine

- Brix26 (a reference to sugar measurement and grape ripeness)

In most jurisdictions, once you have chosen your business name you will also have to file a "Doing Business As" (DBA) application, to register the fictitious name under which you will conduct your business operations. The DBA allows you to operate under a name other than your own legal name.

Filing a DBA usually takes place at the county level, although some states require that you file at the state level, publish your intent to operate under an assumed business name, and sign an affidavit stating that you have done so. However, in most cases it's usually just a short form to fill out and a small filing fee that you pay to your state or provincial government. You can find links at the Business.gov website to the appropriate government departments where you can file your business name at **www.business.gov/register/business-name/dba.html**.

Trademarked Business Names

A trademark database lists all registered and trademarked business names. In the U.S., the essential place to start is with the U.S. Patent and Trademark Office. You can hire a company that specializes in this type of service to do a name search for you, if you choose. However, you can do an online search of the federal trademark database yourself to determine whether a name has already been registered. You can also do this at the county level or at the state level when you file for a DBA using the fictitious names database of the agency you're filing with. The fictitious names database is where non-trademarked business names are listed.

You can check trademarks at the United States Patent and Trademark Office (**www.uspto.gov/main/trademarks.htm**). In Canada, the default database for name searches is the Newly Upgraded Automated Name Search (NUANS). You can search the NUANS database at **www.nuans. com**. There is a $20 charge for each NUANS search.

If you would like to learn more about this subject, you can read an in-depth article about naming your business entitled "How to Name Your Business" at the Entrepreneur.com website. This article includes tips on how to brainstorm ideas for naming your business, as well as establishing trademarks and how to file a DBA. A related article, "8 Mistakes to Avoid When Naming Your Business" offers tips on avoiding some typical business naming mistakes. You can find both of these articles at **www. entrepreneur.com/startingabusiness/startupbasics/index144024.html** (click on "Naming Your Business" in the "Browse by Topic" section).

3.4   Your Business Plan

3.4.1   What to Include in a Business Plan

A business plan is a comprehensive report that lists all information of relevance to your business. A well written business plan is essential if you are looking for investors in your new venture or trying to secure financing, but even if you're not trying to entice outside investors you should still create a business plan in order to formulate marketing strategies and create a blueprint that you can use to model your initial activities and future growth.

There are three main parts of a business plan: the executive summary, the financial plan and the marketing plan, but you should also include any supporting documents that will help to clarify your situation or your qualifications. A good plan will help you over the rough spots by identifying where you might have slow cash flow during certain seasons (e.g. January when the holidays have ended and people are more reluctant to spend money on entertainment). A well-prepared plan will help you learn who your customers and competition are, to understand the strengths and weaknesses of your business, and to recognize factors that could affect the growth of your company.

A good business plan addresses all of the areas of concern for a start-up business, such as what your business objectives are; what kind of business you will be starting; details about running, financing and marketing your business; and includes any additional information about matters unique to your industry and business experience.

The following section details the main parts of a good business plan and offers some sample documents to guide you.

The Cover Sheet

Here you will list the legal names and contact information of all parties involved in the business.

The Statement of Purpose

This is brief statement explaining what is covered in this business plan and what the business objective is. The objective section should be less than one page. You will address all of the issues the outline raises, including the purpose of the plan, whether it is an operations guide or financing proposal.

Table of Contents

A table of contents should follow the statement of purpose in order, organizing the material in an easy-to-read, concise style. Text should always be comfortably spaced and organized with Roman numerals or numbers for large sections, and letters for individual parts. The easiest way to create a table of contents is to wait until you have finished everything else, and then use your finished report as a guide.

Executive Summary

In this section you will provide an outline of the fundamentals of your proposed business. What products will you sell? Who will your customers be? Who owns the business? What do you think the future holds for your business and your industry? If you're applying for a loan, your financier will want to know how much money you wish to borrow, what you will spend the money on and how and when you plan to pay it back. Try to make your summary concise, professional, enthusiastic and as complete as possible.

Description of Your Business (Company Profile)

The description of your business will demonstrate to lenders that your business is well thought out, and on the road to success. Lenders need to be convinced that their money will be wisely invested and need to see your idea presented clearly.

In your business description you will include the following:

- *Products and Services:* Provide a description in detail of what products and services you will be offering, such as wines, liquor, and beer for a retail store or types of drinks, food and other amenities you will be offering in a wine bar (if you're planning both).

- *Customers:* This is the section to give an overview of who you think will be buying your product. Are you planning to sell just to customers who walk through your door or are you opening an online operation, too? Are you selling to collectors of fine wines (if you're a retail operation)? Locals? Tourists?

- *Goals:* What would you like to achieve by opening your business? To be a million dollar per year wine retailer in five years' time and have a chain of wine stores? To offer lectures and wine-tasting events to teach the community about wine? Whatever your goals for your business, this is where to list them.

- *Store Appearance:* Describe how your store will look, from the exterior, to the flooring, to interior decor. Include merchandise display features, how traffic will flow through the store, as well as the total square footage of your business location. If you're planning a wine bar, too, include your bar's theme and how you will decorate and lay out your bar.

- *Unique Features:* What will separate your wine store from others? What strengths will your business have over others in your community or industry sector? What previously unfilled area of the industry are you filling? (This will also be a part of your marketing section.)

- *Management:* In this section explain the business's ownership and legal structure, whether you intend to have employees and who will manage them, and what training you will offer to them.

- *Start Up:* Lenders are particularly interested in how much you need to get you up and running. Provide an overview of your financing requirements including your own investment and sources of other investment capital. Explain your business registration, licenses, and insurance. This will be only a summary, and details will follow in your financial section.

Management Summary

Review your managerial resources and why you are qualified to handle this business venture. Items should include:

- Any and all managerial experience and operational experience you have

- Your management strengths and weaknesses

- Will you hire employees or consultants to assist you?

- Your education and how it will affect your type of business

- Personal data: Your abilities, interests, motivations and physical condition.

Personnel

Include a review of your proposed employees and what your criteria are for selection. Questions to answer:

- What are your employer needs now and what will they be in the future? (3-5 years)

- Do you have a staff assembled now? List them.

- What salaries are they paid and how?

- What are your company's policies on benefits, employment laws and overtime?

- Other resources you have acquired for legal matters and paper-work.

Summary of Your Business Plan

In approximately one page or less, summarize the important points of your business plan and why you are qualified to run a business. Be sure to touch on all the main ideas discussed above.

Marketing Plan

A profile of the market you'll be operating in follows the business description and explains specifics on who needs your product and why. Issues to address include:

- The demographics of your customers and the neighborhood

- The overall size of the market, any growth, and your expected share

- How you will satisfy the market as well as your plans to expand

- How you intend to price your products and what research was involved

- What share of the market you expect to have

- Barriers to your success

List methods of advertising and publicity you have planned, the frequency, and cost. Consider what sort of ads to place and in which magazines, newspapers, and other print media. A good website might help draw customers to you. Estimate your costs to produce an attractive website for your business and acquire a domain name.

The Competition

Businesses—yours included—compete for customers, market share, publicity and so forth. It's smart to know who your competitors are and exactly what they're doing. In order to provide services that are different and better, you need to look carefully at your competitors' products and services, how they're promoting them, and who's buying them.

Start by answering some basic questions about your competition:

Who are your nearest direct and indirect competitors?

List at least five other wine store owners in the area; also list other sources of wine including local grocery stores and liquor stores

How are their businesses doing?

You can discover this by conversing with the merchants, store employees and other knowledgeable wine contacts. A business report may be available online, or you could simply observe which days of the week seem to be the busiest. Take notes for a period of time and determine if their business is steady, increasing or decreasing.

What are they doing right?

What effective strategies do you see, from advertising to marketing to store operations? Why do a steady number of customers already shop at that location? Is it because of convenience or service?

What are they doing wrong?

What could improve your competitor's business? Can you think of something that would be more convenient to customers or encourage more sales?

How do their services, or even their products, differ from what you plan to offer?

Are there any drinks they do not offer, or do they lack a variety of some drinks? Can you think of ways to improve customer relations or even the store's layout and interior decoration?

Keeping a File

Common business plans often include a file of all your competitors by business name, and include all relevant marketing materials from competitors. These may be promotional materials, marketing techniques and pricing history. Over time you will start to notice patterns; perhaps the merchant holds special sales several times a year according to season or offers volume discounts, etc.

Save any promotional materials so that you can get ideas for your own advertising. Are competitors' advertisements or signs short and to the point or descriptive? How do they determine their prices? When they advertise a sale, how much do they discount a product from the regular price? Refer often to the competitor's file and think of every new business day as a new opportunity to compete.

Create a report on your closest competitors and why your business will improve upon their services. Issues to consider will include:

- An analysis of your five nearest competitors—what is their market share?

- The similarities and differences between their operations and yours

- Your competitors' strengths and weaknesses and how you can improve upon them

- How you will keep an eye on the competition in the immediate and distant future

Location of Your Business

This is a description of your business location and why the location is paramount to your plan. Questions will include:

- What are the benefits of your chosen location?

- Is your building located conveniently? Does it have parking for suppliers and customers?

- How will you determine target demographics in your location?

- Are you aware of local laws (zoning, legal) and how they will affect you?

Section 6.1 has additional information about marketing to help you generate ideas for your marketing plan, including different marketing strategies for wine stores and wine bars.

The Financial Summary

Your financial plan follows your marketing plan. This financial data includes important figures and projections for your business. If you are applying for a loan, provide details, including the expected effect of a loan. List other sources of financing.

Financial management is crucial to running a successful business. Your business financial plan should describe both your start-up costs and your operating costs. The start-up budget includes all the costs necessary to get your business up and running. Operating costs are ongoing expenses such as advertising, utilities, rent and so forth.

Remember to include the following items in your budgets. Notice that some expenses overlap on the start-up and operating budgets.

- *Start-up budget:* Legal and professional fees, licenses and permits, equipment, insurance, supplies, advertising and promotions, accounting expenses, utilities, payroll expenses.

- *Operating budget:* Make a budget for your first three to six months of operation, including expenses such as: personnel (even if it's only your own salary), insurance, rent, loan payments, advertising and promotions, legal and accounting fees, supplies, utilities, dues and subscriptions, fees, taxes and maintenance.

Your financial management plan also should address the accounting system you plan to use. Many small business owners conduct their own accounting, using software such as Quicken or QuickBooks, **www. quickbooks.intuit.com**, while others hire someone to set up a system for them.

Supporting Documents

In addition to a comprehensive business plan, include a financial report and any applications for financing. If you are applying for a small business loan then you must include supporting documentation to back up all your statements; these include your personal resume, job descriptions, credit reports, reference letters and letters of intent, contracts, leases and other legal agreements, personal financial statements and any other documents that will lend credence to your business plan.

3.4.2   Start-Up Financial Planning

Financial management is crucial to running a successful business. One of the first important questions you should find an answer for is how you will finance your monthly expenses until you turn a profit. These ongoing monthly costs will include things like mortgage, renting or leasing costs; employee wages; utilities, store supplies and so on. In addition, you'll need to decide how much you will pay yourself and your staff, how much you want to save for unexpected expenses, and how much you will put back into the business to finance growth.

When writing your business plan, be realistic. It is better to overestimate costs and underestimate profit. If you make more than expected in your first few months to a year, then so much the better. You will be in great shape!

Budgeting Basics

If you have ever sat down and calculated how much money you'll need for something like the family vacation by figuring out what your income and expenses are, you already know how to budget. The most difficult part of budgeting for a business is that unlike when you work for a steady paycheck, it's more difficult to project your expected income after you pay all your expenses out of your revenues.

To clarify the situation in your business plan you will need to determine, as best you can, both your start-up costs and your operating costs.

The start-up budget will include all the costs necessary to get your business up and running. Your operating costs will be all of the ongoing expenses once the business is in operation. In your planning, be clear about where the money is going and why, and explain how you came to your conclusions.

For starters, having a buffer of at least six months' finances available to cover your basic expenses is a good idea, just in case the business does not create a profit immediately. Many businesses will take up to a year to see a profit. Your store may show a profit sooner, but it's best to be prepared.

Here are some things you should consider when completing your revenue forecast and financial projections:

- Market trends and cycles

- Any seasonality of the business

- Varied sources of revenue

- Holidays (note that in the sample plan, revenues for December were projected as being higher than the months before and after)

- Unexpected events (such as equipment breakdowns, personal illness, etc.)

- How will you monitor your cash flow?

The financial section of your business plan will include your financial projections, break-even analysis, a projected profit and loss statement (also called an income statement), and information about your personal finances.

As mentioned in the previous section, remember to include the following items in your budgets:

- *Start-up budget:* Legal and professional fees, licenses and permits, equipment, insurance, supplies, marketing costs, accounting expenses, utilities, payroll expenses.

- *Operating budget:* Make a month to month budget for at least your first year of operations, including expenses such as: staff (even if it's only your salary), insurance, rent, loan payments, advertising and promotions, legal and accounting fees, supplies, utilities, dues and subscriptions, fees, taxes and maintenance.

You can get a good idea for the cost of many of these budget items by browsing business supply websites, talking with realtors for rental costs, and basing your wages at minimum hourly wage to start. You may want to pay higher than minimum wage to your staff in order to get more qualified employees. At times, you may have to make an educated guess based upon your research and your chats with other business owners.

List expected profits and/or losses for at least the first year, but preferably for three years. You will want to break this down on a month-to-month basis. Show where the money is going and how much you expect will come in. If the business plan is for a loan, explain how much you need to borrow, why you need that much (exact uses of money), and where you plan to obtain it.

Two sample start-up budgets appear on the following pages. The first outlines the costs involved in building out a new wine store, while the second shows a potential budget for renting a space for your wine store. In the second sample, notice where the changes in start-up expenses came from. Few expenses were eliminated entirely, as there are some costs that you just can't get away from. Air conditioning units and sealing off basements or large rooms for wine storage are necessary expenses, though perhaps you could find a better deal in a smaller town. Most of the cuts in expenses involve reducing the budget of inventory, staffing and marketing, along with plans for exterior construction.

Estimating Your Revenues

Depending on your geographic location, your revenues can be in the tens to the hundreds of thousands. Of course, this amount also varies greatly depending upon the demand for your products, what you pay to your suppliers, and how much you market your business.

Speak with other store owners in your general region of the country but are not competition for you. If you live in Indiana, consult with store-owners in Ohio, Illinois and Kentucky. If you live in California, consult with store owners up the coast, in Oregon or Washington for example. If you live in New York, consult with store owners in New Jersey.

Sample Start-Up Budget for Building Out a New Wine Store

CONSTRUCTION	
Architect	$1,500.00
Building Costs & Permits	$50,000.00
Plumbing & Electrical Work	$10,000.00
Total Construction	**$61,500.00**
LEGAL FEES & INVENTORY	
License & Permits (3 Years)	$5,000.00
Lawyer	$6,000.00
Start-up Inventory	$100,000.00
Working Capital	$10,000.00
Total Legal Set-Up	**$121,000.00**
STORE SET-UP AND DESIGN	
Sign & Exterior Decoration	$5,000.00
Interior Design	$5,000.00
POS & Software	$12,000.00
Security System	$2,000.00
Utilities Set-up	$1,000.00
Air Conditioning & Sealing	$19,000.00
Total Design	**$44,000.00**
MISCELLANEOUS	
Staffing & Payroll Taxes	8,000.00
Advertising	$2,000.00
Total Miscellaneous	**$10,000.00**
Total Projected Costs	**$236,500.00**

NOTE: This start-up budget does not include real property costs, which can vary widely by location.

Sample Start-Up Budget for a
Wine Store in a Rented Location

LEGAL FEES & INVENTORY	
Security Deposit	$1,000.00
License & Permits (3 Years)	$5,000.00
Start Up Inventory	$25,000.00
Working Capital	$5,000.00
Total Legal Set-Up	**$36,000.00**
STORE SET-UP AND DESIGN	
Sign & Exterior Decoration	$5,000.00
Interior Design	$5,000.00
POS & Software	$12,000.00
Security System	$2,000.00
Utilities Set-Up	$1,000.00
Air Conditioning & Sealing	$19,000.00
Total Set-Up Design	**$44,000.00**
RECURRING EXPENSES	
Rent	$2,000.00
Utilities	$500.00
Insurance	$1,000.00
Marketing	$2,000.00
Accountant/Book Keeper	$500.00
Total Monthly Expenses	**$6,000.00**
Total Projected Costs	**$86,000.00**

One way to figure out how much you will need to sell to make a profit is to figure out the average cost of your items. (We'll look at how to figure out a break-even point based on your estimated expenses, including inventory, a little later in this section.) Depending on the suppliers you will deal with, you might be able to get a copy of a wholesale catalogue or get access to wholesale prices on the supplier's website. You may have to open a merchant account with them first, though. Once you have done a little research on who your suppliers will be, you can go ahead and contact them to get more information about your initial inventory costs.

Sales Projections

Before you can start your budget, you must arrive at some reasonable monthly sales projections. Many business decisions will be based on the level of sales that you forecast, so if you're too optimistic, you might find your business in trouble. As mentioned earlier, it's always best to be conservative in your estimates.

Alternatively, if you underestimate the amount of sales, you might make decisions that hold back the growth of your business, such as deciding on a less-than-perfect store location because the rent or building purchase price is cheaper. A certain amount of "guesstimating" is required, but you can learn as much as possible about your market beforehand in order to make the estimates more accurate.

There are two types of revenue forecasting methods: Top Down Method and Bottom Up Method.

Top Down

The Top Down Method is what retail operations most frequently use because you can fairly accurately estimate your total market size and from that the amount of money you can reasonably expect to earn from sales.

To use the Top Down Method you must first estimate what the total sales potential would be. This type of information often can be gathered through the Chamber of Commerce, government census data, or from local, state, or national retailers' organizations. Then, by estimating what share of that market you can reasonably expect, you arrive at your possible sales for the year.

Calculation for Top Down Forecasting

Step 1:   Total market size x average annual spending (by customers in businesses like yours) per family or per person = total market potential

Step 2:   Total market potential (from Step 1) x number of competitors = average market share

Step 3:   Average market share (from Step 2) x your estimated percentage of market share = potential annual sales

Bottom Up

The Bottom Up Method is most often used when forecasting revenues from delivering a service. Depending on your business, you might need to use both Top Down and Bottom Up.

The Bottom Up Method is what you will use to calculate revenues from offering services only. Service revenues are limited by the number of hours you can reasonably work. You must first calculate your rate per hour (if you have several services you're offering, use an average price per hour and average production time to make the calculations easier).

Calculation for Bottom Up Forecasting

Step 1:   Hourly rate x number of hours available to work in a day = average daily sales

Step 2:   Average daily sales (from Step 1) x number of days you can work per year = possible annual sales

Step 3:   Possible annual sales (from Step 2) x expected rate of efficiency = projected annual sales.

NOTE: Rate of efficiency is usually about 50% in the first year. Any guaranteed contracts would have a 100% efficiency rate.

Operating Budgets

The first step in creating an operating budget is to determine what your monthly costs are. Take any bills, such as insurance and taxes, that occur either quarterly or yearly, and divide them by 4 (quarterly) or 12 (yearly) to find out how much you pay for those expenses each month.

Sample Budget Analysis for a Wine Store

Step 1: Data collected for the year projections

Description	Expenses	Revenues
Yearly projected revenue		$112,500
Lease	22,200	
Wages	18,000	
Loan repayments	8,000	
Office expenses	1,400	
Utilities	3,600	
Cost of Goods Sold*	27,900	
Taxes and membership fees	3,000	
Equipment & maintenance	5,000	
Advertising	4,425	
Totals	$93,525	$112,500

Yearly Net Profit = $18,975

Step 2: Monthly Budget Analysis

Description	Expenses	Revenues
Yearly projected revenue		$9,375
Lease	1,850	
Wages	1,500	
Loan repayments	667	
Office Expenses	117	

Utilities	300	
Cost of Goods Sold*	2,325	
Taxes and membership fees	250	
Equipment & maintenance	417	
Advertising	369	
Totals	$7,795	$9,375
	Monthly Net Profit = $1,580	

NOTE: The accounting definition of Cost of Goods Sold (COGS) is: opening inventory + cost of purchases – closing inventory. If you use inventory tracking software, you can get a good idea of your COGS on an ongoing basis, although this is not as accurate as doing regular physical inventory counts.

With these annual and average monthly figures projected, the retail owner can now take a look at where the money is being spent and make some informed decisions about how to cut back on some of the expenditures in order to grow profits. Coming up, we'll show you how to calculate a break-even point for your retail business based on the projections you have already made for your operating expenses.

If you'd like more information about budgeting for your business, check out the article, "Basic Budgets for Profit Planning", on the U.S. Small Business Administration website. The web page address is **www.sba. gov/idc/groups/public/documents/sba_homepage/pub_fm8.pdf**.

TIP: Every month, take a look at your expenditures and your sales, and update your budget and financial statements. A large setback, say purchasing an item that won't sell, or a repair to your vehicle, will mean you must redo your projections and budgets.

Calculating Your Break-even Point

Break-even analysis is a good way to find out how much you must sell in order to cover your costs. (You can compare the result with your projected revenues to see how they match up.) This is without profit or loss; profit comes after the break-even point. Figuring out your break-even point involves a fairly straightforward calculation. You must, however, have all the figures ready in advance before you can get an accurate number. In addition, in order to calculate the break-even point, you'll first need to break out fixed (non-controllable) costs like rent from variable costs like supplies.

Sample Break-Even Point

The formula is:

Break-even point = Total fixed costs ÷ (1 – total variable costs ÷ revenues)

Using the numbers from the sample budget analysis we did earlier, let's say your store has fixed expenses of $22,200 for lease payments and $8,000 for loan costs (totaling $30,200) during the first year. The rest of the budget expenses are variable costs, totaling $63,325. Based on revenues, variable costs are 56% (or in other words, for every dollar in sales, 56 cents is variable costs).

Here's how to calculate your break-even point:

Break-even point = Fixed costs [$30,200] divided by (1 minus variable costs [$63,325] divided by revenues [$112,500])

30,200 ÷ (1 - 63,325 ÷ 112,500)

30,200 ÷ (1 - 0.56)

30,200 ÷ 0.44

Break-even point = $69,000 (rounded)

The store will have to earn gross revenues of about $69,000 each year in order to break even. This company is operating at 112,500/69,000 or 163 % of break-even, meaning it is profitable. With these figures determined, you can now look at ways of reducing your variable costs as well as increasing your revenues to try to widen the gap between gross revenues and your break-even point. It's also a good way to see if your projected revenues are realistic when balanced against known expenses.

When Can You Expect to Turn a Profit?

This varies widely from region to region, store to store, and owner to owner. Most stores break even sometime during the first year. You can reasonably expect to start making profits after that time period.

A lot will also depend on your overhead costs. If you are running an Internet store with low overhead costs, you may turn a profit very quickly. Or if you are running the business out of your home and have no rent, then you may turn a profit more quickly than someone leasing space in a strip mall.

One idea might be to start small with an Internet or home-based store and then move to a larger space as your business grows. This way, you'll see a profit much quicker without the risk involved in investing your own or someone else's money.

3.4.3   A Sample Business Plan

Keep in mind that this is a somewhat simplified business plan. You will need to provide more detailed information in some areas, particularly in the financial section (including financial statements) of your plan.

Sample Business Plan: Life is a Cabernet

Cover Page

(Include the title, your name and contact information.)

Executive Summary

This business plan is the five-year operational blueprint for a unique new wine store, Life is a Cabernet, to be located at 123 Oak Street West, Mytown. The owner and sole proprietor plans to open during the fourth calendar quarter (October 1) to take advantage of the approaching holiday season's wine and spirits sales.

The store will occupy 1,400 square feet of retail strip mall space, with an additional 600 square feet in storage area equipped with a cooling unit to maintain fine wines at their optimum temperatures for short-term or longer-term storage. A two-year lease will cost $2,000 per month plus utilities.

Start-up costs of $75,000 will come from the owner's personal savings and a bank loan, and will include $45,000 for operating capital, store fixtures, cooling units and retail equipment such as cash register/inventory software, POS equipment, etc., and a starting inventory valued at $30,000. In addition to personal savings of $45,000 the owner will require $30,000 to cover costs of equipping the store.

The store will specialize in North American wines, with special attention to marketing to and educating its customers on the distinctive pleasures of domestic wines. In addition, the store will offer for sale wine-related items such as cork screws, gift bags, hats, books and other items of interest to wine enthusiasts. However, the store's main mission is to promote the sale of and educate customers about domestically produced fine wines.

Advertising and marketing efforts have been designed to bring attention to the store's unique business concept as well as to attract prospective wine enthusiasts from around the city, state and country. The store will sponsor wine-tasting events several times a year with the assistance of the local Tourism Board and the nearby Wine Valley Growers Association. With no other local wine store in the area offering a large and exclusive selection of North American wines, this is virtually an untapped market.

The store will be managed by owner Walter Wineseller. Mr. Wineseller has 12 years' experience managing a big-box liquor store in Big City, Oregon. In addition, he has completed a number of continuing education courses, including courses in entrepreneurship, marketing, bookkeeping and accounting. Assistant manager, Ima Winelover, who has worked as a professional sommelier at a variety of wine boutiques around the state over the past 10 years, will provide additional management experience. The store will hire full- and part-time staff as required and as growth allows.

The store can be operated with 2-3 staff members, including the manager or assistant manager. It will require only 3-4 staff during the busiest of times, and one or two most others. As it is highly computerized, inventory tracking and the creation of a customer database will be simple and effective.

With no similar wine store in our planned local area, we expect to turn a profit within the first year of operations. We estimate that, with the high volume of wine sales in our area and the lack of immediate competition, coupled with our unique business concept, we will capture approximately 10-15% of the local wine market in the first year. This translates to more than $100,000 in sales.

Both the location and the timing are perfect for starting this type of business in our community. We have identified a lucrative market niche that has gone unfilled before now. No other liquor store in the area offers the kind of products and services that we do. With the extensive experience and savvy business acumen of its management, Life is a Cabernet will be one of the most profitable wine retail stores in the area.

Table of Contents

(To be completed last.)

Business Location

Life is a Cabernet is situated in a strip-mall near the intersection of two main roads through town. The area is bordered by four residential areas mostly populated by young to middle-aged professionals. The strip-mall is always a very busy spot due to a chain discount supermarket, an organic food store, two busy restaurants, and numerous other businesses frequented by the local populace. The nearest large mall is located nearly 2 miles away, and our location is convenient for the local residents.

Description of the Business

Life is a Cabernet is planned as a wine boutique. As such, we will cater to the discriminating palate of the wine connoisseur, as well as to people interested in learning more about wine and trying new wine styles. We also plan to sell some wines that will appeal to occasional wine drinkers who don't wish to spend more than $15-20 on a bottle of wine.

The building is easily accessible by foot traffic from the nearby subdivisions, and the shopping center has a large public parking lot. Several shuttle buses that serve the surrounding housing developments are located just down the street with the last leaving at approximately 7:30 p.m. This is a situation very conducive to people coming from the downtown business areas doing some last minute shopping before heading home on the last shuttle bus.

The interior is essentially a large rectangle and currently has only a wall dividing the former retail store's storage area, and washroom. Therefore, extensive interior remodeling will need to be done. We plan to keep a portion of the rear of the store as storage space, but also assign about half the store to a walk-in refrigerator, a custom-built wine cellar, and wine racks.

The floor will be redone in laminate flooring throughout the sales floor area. This will make for easy clean-up, and the flooring is quite durable. We plan to purchase several display islands for our higher-end wine. The remainder of our wines will be displayed in shelving along the walls. We will also have a walk-in refrigerator for a small selection of premium beers, chilled wines, ciders, and coolers. The cash desk will be located near the front of the store.

The store will be open 7 days a week from 11:00 a.m. until 9:00 p.m. from Monday-Thursday and open until 10:00 a.m. Friday and Saturday nights. We will open limited hours on Sunday from 11:00 a.m. until 5:00 p.m. These hours are dictated by our liquor license.

Unique Features

The store will offer customers a unique atmosphere for trying and purchasing new wines. Its unique inventory will make the store a destination shopping for wine lovers from across the city. Our resident sommelier, Ima Winelover, will be on hand every Friday and Saturday to offer wine workshops, wine tastings, and other special events as our schedule allows.

We will also offer a special "Connoisseurs Club", to our customers. The Connoisseurs Club will meet once per month and will attract serious wine lovers as well as encourage new members to join who want to try new wines and learn more about wine in general.

Description of the Industry

According to figures from the Wine Institute, the average American in 2009 drank 3 gallons of wine per year. This is an increase of 4% from the previous year and an increase of 44% over a 10-year period. The most recent economic census data from the U.S. Census Bureau show that, while the number of establishments selling alcohol has decreased by 8%, sales per individual store have actually increased by 32%. This indicates that the retail wine industry has seen significant growth in sales over that period. Concurrent with the increase in sales has been the increase of Americans choosing wine as their beverage of choice.

Another factor in our favor is the fact that only seven establishments exist within a 20-mile radius whose primary business is as a liquor store, and none that sell primarily wine, while most other establishments that sell wine are grocery stores. With the selection of quality wines so limited, we believe that our business concept is well-placed to reap the benefits of a demand for a unique store with such a pleasant atmosphere to learn about and buy wines. A survey of wine enthusiasts by *Wine America Magazine* suggests that these consumers prefer an establishment dedicated to wine with excellent customer service when considering purchasing their wines. Our area has several clubs dedicated to wine tasting and appreciation whose members we believe will welcome our concept.

(*Wine America Magazine* is a fictional publication. A real business plan needs real data sources, which you can find online through resources such as the U.S. Census report on Statistics of U.S. Businesses at www.census.gov/csd/susb/susb.htm or through industry magazines and organizational reports. Each industry has its own organization.)

Business Legal Structure

Life is a Cabernet wine store is licensed as a Sole Proprietorship. We have chosen this business legal structure because the cost for incorporation or registering as a LLC are too high at this time. The additional reporting required is also considered burdensome.

(*Note to reader:* This may not be the best choice for you. Please read section 3.6.1 on legal structure and consult with a lawyer or other professional, if you are still uncertain.)

Target Market

The store's target market includes young urban professionals, occasional wine drinkers, and wine connoisseurs. According to the U.S. Census Bureau, an estimated 25,000 young urban professionals reside within a fifteen minute drive of our location, with an additional 300,000 suburbanites living a 15-minute drive away, many of whom fit the target demographic and pass by the area during the day.

The median income of those living in the area is $65,000 per year, and the median age of the target demographic is 37, with 55 percent of the total population over 35, 15 percent under 18, and 30 percent between 19 and 34. The store's location near a heavily populated area is ideal for attracting this group since there is no other outlet selling wines as varied as ours in this area. Other outlets that sell wine are selling primarily wines in the $5-$20 range, with an average selling price of about $10.

Marketing strategies will include promoting the store in conjunction with the local Chamber of Commerce's efforts, as well as hosting community wine tasting events, the Connoisseur Club, and a tasteful and informative website.

Products and Services

Life is a Cabernet will sell fine wines from around the world, and specialize in high quality domestic wines. The store will cater to the discriminating connoisseur as well as to the novice wine taster.

Each week a new wine special will be offered featuring a wine from a specific geographic region or featuring several characteristic wines of a type from different wineries and vintages. Wines from Europe, Australia, South America and North America will be featured.

The store will also host wine tasting events and establish a "Connoisseur Club" which will meet once each month to try a variety of wine varietals from around the world. We also plan to have guest speakers from wineries in our region, as well as well-known wine writers, come to the store to talk with our customers about wine in special workshop and wine tastings settings.

Modifications to our inventory will follow the interests of customers.

Promotion

We will run advertising in the local newspapers, through direct mail, and community announcement areas such as local radio, bulletin boards, and large signs. We will also develop a website and an email newsletter as cost effective methods of keeping in touch with customers. Database software will help us keep track of customers so we can send them promotional offers and news. In addition, we will hold events like wine tastings, wine writer appearances, etc., to draw new customers into the store.

Competition

While there are several liquor stores in the area offering a selection of wines, none offer the large and varied selection we will offer. Our only real competition in the fine wine sector is Mytown Wine Bar. Mytown Wine Bar opened approximately twelve years ago and with minimal advertising have developed a 30% market share. Although primarily a wine bar and restaurant, they do have a 300 square foot retail outlet attached to the business. However, they are located near the waterfront in the downtown core, and do not compete directly in our local area.

The other establishments selling wine are liquor store located about half a mile from us, the grocery store in the shopping complex, and several neighborhood liquor stores selling mainly beer and liquors. We don't see these as direct competition, since their target demographic is completely different from ours. Other indirect competitors include convenience stores nearby and several national chain grocery stores selling wine. However, these only compete against us in a limited way, since their primary focus is on food.

A Competitor Analysis table appears on the next page.

Table 1: Competitor Analysis

Factor		Strength	Weakness	Competitor:	Importance to Customer
	Life is a Cabernet			*Mytown Wine Bar*	
Products	Emphasis on world wines	X		Emphasis on domestic wines	High
Price	Slightly higher		X	Charges less	Medium
Quality	High	X		High	High
Selection	Greater selection	X		Lesser selection, mainly domestic	Medium
Service	More personalized service plus guidance on customer selections if desired	X		Service efficient Less guidance on selections	Medium-High
Reliability	Extremely reliable	X		Less reliable; not all staff as knowledge-able about wines as ours	High
Stability	Low - if we do not do well in the beginning success is threatened		X	Very stable and well established	Medium
Expertise	Very high; all staff knowledge-able about wine	X		Some staff are not wine experts	Somewhat high
Company Reputation	None		X	Good reputation in their market	High
Location	Prime location with lots of traffic	X		Prime location. Lots of traffic	Medium

Table 1: Competitor Analysis, continued

Factor	Life is a Cabernet	Strength	Weakness	Competitor: Mytown Wine Bar	Importance to Customer
Appearance	Professional and pleasant. Great atmosphere	X		Professional, clean, nice atmosphere, but busy at nights	Medium
Sales Method	Targeted advertising	X		Targeted advertising	Medium
Credit Policies	Accept credit cards, cash, debit cards	X		Same	High
Advertising	Well thought out, targeted advertising campaign	X		Does some advertising	Medium
Image	Upscale boutique; serving a wide customer base	X		Caters to a younger crowd	High

Management and Staff

The owner, Walter Wineseller, will oversee all responsibilities for financial management and major administrative functions.

Sommelier Ima Winelover will be hired to act as assistant manager and resident wine expert at a salary of $30,000 per year to start. This person will be responsible for overseeing store management when the owner is off duty.

In addition, two part-time staff will be hired immediately and additional part-timers will be hired as needed. Each staff member will be paid minimum wage or a slightly higher depending on their level of experience and value to growing the business. All staff will be fully trained in the store's business concept, knowledge of wines, beers and spirits, liquor laws, and in the use of the computerized cash register.

Financial Information

The owner will provide starting capital of $45,000 to pay for start-up costs. Little in the way of interior architectural redesign is required as this location previously housed a retail store. However, additional equipment needs to be purchased, such as cooling units and walk-in refrigerators. Therefore, $35,000 will be required to purchase this, as well as POS equipment, store fixtures and to decorate the interior. The owner is seeking additional start-up capital of $30,000 in the form of a loan or investment capital to commence operations.

The owner will also use his own computer for office purposes, but will purchase bookkeeping software.

Additional costs include office supplies, printing of business cards and menus, business and liquor licenses, annual liability insurance, worker's compensation insurance, attorney fees, and advertising. Internet access, web hosting, and telephone expenses are also included in the start-up costs.

Start-up costs will be paid using the owner's personal funds and investment capital or loan, and income from sales will be used to purchase new inventory, return the investment capital and dividend or pay down the loan, pay salaries and hire additional staff as required.

Risks

As with any business venture there are risks associated with opening this store. One possibility is that our main competitor, Mytown Wine Bar, might decide to incorporate a greater selection of wines in their menu. However, we see this as a remote possibility since they would need a larger retail store in order to do this. As the wine bar is well established it is doubtful they would move to another location.

Another risk might be that Mytown Wine Bar might lower its prices and try to undercut us. Since our prices will be higher than theirs to start with, this may impact us if their profit margins are a bit wider than our own. We cannot afford to take a smaller profit margin. On the other hand, we are also in a higher traffic area than they are and we still expect wine enthusiasts to prefer our greater selection and convenient location.

We believe that our sales targets are realistic based on our market research, but there is always the possibility that our target sales will not be achieved for the year. We will closely monitor revenues on a daily, weekly and monthly basis to ensure that our sales targets are being reached, and if they are not, we will make every effort to discover why not and correct any issues we discover. Start-up capital will carry the store's expenses through the first six months of operations.

[You should include any additional risks that you can think of that might affect your business.]

Cash Flow

Excluding the spike in cash flow for holiday sales increases, we project positive cash flow beginning in April of next year. Following are our cash flow projections for the first six months of operations.

Life is a Cabernet Cash Flow Projections: 1st Six Months of Operations

	Sept	Oct	Nov	Dec	Jan	Feb
Cash on Hand	$75,000	$4,900	$3,600	$4,013	$9,607	$5,757
Sales Revenues	10,000	17,250	21,563	32,344	11,500	8,000
Total Cash and Sales	**85,000**	**22,150**	**25,163**	**36,357**	**21,107**	**13,757**
START-UP EXPENSES						
Construction	$20,000					
Computer and POS	5,000					
Furniture & Fixtures	20,000					
Opening Inventory	25,000					
Total Start-up Costs	**70,000**					

Life is a Cabernet Cash Flow Projections: 1st Six Months of Operations, continued

	Sept	Oct	Nov	Dec	Jan	Feb
ONGOING EXPENSES						
Rent	$2,000	$2,000	$2,000	$2,000	$2,000	$2,000
Advertising	200	200	200	100	100	100
Accounting	300	300	300	300	300	300
Legal	300	150	150	150	150	150
Telephone	100	100	100	100	100	100
Utilities	750	750	750	750	750	750
Wages	4,000	4,000	4,500	5,000	4,000	4,000
Taxes	800	800	800	800	600	600
Office supplies	200	100	100	100	100	100
Inventory purchases		8,700	10,800	16,000	5,800	4,000
Loan repayment	1450	1450	1450	1450	1450	1450
Total Ongoing Expenses	**10,100**	**18,550**	**21,150**	**26,750**	**15,350**	**13,550**
Cash Ending	**$4,900**	**$3,600**	**$4,013**	**$9,607**	**$5,757**	**$207**

[You should create a month by month cash flow projection sheet for the entire year to include in your business plan, rather than the six months in our example.]

Statement of Net Assets

Following is the statement of net assets representing the personal assets and liabilities of Walter Wineseller.

Personal Assets & Liabilities of Walter Wineseller

ASSETS	
CURRENT ASSETS	
Cash	$45,000
Investments (401K)	$10,000
TOTAL CURRENT ASSETS	**$55,000**
LONG-TERM ASSETS	
Automobile	$12,500
Home Equity	$125,000
TOTAL LONG-TERM ASSETS	$137,500
TOTAL ASSETS	**$192,500**

LIABILITIES	
CURRENT LIABILITIES	
Car Loan Payment	$400
Mortgage Payment	$650
Utilities and Other Expenses	$750
Property Taxes	$1,500
TOTAL CURRENT LIABILITIES	$3,300
LONG-TERM LIABILITIES	
Car Loan	$9,000
Mortgage	$150,000
TOTAL LONG-TERM LIABILITIES	$159,000
TOTAL LIABILITIES	**$162,300**

TOTAL NET ASSETS	**$30,200**

[For a start-up company, one without business assets and liabilities, you should create a balance sheet like this to represent the owner(s) total personal assets and liabilities.]

Other Items

In addition to the items listed above, your business plan might include things such as a statement of personal finances (this can include a print-out of your credit history and tax returns), a resume, reference letters, and other items. It is up to you if you want to include these things. Always err on the side of giving more information, especially if you are unsure if you can secure a loan based on the information you're providing to lenders.

Another item you might want to add is a loan proposal or request for funding. In the example financial statements above, the owner will need an additional $30,000 in start-up funding to add to the owner's $45,000 cash in personal assets to carry the business through the first six months of operations.

A lender or investor will want to see a loan proposal or request for funding detailing how much money you want to borrow, what you plan to spend the money on, and how you plan to pay it back. Under this heading, state the amount of money you are asking for, whether it is a debt or equity funding request (i.e. if you are borrowing money, that is debt funding; if you are asking someone to invest in your business as a shareholder or minority partner, that is equity funding), how you plan to repay a loan, or what an investor gets out of investing in your company.

Your loan proposal should include:

- How much money you want

- How long it take you to pay it back

- Details of how you plan to spend the money

- How you will get the money to pay back the loan

- A description of your own personal assets and other collateral that you can use to secure the loan

If your business will need start-up financing, section 3.5 coming up will tell you how to go about finding it.

3.4.4   Business Plan Resources

You can find a free sample business for a wine store business at **www.bplans. com/wine_store_business_plan/executive_summary_fc.cfm**. Here are some additional resources that you might find useful in helping you to write your business plan:

- *SBA: Writing the Plan*
  www.sba.gov/smallbusinessplanner/plan/ writeabusinessplan

- *Canada Business: Preparing a Business Plan*
  www.canadabusiness.ca/eng/86/

- *SCORE: Business Plan Templates*
  www.score.org/template_gallery.html

- *BDC (Canada) Business Plan Template*
  www.bdc.ca/en/business_tools/business_plan/default.htm

TIP: When writing your business plan, pay close attention to spelling and grammar, and try to write clearly and concisely. You don't want to make reading the plan a chore.

3.5   Start-Up Financing

This section covers sources of start-up financing, and what you'll need to present to lenders in order to apply for funding. Additional advice on all aspects of financing your business can be found at the SBA's Small Business Planner website at **www.sba.gov/smallbusinessplanner** (under "Start Your Business", click on "Finance Start-Up" then choose "Financing Basics"). In Canada, visit **www.canadabusiness.ca/eng/125/142**.

3.5.1   Getting Prepared

When looking for funding, you must first be well prepared before approaching any potential loan or investment sources. You will need the following things:

- *A Business Plan:* As you learned in the previous section, a business plan is the document that lenders will review to decide whether or not to give you a loan. This document is absolutely necessary for banks or other lenders, and even if you are getting the start-up money you need from a rich aunt, you should prepare your business plan and present it so the person lending you money can see that you have a clear and organized plan. (If you haven't read it already, see section 3.4 for advice on creating a business plan.)

Your financial statements are a particularly important part of your business plan.

- *A Personal Financial Statement:* This should be prepared as part of your business plan. It is important because you need to have a clear picture of your own financial state to know exactly where you are financially before you begin. This financial statement will tell you:

  - How much money you need every month to pay your bills

  - What kind of resources or assets you have

  - What kind of debt you carry. How will you repay this debt while you are putting your total effort into opening your store?

- *A Start-Up Survival Nest Egg:* Many financial consultants think that having a nest egg to live on while you are starting up your store is one of the most important things you can have. Some suggest at least six months' of living expense money — that is, all the money you will need monthly to pay all your personal living expenses, bills, and debts, so you can focus on your new retail business without stress. This is apart from any reserve start-up capital you might need for the business itself.

Asking for Money

Keep these tips in mind when you ask someone for funding:

- Get an introduction or referral. If you can get someone who is respected in the community to introduce you to a potential lender, it gives you credibility and that's a big advantage.

- Have an extra copy of your business plan available for the potential lender's inspection, and be able to speak clearly and concisely about your plans. Be able to discuss all aspects of your business plan, your long-range goals and your prospective market.

- Be professional. Shake hands, speak with confidence and look the person you're talking to in the eye.

- Dress to impress. You're going to be a business owner. Be sure you look the part.

- Be receptive. Even if you don't end up getting any money from a prospective lender or investor, you may be able to get ideas and suggestions from them. Perhaps they'll have some pointers regarding your business plan, or some suggestions about steering your business in a particular direction. Don't be afraid to ask questions, either.

Remember that if someone agrees to loan you money or invest in your business, they're doing so because they believe in you and what you can do. When you ask someone for money, you need to sell yourself and your ideas. Make sure you have a great sales pitch.

There are a number of online resources to help you find out more about financing options for your business. The SBA link noted above is a good place to start in the United States. In the "Start Your Business" section of the Small Business Planner, open the "Finance Start-Up" link and scroll down to find Loan and Funding information. In Canada, you can try Industry Canada's "Search for Financing" page at **www.canadabusiness.ca/eng/82/**.

Now that you know the basics, you are ready to determine who you will approach for your funding.

3.5.2   Equity vs. Debt Financing

In business, there are two basic kinds of financing: equity financing and debt financing. Essentially, equity financing is when you agree to give someone a share in your business in exchange for an agreed amount of investment capital from that person. Debt financing is, as you probably already know, borrowing money at interest that you pay back in installments over time or in a lump sum at a specified future date. (Or repayment could be a combination of these; the point is, you'll pay interest). The decision to choose debt or equity financing usually will be based on your personal financial position and how much additional money you need in order to get your business started.

One form of equity financing is investment capital provided by venture capitalists. You'll want to look for an individual or investment firm that is familiar with your industry. You'll have less explaining of your business concept to do and they might be more open to investing in a company such as yours whose premise they already understand.

While a venture capital investor won't expect you to pay interest and regular monthly installments, they will expect some kind of return on their investment. This could include dividends paid out of your net income, the right to interfere with operations if they think they could do better, or the right to resell their interest to someone else for a higher price than they originally paid for their share of your company. Make sure that you are comfortable with the terms of any investment capital agreement, and that it clearly specifies what your obligations are. Check with a lawyer if you're not sure.

Another form of equity investment comes from your circle of friends and your family. You might be able to get a no-interest loan from a family member or a close friend, with the promise to pay them back at a time in the future when your business is self-sustaining. This is an ideal situation for you so long as the lender has no expectation of "helping" you run your business if you're not comfortable with that. You may also decide to bring in a friend, business acquaintance, or family member as a partner if they have some capital to invest to help cover start-up costs.

Debt financing is any form of borrowing, including a loan, lease, line of credit or other debt instrument on which you must pay interest in order to finance the original principal amount. Sources for this kind of financing include banks, credit unions, credit card companies, suppliers, and so on. If you buy a computer system for your company and pay for it in monthly installments over a couple of years, that is a form of debt financing since you will pay interest on the amount you finance. In the following sections we'll look at some of the sources of each type of financing and the advantages and disadvantages to each.

3.5.3 Borrowing Money

You can choose to utilize any mixture of the financing suggestions that follow. Many new business owners choose a mix of some of their own savings, a family loan, and a small business loan. Only you can decide which financing sources will be the best ones for your business and your personal situation. The most important thing is to make sure you agree to loan repayment terms that you can live with and that are realistic for you.

Commercial Loans

Commercial loans are loans that you can get from a financial institution like a bank or a credit union. You can go to your neighborhood bank around the corner to set up all your small business banking needs, or you can shop around for a bank that will offer you the best loan terms possible. The terms of your loan will depend upon several things:

- Your credit score

- Your collateral

- Your ability to pay back a loan

There are a number of different loan types you can enter into with these financial institutions. They offer both long-term and short-term loans. For example, you might choose an operating term loan with a repayment period of one year. This will help you finance your start-up costs such as buying equipment and inventory or pay for any renovations you might need to do.

> **TIP:** If you're looking for a long-term loan of less than $50,000 the bank will probably consider it a personal loan. As a result, they will be more interested in your personal credit history, and they may require you to put up personal assets such as real estate as security.

You might also choose a business line of credit if your situation warrants such an arrangement. In this setup, the bank will grant you what is in essence a revolving loan in a specified amount, and will honor any checks you write to pay for your ongoing business expenses. You will pay interest on any amounts outstanding under the line of credit.

Remember that lines of credit are to be used to pay for operating expenses as needed. Don't abuse the privilege by going out and buying thousands of dollars worth of office equipment or a new car for the business. If you do, then you won't be able to meet the projections you gave the lender when you presented the business plan to them. Those projections are why you got the line of credit in the first place.

Operating term loans and lines of credit, particularly if they are unsecured by assets (or other collateral), will have higher rates of interest attached. In some cases, the lender may require that you offer some sort of security for the loan, such as having a co-signer or putting up your personal assets against it. Some lenders may accept inventory (usually at 50% of your cost to purchase it) as a portion of collateral. Another consideration is that your interest rate will change as the bank's interest rates fluctuate.

You might choose a long-term loan, rather than short-term financing, if you need to do major renovations or building, or take out a mortgage if you intend to purchase a building as your retail location. One advantage to this type of financing is that the interest rates are usually lower. This is because the loan is paid back over a longer period of time than an operating term loan or line of credit, and you pay interest at a fixed, instead of a variable, rate. Another reason interest is lower is that the loan is backed by the value of the asset you're purchasing. This makes repayment of the loan more likely. (The lender can always sell an asset like a building if you default on the loan.)

One major disadvantage to a long-term loan is that you will have a debt burden that you will need to carry for a number of years. This can affect your company's growth because you might not have the liquidity you need to pay for expansion or to pursue new lines of merchandise. You might also have to pay a financial penalty if you decide to pay back the loan earlier. Consider all your options carefully before you enter into any kind of long-term debt arrangement. Speak with an accountant and a lawyer first.

Personal Loans

One of the greatest resources for your start-up money will always be the people you know who believe in you and your ideas—your family and friends. Very often they will help you with money when all other resources fail you. They usually will agree to payback terms that aren't as strict as commercial lenders, and they are usually pulling for you, too. As with any other kind of loan, it is important to make sure that you and the other parties completely understand and agree to the terms of the loan. Also, make sure to put everything in writing.

Another possibility is to ask a family member to co-sign a commercial loan for you. Co-signing means that this person agrees to take on the financial responsibility of the loan if you should fail. Family members are often willing to help you out this way. Make sure, before friends or family members help you out by co-signing a loan, that they are really comfortable doing so.

3.5.4   Finding Investors

Venture Capital and Investment Capital Investors

Depending on the type and size of your business, you might consider finding investors to help you with your start-up capital. You find may find that some investors are not willing to invest venture capital in a small, single-location retail store, however, many small retailers have gone on to grow their companies into regional or national chains. So this type of investment may well be something you'll want to look into for the future. As you'll see later in this section, there are ways to find investors willing to put money into small businesses.

Remember that investors are looking to make money by investing their capital in your business. They may or may not be people you know, but they will want you to show them how they will make a profit by helping you. You have to assure them that they will get something out of it, because for them investing in your store isn't personal (like it might be when a family member invests in your business), it is business.

Investors work one of two ways:

- They want to see their initial money returned with a profit
- They want to own part of your business

While investment capital might seem like a great idea, be aware that many entrepreneurs have been burned when venture capital vanished when the start-up money was needed. As mentioned earlier, the investment agreement could contain unsavory terms that give too great a portion of control to the investor instead of leaving it in the hands of the company owner.

However, on the plus side, private investors can be more flexible to deal with than lending institutions like banks. They may not want to get too deeply involved with the day-to-day management of the company. They might also be more willing to accept a higher level of risk than a bank, trusting in your skills and knowledge of the industry and leave your assets unencumbered.

To find venture capital investors beyond your immediate circle of family and friends, you can investigate some of the resources found at the websites listed below.

- *VFinance*
  www.vfinance.com

- *Angel Capital Association Member Directory*
  www.angelcapitalassociation.org/dir_directory/directory.aspx

- *Venture Capital in Canada*
  www.ic.gc.ca/eic/site/ic1.nsf/eng/h_00073.html

You can also find investment capital through the Small Business Administration's Small Business Investment Company (SBIC) program. While the SBA does not act as an intermediary on behalf of entrepreneurs, they do have a wealth of information about the process of finding investors on their website at the "SBA Entrepreneurs Seeking Financing" link below. You can use their services to help you put together a business plan and a request for funding package (see more about this in section 3.5.5), which you can then submit to SBICs that might be interested in providing you with investment capital. You can search for SBICs to match your needs at **www.sba.gov/aboutsba/sbaprograms/ inv/esf/INV_DIRECTORY_SBIC.html**.

- *PrivateEquity.com*
  (Click on "Private Equity Firms".)
  http://privateequity.com

- *National Association of Investment Companies*
  www.naicvc.com/Home/FullMembers.aspx

- *The National Association of Small Business Investment Companies*
  www.nasbic.org/?page=SBIC_financing

You have to decide what you want. Do you feel you will be able to meet the investor's terms? Do you want to share ownership of your business with another person? For some new business owners, the perfect solution is to find a person who wants to partner with them, share the responsibility of their new store, and bring some money to invest.

Partners

One of the simplest forms of equity financing is taking on a partner. Having a partner in your business brings additional skill sets, business contacts and resources to the venture. Most importantly, a partner can bring money to help pay for start-up costs and assist with ongoing operations. You'll need to decide whether your partner will be active in the running of the company or just a silent partner who invests the money, receives income from the business, but has no say in how things are run. (You can read more about Partnerships as a form of business legal structure in section 3.6.1.)

You as an Investor

Never forget that you might be your own best source of funding. One nice thing about using your own money is that you aren't obligated to anyone else or any other organization—it is yours to invest. This can be an excellent solution for individuals with some credit problems. To raise your own capital, you can:

- Cash out stocks, bonds, life insurance, an IRA, RRSP, or other retirement account

- Increase your credit on charge cards (remember that you will pay high interest rates on these)

- Use personal savings

- Take out a second mortgage or home equity loan on your house or other property

- Sell something valuable, like a car, jewelry, real estate, or art

3.5.5   Government Programs

Small Business Administration Loans

The Small Business Administration (SBA) doesn't actually lend you money. However, they have a program called the "7(a) Loan Program" in which they work with banks to provide loan services to small business owners. The SBA guarantees a percentage of the loan that a commercial lender will give you, so that if you default on your payments, the bank will still get back the amount guaranteed by the SBA. Both the bank and the SBA share the risk in lending money to you. As the borrower, you are still responsible for the full amount of the loan.

When you apply for a small business loan, you will actually apply at your local bank. The bank then decides whether they will make the loan internally or use the SBA program. Under this program, the government does not provide any financial contribution, and does not make loans itself.

The SBA also provides a pre-qualification program that assists business start-ups in putting together a viable funding request package for submission to lenders. They will work with you to help you apply for a loan up to a maximum amount of $250,000. Once the loan package has been submitted, studied, and approved by the SBA, they will issue a commitment letter on your behalf that you can submit to lenders for consideration.

In essence, the SBA gives lenders the reassurance that they will pay back the loan if you don't. They provide the extra assurance that many lenders need to get entrepreneurs the financing they need. You can read more about the process at **www.sba.gov** (click on "Services" then on "Financial Assistance").

The SBA also has a "Micro-Loans" program, which offers loans to start-up and newly established businesses through non-profit entities at the local level up to a maximum of $35,000. The average loan is about $13,000. Interest rates for these small loans vary between about 8 to 13 percent. You can find out more about these loans at the SBA website.

Government Programs in Canada

If you are planning to open a retail business in Canada, you might be interested in the Business Development Bank of Canada (BDC) or the Canada Small Business Financing Program (CSBF). The BDC is a financial institution owned by the federal government that offers consulting and financing services to help get small businesses started. They also have a financing program aimed specifically at women entrepreneurs. You can learn more about the Business Development Bank of Canada (BDC) and its financing resources at **www.bdc.ca**.

The Canada Small Business Financing Program is much like the SBA 7(a) Loan Program mentioned earlier in this section. The maximum amount you can borrow is $250,000, and the funds must be used to purchase real property, leasehold improvements or equipment. The CSBFP works with lenders across the country to offer loans at 3% above the lender's prime lending rate. To find out more, visit **http://strategis.ic.gc. ca/epic/site/csbfp-pfpec.nsf/en/la00049e.html**.

3.6   Legal Matters

3.6.1   Your Business Legal Structure

One of the most important aspects of starting your own business is deciding the best legal structure for your new company. This is important because your business structure will directly affect your income and even your assets, should the company suffer losses. There are five business structures to choose from in starting a new wine company.

Sole Proprietorship

A sole proprietorship is any business operated by one single individual without any formal structure or registration requirements. A sole proprietorship is the simplest and least expensive business legal structure when you are starting out. It is also the easiest because it requires less paperwork and you can report your business income on your personal tax return. One drawback to this type of business is that you are personally liable for any debts of the business.

As a sole proprietor you can start your business simply by getting your store open. However, local municipalities require business licenses and permits. The costs of these licenses are usually minimal, but be sure to check with your local municipal licensing office.

Here are some of the advantages and disadvantages of starting your wine business as a sole proprietor:

Advantages

- Easy to start

- Low start-up costs

- Flexible and informal

- Business losses can often be deducted from personal income tax

Disadvantages

- Unlimited personal liability: the sole proprietor can be held personally responsible for debts and judgments placed against the business. This means that all personal income and assets, not just those of the business, can be seized to recoup losses or pay damages.

- All business income earned must be reported and is taxed as personal income.

- More difficult to raise capital for the business

Partnerships

Another business structure that some business owners choose over sole proprietorship is the partnership. A partnership is precisely as its name implies, a business venture entered into by two or more people with the intent to carry on business and earn profits. Partnerships can be beneficial since the workload and finances can be shared, and partners with differing areas of knowledge can increase business opportunities.

You must register your partnership with a corporate registry. This does not mean that you must incorporate, only that you are making a formal declaration of entering into business with another person or persons. Be sure to consult your local business registry and a lawyer specializing in business registry. The primary purpose for doing this is for all partners to protect themselves concerning issues such as sharing profits, liability and dissolving the partnership equitably.

Beyond any legal issues, before going into business you should spend some time talking with your partner(s) about how you will work together, including:

- What each of you will be responsible for
- How you will make decisions on a day-to-day basis
- What percentage of the business each of you will own
- How you see the business developing in the future
- What you expect from each other

During your discussions you can learn if there are any areas where you need to compromise. For example, one of you may want to start your business as a part-time job, while the other wants to work full-time and eventually build a business that will employ a dozen or more people. You can avoid future misunderstandings by putting the points you have agreed on into a written "partnership agreement" that covers any possibility you can think of (including one of you leaving the business at some point in the future).

Below are some of the advantages and disadvantages to partnerships:

Advantages

- More initial equity for start-up costs
- Broader areas of expertise can lead to increased opportunities
- Lower start-up costs than incorporation
- Some tax advantages

Disadvantages

- All partners are equally liable for the others' mistakes with the same liability as a sole proprietorship
- Profits and losses must be shared
- The business must be dissolved and reorganized when a partner leaves

Incorporation

Incorporation of a business means that a separate, legal corporate entity has been created for the purpose of conducting business. Like an individual, corporations can be taxed, sued, can enter contractual agreements and are liable for their debts. Corporations are characterized by shareholders, a board of directors and various company officers. In this model, ownership interests can be freely transferred.

Creating a corporation requires filing of numerous documents to legalize your business, as well as formally naming a president, shareholders, and director(s), all of whom can be a single person as set out in the company charter. Since the rules and forms required for incorporation vary from jurisdiction to jurisdiction, it's best to consult your local business licensing office or a local lawyer specializing in incorporation.

Here is a list of some of the advantages and disadvantages to incorporating:

Advantages

- Protect personal assets and income from liability by separating your business income and assets from your personal.

- Corporations get greater tax breaks and incentives

- Ownership can be sold or transferred if the owner wishes to retire or leave the business

- Banks and other lending institutions tend to have more faith in incorporated businesses so raising capital is easier

Disadvantages

- Increased start-up costs

- Substantial increase in paperwork

- Your business losses cannot be offset against your personal income

- Corporations are more closely regulated

An S Corporation is similar to the corporation in most ways, but with some tax advantages. The S Corporation can pass its earnings and profits on as dividends to the shareholder(s). However, as an employee of the corporation you do have to pay yourself a wage that meets the government's reasonable standards of compensation just as if you were paying someone else to do your job.

Limited Liability Company

A Limited Liability Company is a newer type of business legal structure in the U.S. It is a combination of a sole proprietorship (where there is only one member of the LLC) or partnership and a corporation, and is considered to have some of the best attributes of each, including limited personal liability.

An LLC business structure gives you the benefits of a partnership or S Corporation while providing personal asset protection like a corporation. Similar to incorporating, there will be substantial paperwork involved in establishing this business structure. LLCs have flexible tax options, but are usually taxed like a partnership.

Here are some of the advantages and disadvantages of LLCs:

Advantages

- Limited liability similar to a corporation
- Tax advantages similar to a corporation
- Can be started with one (except in Massachusetts) or more members like a sole proprietorship or partnership

Disadvantages

- More costly to start than a sole proprietorship or partnership
- Consensus among members may become an issue
- LLC dissolves if any member leaves

In the end, choosing a business legal structure for your company is a personal choice, and the advantages and disadvantages should be considered thoroughly. Many small business owners begin their independent venture as a sole proprietorship because of the low costs, and incorporate as the business grows and becomes larger and more complex.

For more on business structures take a look at the resources available at FindLaw.com (**http://smallbusiness.findlaw.com/business-structures**). For some additional government resources to help you decide which structure to choose, try the SBA Small Business Planner at **www.sba. gov**. In the "Start Your Business" section, open the "Choose a Structure" link. In Canada, you can find more information about business structures at the Canada Business Services for Entrepreneurs website (**www. canadabusiness.ca**). Click on "Starting a Business," then on "Getting Started, "and choose the "Forms of Business Organization" Fact Sheet.

3.6.2   Business Licenses

Regardless of what form of legal structure you choose for your business, you'll need to obtain business licenses. This is not a difficult task. All it normally entails is filling out some forms and paying an annual license fee. Contact your city or county clerk's office for more information about registering your business. Contact information can be found in your phone book or online through resources such as Business.gov at **www.business.gov/register/licenses-and-permits**.

There may also be a number of other permits and licenses you will need:

- EIN (Employer Identification Number) from the IRS or a BN (Business Number) in Canada. All businesses that have employees need a federal identification number with which to report employee tax withholding information.

- Retail businesses that collect sales tax must be registered with their state's Department of Revenue and get a state identification number. In Canada, you will need to register to collect the Goods and Services Tax (GST), as well as provincial sales tax (except in Alberta), or Harmonized Sales Tax (the HST blends provincial sales tax and GST together in one tax).

- If you are putting up a new building for your store, you will need to ensure you have appropriate permits and comply with any requirements for zoning or access for people with disabilities (see section 4.1.2).

- Occupancy Permit You'll need this permit if you are starting up a wine store in a building that has never been zoned for that use before, particularly if you're adding a wine bar to your operation. You'll need to meet all the requirements of zoning, fire code, customer capacity, etc., in order to be approved. Inspections are required. Check with your local zoning board or city hall. (See section 4.1.2 for more about zoning issues.)

Finding Information about Licenses and Permits

For information about local, state, and federal requirements in the U.S. visit the SBA Small Business Planner (**www.sba.gov**) and choose "Get Licenses and Permits" in the "Start Your Business" section.

In Canada, business licenses are issued at the municipal level so check with your local municipality for help with acquiring a business license. For a province-by-province list of Canadian municipalities and their websites, visit the BizPal website at **www.bizpal.ca/part_partners. shtml**. Many municipalities offer business license applications right on their websites.

3.6.3   Licenses to Sell Alcohol

You will need a license to sell alcohol, whether you focus on just wine or want to include liquor or beer sales. The requirements for licensing will differ from state to state, and depending on municipality. Some cities don't accept new applications for alcohol licenses, so the only way you'll get one is to buy it from an existing business. You'll need to check with your state and local liquor licensing boards to find out what is required in your area. You can find links to state liquor licensing boards at **www2.potsdam.edu/hansondj/stateandlocallaws/1137435991.html**.

Many municipal codes by state are available at **www.ordlink.com/codes. htm** (when you find your municipality, look for a business licenses link). Your liquor license has to be prominently displayed at all times. Expect a 3-6 month wait for approval of this license, although you might receive it faster (or slower) than that.

For the most part, state licensing is provided to merchants based on the kind of business they run. Many states will separate the alcohol license according to wine, beer and spirits. Wine and beer licenses are always less expensive than a liquor license, and bar or restaurant licenses where liquor is served on the premises are the most costly.

The following licenses may be required depending on the design of your store.

Licenses You May Need

Eating place or restaurant license

This could include licenses for beer, wine or both. This primarily means that beer or wine could be consumed on-premises or be sold for off-premises consumption. Sometimes the state license may require that alcohol is not your primary revenue source, in which case you would not need this license. However, other states may require a restaurant license or a restaurant-brewer license if you plan on serving beer for on- or off-premises consumption.

Club licenses for beer, wine and liquor

These are for private on-premises consumption of alcoholic beverages. This license may be required if you plan on having special events in which drinks will be consumed, but that are not available to the public.

On-premises license for beer, wine and liquor

This is the usual license required if you want to serve drinks on-premises. Wine and beer licenses cost less than a full-scale liquor license. This may also be broken down into a tavern license (for wine and beer) or may require that some food to be served along with alcohol.

Liquor, beer and wine retail store license

Wine and beer licenses are less expensive than liquor licenses, but a standard wine or liquor license may not give you the right to sell beer. In any event, this retail license applies to alcoholic beverages sold for off-premises consumption. However, if the right is available in your state, you could buy a special on- and off-premises retail license allowing your customers to sample drinks. The law also may regulate wine supplies sold in stores.

Other alcohol related licenses and permits

Your state may require special licenses for:

- Transporting alcoholic beverages for commercial purposes

- Importing wines from overseas or other states for the purpose of resale (might apply if you plan to find your own unique wines for sale rather than relying on one domestic wholesaler)

- A staff training permit, allowing your employees to legally serve alcohol (if you're planning to add on a wine bar) after completing a training program

Laws Affecting Wine Stores

There are many laws that regulate retail wine and liquor stores over and above the minimum age requirement. For one thing, in most states private consumption of alcoholic beverages by minors is tolerated. Some states allow minors to be present in alcoholic beverage stores (or even work in such a store) so as long as they do not consume or handle an open beverage. Similar regulations are in place in Canada.

State Prohibitions

The state may also restrict when and how you sell your drinks. A state can set your schedule for you, forbidding sales of alcohol for off-premises consumption on certain days, holidays, or specific hours of the night. Many states forbid sales of alcoholic beverages on Sundays, whereas others will require that Sunday sales be postponed until noon or later.

In some states you will be legally restrained from selling certain drinks depending on the type of store you have. Specialty liquor stores might be state-controlled, meaning beverages over a certain amount of alcoholic content cannot be sold by a private retail wine store. Some counties may ban certain drinks or deny new liquor licenses based solely on a town's population. For links to state and provincial Alcohol Beverage Control Boards in the U.S., Canada and Puerto Rico, visit the Alcohol and Tobacco Tax and Trade Bureau website at **www.ttb.gov/wine/control_ board.shtml**.

Dry County Laws

Dry counties are counties that will not tolerate wine or wine store own-ers and prohibit completely the sale of alcoholic beverages. These juris-dictions are a throwback to Prohibition days, and thankfully are not to be found on a state level. Some dry counties may prohibit the sale of al-cohol, but not private consumption. Also, some counties, though being classified as dry, are really "moist" in that they allow the sale of alcohol to take place if the merchant follows strict guidelines. Some guidelines include:

- Stocking beverages such as beer or wine that are less than a speci-fied percentage alcohol content.

- Arranging a private club membership at a restaurant that allows customers to order alcoholic beverages.

- Closing on Sunday or at night in respect to the religious commu-nity

Some county laws may sound contradictory or even bizarre to the aver-age wine store owner, but government officials have already approved these laws and they mean business. Selling alcoholic beverages in a dry town is illegal and a violator could be charged with a misdemeanor or even a felony depending on the location.

Keep in mind that prohibition in dry counties applies not only to selling alcoholic beverages, but even in transporting sealed alcoholic bever-ages. Make sure you know the laws of your community and do what's best for your business—that is, moving away from the dry county!

The Legal Drinking Age

The first rule to consider if you're selling alcoholic beverages is the minimum age for drinking and purchasing them. There are different laws regulating the purchase of alcoholic beverages as well as private consumption. The National Minimum Drinking Age Act (1984) in the U.S. sets the minimum age for the purchase and public possession at 21 years of age, although the Act does not specify a minimum drinking age. Individual states have dif-fering laws for the consumption of alcohol. Check your state to see what regulations apply to your business.

In Canada, the legal age for purchase and consumption of alcohol varies by province, but the range is 18-21 years. Are you thinking of opening a wine store in France? You can actually serve 16 year olds and not be in violation of alcohol laws. There are some countries that forbid the sale, purchase and consumption of alcohol and other countries with no regulations whatever. Check the laws regulating alcohol purchase and consumption in your area to be sure you are in compliance.

In some states, under certain circumstances, alcohol can be purchased by a legal guardian for a person less than 21 years of age. The National Institute on Alcohol Abuse and Alcoholism (**www.niaaa.nih.gov**) reports that 31 states have exceptions to laws about underage persons purchasing alcoholic beverages.

However, the general rule is that minors must be accompanied by a legal guardian when entering your premises or may be banned altogether. Always verify a customer's age information if there is any doubt since merchants can be held criminally liable for underage sales.

Most states have a statutory defense available to merchants who have been duped by a minor who created a fake driver's license or some other form of ID. Nothing is for sure in life, however. Remember that you as a merchant have the right to refuse service to any customer based on suspicious evidence provided.

Other Regulations

Your state or province may demand that retail stores selling alcoholic beverages be placed a specified distance from a nearby church, hospital or school. This is why it's important to make sure you choose a contractor who is familiar with building codes and immediately inform the city of your blueprints as soon as you're serious about building a new wine store.

There may be sign requirements including a 51% sign that explains that the possession of a concealed weapon on the premises is illegal. (The 51% means that alcohol sales constitutes more than half of the total gross receipts; hence any wine or liquor store). Another sign that may be required is the consumption warning sign stating it's a misdemeanor to consume alcoholic beverages on the premises, provided you do not have a special retail license exempting your business. Contact your state alcohol beverage control board for more information on sign laws.

Fees

Fees for licenses are determined by local municipalities which are governed by the limits set by state or provincial law. Some licenses can be very expensive with one-time fees over $10,000, along with renewable license fees perhaps as much as $20,000. Some jurisdictions may actually have a moratorium on new license applications, so the only way you'll get a license is to purchase an existing store or purchase the license of a store going out of business. Licenses in this type of situation can be expensive due to their limited availability.

How to Apply

Don't apply electronically unless you know you are dealing directly with the state. The standard way to apply is to contact the city or town clerk to begin opening paperwork, as well as to check your state Alcoholic Beverage Commission for further requirements. If you're counting on a successful grand opening with no licensing problems then hire a reliable attorney to guide you through the process.

3.6.4   Small Business Taxes

Knowing your tax responsibilities and staying on top of them is an absolute must when you operate a wine store. Understanding the tax system for small businesses is essential and enlisting the services of a good tax professional will help you meet your business tax obligations in a timely manner.

Get Informed First

The best thing you can do to be sure of your personal and business tax obligations is to find the information you need before you start your new store. The Internal Revenue Service (IRS) has a number of informative documents online that you can look at today to learn the basics about everything you need to prepare for your taxes as a small busincss owner. If you read these documents and understand them, you will have no surprises at tax time.

One helpful document is the Tax Guide for Small Businesses that outlines your rights and responsibilities as a small business owner. It tells you how to file your taxes, and provides an overview of the tax system for small businesses. You can find this document at **www.irs.gov/pub/ irs-pdf/p334.pdf**. For more general information for small business owners from the IRS visit their website at **www.irs.gov/businesses/small/ index.html**.

For Canadian residents, the Canada Revenue Agency also provides basic tax information for new business owners. This includes information about the GST, how to file your taxes, allowable expenses and so on. You can find this information and more helpful documents at **www.cra-arc. gc.ca/tx/bsnss/menu-eng.html**.

It is also important to be informed about your tax obligations on a state and local level. Tax laws and requirements vary on a state-by-state basis and locally, too. Make sure that you find out exactly what you are responsible for in your state and city. In addition, it is important to find out about sales tax in your area.

The Federation of Tax Administrators website provides information on a state-by-state basis for personal, sales and other taxes. Visit **www.tax admin.org/fta/link**. Look for a "Businesses" or "Small Business" link (or something similar) on your state's revenue agency website. Canada Revenue Agency has a linked directory of government websites at **www. cra-arc.gc.ca/tx/bsnss/prv_lnks-eng.html** where you can find tax information on a province-by-province basis.

Tax Preparation

Once a year it's tax time and that means income tax on top of self-employment tax. Depending on your finances, income tax could be anywhere from 15% to nearly 40% of your gross income. Self employment tax for social security can be another 15%. The more money you make the fewer exemptions and deductions you can claim.

The fact that you will be charged according to your gross personal income (meaning your take-home profit) is somewhat satisfying, though it doesn't change the fact that you will probably pay more than you need to if you don't know how to file your income tax. Well, of course anyone could read the instructions and figure out the paperwork. But do you truly know what you're doing according to IRS regulations? Do you know what's deductible and what isn't and the rights you are entitled to?

You probably don't, unless you're a certified public accountant, who certainly do make a lot of money but who don't have the honor of handling fine wine ten hours a day. It's best to hire a CPA to do your tax preparation for you—particularly if they have experience in handling accounts from wine and liquor stores. You could choose to file on your own, though this would take considerable time researching the laws applicable to you at the IRS website.

Business Legal Structure and Tax Benefits

You may be surprised at the tax benefits offered to you depending on your chosen business structure (see section 3.6 for more on types of legal business structures to choose from). For example:

Sole Proprietorships

If you hire family members you may be exempt from certain payroll taxes and child labor laws. There are also a few legalities on hiring your spouse and borrowing money in his or her name, that may help save you money.

S Corporations

Filing as an S corporation entitles you to take large amounts of money from the business while still receiving liability protection. S elections allow the corporation to be exempt from corporate income tax in exchange for the tax burden devolving to its shareholders.

C Corporations

Some advantages of a C corporation are increased fringe benefit plans and investment privileges. Companies with profits totaling more than $1 million usually find it more beneficial to file as a C corporation. It is the ideal choice if you want to put away money for savings.

Limited Liability Companies

LLCs can be very flexible in choosing tax classifications and planning. However, they are also known to be confusing to owners and accountants alike. You can also change your company from an LLC, which is a friendlier structure for offsetting first year losses, to an S corporation status when you start to make a profit.

Documenting Profit And Loss

Every business operates under the same basic principle in profit and loss: you record every single sales transaction that takes place and document your totals for the day. You document sales tax as well as your income tax and this may involve totaling receipts by the month, the year or quarterly. Keep all your receipts and be ready to explain large deductions such as travel expenses, entertainment, home office expenses and automobile usage to your accountant as well as the IRS.

The old-fashioned way of tracking income was to simply record all of your daily income on a bank deposit slip, make regular deposits, and then figure out the specifics at the end of the year. However, classifying the different types of income early on will simplify all of your tax season paperwork. Whether you sort out these figures yourself or if you pay a CPA by the hour, it will save you time and money to get organized early in the year.

Other Important Tax Reminders

If you get behind in taxes owed, you can make installment payments. This is usually done over a 12-month period, and you must pay off one installment agreement before the IRS will grant you a second. You are also expected to make installment payments regularly or else the IRS could cancel the arrangement and demand full payment.

On the other hand, the IRS is not so quick to stretch out payroll taxes over time. The IRS also has a program for discounting tax debts for companies that are in serious financial trouble, called an Offer in Compromise. Ask your accountant about it rather than assuming your career is over at the first sign of trouble.

Report all income including any barter income. When in doubt, report all of your money or trades to your accountant who knows the best way to report it.

Mail out 1099 forms (miscellaneous payments to non-employees) to recipients. Failure to do this can result in large penalties.

Getting Assistance

If you decide you would prefer a qualified tax professional to help you handle your taxes, you will find you are in good company. Many small business owners decide to have a professional handle their taxes. An accountant can point out deductions you might otherwise miss and save you a lot of money.

One resource that may assist you in choosing an accountant is the article "Finding an Accountant" by Kevin McDonald. It offers helpful advice for finding an accounting professional whose expertise matches your needs. The article is available at **www.bankrate.com/brm/news/advice/19990609c.asp**.

Once you've determined what your accounting needs are you may be able to find a professional accountant at the Accountant Finder website (**www.accountant-finder.com**). This site offers a clickable map of the United States with links to accountants in cities across the country. Alternatively, the Yellow Pages directory for your city is a good place to find listings for accountants.

You will also need to understand payroll taxes if you plan on hiring employees. Each new employee needs to fill out paperwork prior to their first pay check being issued. In the U.S. this will be a W-4 and an I-9 form. In Canada, the employee will have to complete a T-4 and fill out a Canada Pension form.

Both the W-4 and the T-4 are legal documents verifying the tax deductions a new employee has. The amount of tax you will withhold as an employer varies and is based on the required deductions an employee has as specified by the federal government. Make sure you retain the forms in a folder labeled with their name and store them in a readily accessible place such as a filing cabinet in your office.

Check with your state or province's labor office to make sure you are clear about all the forms employees must fill out in order to work for you. The sites below give more information on legal paperwork, including where to get blank copies of the forms your employees will need to fill out.

- *SmartLegalForms.com*
  (Sells employee forms online)
  www.hrlawinfo.com/index.asp

- *GovDocs Employee Records and Personnel Forms*
  (Click on "Employee Management")
  www.hrdocs.com/Posters/hrproducts

- *Canada Revenue Agency*
  (Download and print any form you need)
  www.cra-arc.gc.ca/forms/

3.6.5 Alcohol-Related Taxes

There are various alcohol-related taxes you need to be aware of when you start your wine store.

Special Occupational Tax (SOT)

Opening a new establishment that sells any alcoholic beverage will require a special occupational tax paid at the federal level. This tax is owed even if you don't make a profit or are exempt from certain income taxes. Visit the Alcohol and Tobacco Tax and Trade Bureau of the U.S. Treasury at **www.ttb.gov/tax_audit/fed_tax_stamp.shtml** for forms and more information.

Federal and State Excise Tax

Excise tax is different from sales tax in that it is charged on the actual product purchased or manufactured and not simply on total sales. State excise tax is charged differently for wine, beer and spirits. Visit the TTB's page on excise tax at **www.ttb.gov/faqs/genalcohol.shtml#g2**.

Visit the Federation of Tax Administrators at **www.taxadmin.org/fta/rate/tax_stru.html** for more information and to review state excise tax rates. You can see state wine tax rates at **www.taxadmin.org/fta/rate/wine.html**.

Direct–to-Consumer and Interstate Shipping

Some states are very friendly towards interstate and direct-to-consumer sales, while others consider it a felony. As a direct-to-consumer seller you could also owe special taxes to those states that tightly regulate interstate alcohol sales. Visit the TTB website at **www.ttb.gov/publications/direct_shipping.shtml** to read more about direct shipping laws and the National Conference of State Liquor Administrators' website (**www.ncsla.org/states.htm**) to find state-by-state laws.

Local State Laws

Paying your primary retail tax on alcohol will depend upon which state you live in. Every state has specific requirements for the sale of alcoholic beverages. Your first point of contact, after the Revenue Department for taxing issues, will be with the State's Alcohol Beverage Board (ABB). Different states have different identifiers for these offices including "Department of Liquor Licenses Control" and "Alcoholic Beverage Regulation Administration."

The TTB provides a list of ABB contact information for all 50 states (and areas in Canada) at **www.ttb.gov/wine/control_board.shtml**. Contacting the state beverage board is the best and easiest way to ensure you legally establish your business.

3.6.6   Insurance

Insurance can help protect the investment you make in your company from unforeseen circumstances or disaster. Types of insurance for a retail business include:

Property Insurance

Property insurance protects the contents of your business (e.g. your computer, your merchandise, etc.) in case of fire, theft, or other losses. If you lease space, you may need property insurance only on your own merchandise and equipment if the owner of the building has insurance on the property.

If your store is robbed and your wine is damaged or stolen, property damage insurance may or may not cover all of your lost wine expenses. Ask your insurance agent if all of your wine products are covered in your property insurance or if you're expected to pay for any losses out of your own pocket. Some more expensive bottles of vintage wines might need to be insured separately.

Liability Insurance

This insurance (also known as Errors and Omissions Insurance) protects you against loss if you are sued for alleged negligence. It could pay judgments against you (up to the policy limits) along with any legal fees you incur defending yourself. For example, if a customer is somehow injured inside your store, or gets into their car and drives away drinking the bottle of wine they just purchased from your store and gets into an accident.

> TIP: For some small businesses, getting a Business Owner's policy is a good place to start. These policies are designed for small business owners with under one hundred employees and revenue of under one million dollars. These policies combine liability and property insurance together. Small business owners like these policies because of their convenience and affordable premiums. You can find out more about these policies at the Insurance Information Institute (**www.iii. org/insurance_topics/**).

Car Insurance

Be sure to ask your broker about your auto insurance if you'll be using your personal vehicle on company business.

Business Interruption Insurance

This insurance covers your bills while you are out of operation for a covered loss, such as a fire. This type of insurance covers ongoing expenses such as rent or taxes until your business is running again.

Life and Disability Insurance

If you provide a portion of your family's income, consider life insurance and disability insurance to make certain they are cared for if something happens to you. If you become sick or otherwise disabled for an extended period, your business could be in jeopardy. Disability insurance would provide at least a portion of your income while you're not able to be working.

Health Insurance

If you live in the United States and aren't covered under a spouse's health plan, you'll need to consider your health insurance options. You can compare health insurance quotes at **www.ehealthinsurance.com**, which offers plans from over 150 insurance companies nationwide.

Canadians have most of their health care expenses covered by the Canadian government. For expenses that are not covered (such as dental care, eyeglasses, prescription drugs, etc.) self-employed professionals may get tax benefits from setting up their own private health care plan. Puhl Employee Benefits (**www.puhlemployeebenefits.com**) is an example of the type of financial planning company that can help you set up your own private health care plan.

Association Member Policies

Some insurance companies offer discount pricing for members of particular organizations. When you are looking for organizations to join, whether your local Chamber of Commerce or a national association, check to see if discounted health insurance is one of the member benefits.

State beverage license associations often offer group liability coverage for their members. You can see an example of the policy offered by the Colorado Licensed Beverage Association at **http://myclba.com/member-benefits/103**. Many other state associations offer similar coverage with discounts to members.

Workers' Compensation Insurance

Another type of insurance to consider if you plan to hire employees is workers' compensation insurance. Most states in the U.S. and provinces in Canada require businesses to have workers' compensation insurance to help protect their employees in case of injury on the job.

To find what workers' compensation laws govern your business in your state check out the Southern Association of Workers' Compensation Administrators' site (**www.sawca.com/workerscomplinks.htm**). It has links to the various states' workers' compensation sites. In Canada you should visit the Association of Workers' Compensation Boards of Canada website where you can find information about the WCB for your province. Visit them at **www.awcbc.org**.

More Information

There are other types of insurance and different levels of coverage available for each type. An insurance broker (check the Yellow Pages) can advise you of your options and shop around for the best rates for you. You might want to check out the SBA's in-depth risk management guide that covers most aspects of insurance planning for small business. You can read it on their website at **www.sba.gov/tools/resourcelibrary/publications/index.html** (click on "Management and Planning Series", then scroll down to #17).

4. Setting Up Your Wine Store

4.1 Finding a Location

You have probably heard it before and it's true: location can make or break your store. Finding a space that suits you can take a little work, but once you have the perfect location, the thrill of opening your own wine store will be that much closer!

4.1.1 Possible Locations

Although you're really only limited to opening your wine store in areas where you know you can obtain a liquor license, there are several options for choosing a particular type of building to house your new business. While some wine stores are located in malls these are often outlets of large regional or national wineries selling their own brands. Still, there may be opportunities in your area for locating your wine store in this type of setting, so do your homework to see what is available if this type of location appeals to you.

Traditional Retail Space

Retail space can be found in numerous locations throughout any community. Options for wine stores include storefronts, shopping malls, strip malls, factory outlets, and stand alone buildings. Your store type and niche may dictate where you want to set up your store.

Fine wine boutiques often are found in historic and high-end retail districts of cities, in tourist shopping districts, specialty retail centers, and in upscale neighborhoods. Mom and pop wine stores may be found near tourist shopping districts, downtown city locations, and suburban malls or strip malls.

While location can mean the difference between success and failure, you also have to consider your budget. How much rent can you afford? Prime locations often have a prime price tag on them as well. You may have to start smaller and work your way up to the store you can afford. Following are some ideas for starting off in a smaller location.

Downtown Building

Downtown or "Main Street" locations are popular among wine store owners.

The advantages to this kind of location are several:

- Increased foot traffic

- Higher visibility

- Access to a larger customer base

As you might expect, there are certain disadvantages, too:

- Higher rents

- Higher incidence of crime

- Transient customer base (e.g., tourists who are only around at certain times of the year)

Rents are higher in these highly visible locations. However, along with those higher rents come higher revenues. This is because, as a result of the higher density of stores, more people frequent the area during peak hours than if you were located in a more distant neighborhood. If you're in a city where tourism is a strong industry, you'll likely see even more customers during times when tourism is strongest.

This type of location is a bit of a trade-off, and you should research other wine store in the area, if possible, to be certain that your business model will work well there. Talk to other wine store owners. Visit stores in the area during peak hours to see what the traffic is like, and talk to people you meet in stores to try to get a sense of what kinds of establishments they would like to see there. Be sure to look at the parking facilities in the area, too.

Strip Mall

Strip malls can be a good location choice for your wine. While the interior spaces available in a strip mall, anywhere from about 800 to 1,500 square feet are perfect for a wine store.

There are a number of advantages to strip mall locations. One advantage is lots of free parking. Spaces in strip malls are usually widely available in most towns and cities. The rents are generally more reasonable than in the downtown area. They're also usually close to residential areas, within easy walking distance. In addition, renovations can be much less expensive than if you're locating in an older building or one that has had other prior usage, because the space is usually all on one level and more or less rectangular. This makes layout and remodeling somewhat simpler.

Another aspect is that you will likely develop a devoted customer base, particularly if you're the only wine store in the immediate area. If the strip mall is located near a high density suburb, you'll likely attract a good following from residents there. If you're thinking of opening in a strip mall in a suburban community, this is a good time to do some research into local demographics so you can appeal to as wide a range of people who live nearby as possible.

One disadvantage to opening your wine store in a strip mall is the very fact that you are dependent on the local population for the most part. This can be an advantage if you're in the right spot, but if your wine store concept doesn't work for the demographic, you'll be hard pressed to bring in customers. For example, if you locate a fine wine boutique in a community whose population would really prefer a selection of wines under $20 or just a liquor store with a varied assortment, chances are you won't get a lot of customers.

Store Within a Store

You might consider having a small "store within a store" where your products are sold in a special area or corner set aside for your goods. This can be a good way to start your business, or to expand your business later by setting up mini stores and grow your business that way. Some franchising companies use this same concept to expand their brands.

Under this arrangement, you will pay rent for the space your business occupies and/or a portion of your profits per month, depending on what you negotiate with the store. If you are just starting out, this can be a good way to develop a customer base and brand recognition while saving a significant amount on rent. However, the ability to run your business from this small space (e.g., limit in the numbers of products you can carry, lack of storage, office space , etc.) should be balanced against the savings in rent.

4.1.2   Points to Consider

You probably have some idea about where you envision your store's location and what sort of a space you are looking for. But to make sure that you don't get stuck with something you are unhappy with, be as definite as possible about all the particulars you are looking for in a space before you begin your search.

As you begin to consider what you need in a space, think about three things:

- Things you must have

- Things you would like to have but can live without

- Things that you definitely want to avoid

Very likely, the first "must have" will be a particular amount of space.

How Much Space Do You Need?

Around 1,000 square feet of floor space is adequate for most retail operations. This gives you enough room to have a good selection and allows one or two people to operate it. However, many new business owners start out in much smaller spaces such as 600-800 square feet. Anything smaller than this and your store will start to feel too cramped for your customers' comfort.

If you have too little space, inventory could end up being crammed into every nook and cranny. Have you ever been in a store where there is no room to move? It is stifling—most customers don't feel comfortable spending much time in stores set up in this manner. However, when they enter a well-organized store that is easy to navigate, they tend to take their time and browse.

Space is often costly, though, because many retail property owners charge rent by the square foot. You may wind up having to compromise and, if you do, it can be important to limit your inventory accordingly so you do not "overstuff" your store. (Tips on using space are covered in section 4.2)

Legal Requirements

Another vital issue is ensuring the space meets all the legal requirements for running your store. Consider the following issues as you begin your search for your new store location.

Permits and Zoning

If you are going to make improvements to your space, you will need to make sure that you check your local city, county, and state regulations and get the proper permits to proceed. Another thing to ask your potential landlord or your local government's zoning department is whether or not the space you are considering renting is zoned as a retail space.

The difference between zoning and the need for a permit is relatively simple. Zoning indicates where a business is allowed by local law to be set up, while permits designate whether a business can operate or not. (For example, many municipalities allow retail pet shops in areas that are zoned for retail, but one selling prohibited exotic species would never get a permit to operate.)

Many jurisdictions also require new business owners to obtain a Certificate of Occupancy. The requirements vary from area to area but many cities require inspections before issuing the certificate.

Access for People with Disabilities

As part of the Americans with Disabilities Act (you can read about the requirements of this legislation at **www.ada.gov**), businesses are required to provide access for people with disabilities. Similar laws exist in Canada (check with your local municipality). Accessibility requirements may include:

- Floor aisles wide enough for wheelchairs
- Wheelchair ramps
- Wheelchair elevators if steps are present
- Rails in handicapped restrooms

Make sure to discuss this with any landlord you are considering renting space from.

Other Points to Consider

Here are some additional questions to ask:

- In what part of town would I like to locate my store?
- Are any nearby stores similar enough to my store to be direct competition?
- Are any large discount, or big box retail stores, that would affect my business close to the area where I would like to locate my store?

- Are there other businesses or services nearby that might attract customer traffic to my store. (For example, a good location for a wine store might be near a gourmet food store or other specialty grocery outlet.)

- Have I observed car traffic near my store at different times of the day?

- How much foot traffic does this location get?

In addition to these questions, you should consider the following points when looking for your retail space:

- *Parking:* Make sure the parking is close enough to your shop for customers to carry their goods to their cars. If they need to pay for the parking, can you offer a validation service? Another issue is that if parking is too far from your store, your customers will not want to purchase wine by the case from you. Wine is heavy.

- *Price:* Sure that spot on Main Street is ideal, but how much will you have to sell in order to afford it? Don't put yourself in financial distress right out of the starting gate; be realistic.

- *Projecting costs:* Calculate how much this space will actually cost. Ask about utilities, taxes, any extra fees you might have to pay.

Considering all these issues should help you narrow down the list of places to consider. The checklist below has a longer list of questions to help you assess the places you decide to check out.

Keeping Track of Places You've Seen

As you look at properties for the perfect potential space for your new store, keep track of where you have been, what each potential space looked like, and the positives and negatives of each space.

Consider taking along a digital camera on your space-hunting trips to take a picture of each space's exterior and interior so you can more easily remember details of each location later.

To make the process easier, use the checklist provided below for each of your space hunting excursions. This checklist, along with a picture or two, will help you to be really clear about each potential location you visit so you can make an informed decision.

Finding Your Perfect Space Checklist

Date: _____   **Location:** _____

Pictures

❑ Exterior front

❑ Interior

❑ Notes on pictures: _____

Space Location Checklist

❑ Does the space have easy freeway access? Which ones?

❑ Does the space have handy public transportation? Where and what?

❑ Is the quality of the neighborhood good?

❑ What possibly helpful businesses are nearby?

❑ What possibly detrimental businesses are nearby?

Exterior Checklist

❑ How is the overall appearance of the building exterior? Does it need any obvious work? What?

❑ Is the building a storefront location?

❑ Is there a garden or parking strip area? Who maintains it?

❑ Where is the trash area? Is trash pick up included as part of the lease agreement?

❑ Is the tenant responsible for sidewalk maintenance? Shoveling snow? General clean up of trash and debris?

Interior Checklist

❑ How is the overall appearance of the building's interior? Does it need any obvious work? What?

❑ What is the square footage of the space? Is there any room to grow?

❑ Are the windows functional? Are there enough windows?

❑ Is there adequate light?

❑ Are the air conditioning and heating systems shared or private for each tenant?

❑ Is the ventilation system shared or private for each tenant?

❑ Is the space technology-ready?

❑ Will you be able to use your own already existing Internet Service Provider if you have one?

❑ Is the space wired for cable modem or DSL?

❑ Is the space wired for phone lines? How many?

❑ Does the space have private or shared restroom facilities? What is the overall state of the existing restroom facilities? Are they wheelchair accessible?

❑ Does the space have hot and cold running water?

❑ Are there existing janitorial services and is the cost for this service part of the lease price?

❑ Does the space have a workroom or break room?

❑ Does the space have a kitchen?

Extra Charges

❑ What services and utilities are included in the lease price?

❑ What services and utilities are provided by the landlord for a fee?

❑ What services and utilities are the responsibility of the tenant?

Shared Tenant Services, Spaces, Costs, Responsibilities

❑ Are there any shared tenant spaces?

❑ Are there any shared tenant responsibilities?

❑ Is there a mandatory tenant association?

❑ Are there any costs that tenants are required to share?

Extra Benefits and Features

❑ Are there any extra benefits or features that make this space especially desirable?

Notes:

_____

_____

_____

_____

_____

_____

_____

4.1.3 Signing Your Lease

Signing a lease for your store space is quite a bit more than putting your signature at the bottom of a legal document. There are a variety of different lease options you can have and a number of things to consider when putting together the details in your lease.

Be sure the following things are clearly stated:

- Who is responsible for what repairs?

- What types of signs can you use? Are there any restrictions on sidewalk sales or signs to draw customers into the store?

- Can you change the colors and décor of the store? (Some malls have very specific rules.)

- Can you make alterations to suit your needs?

- Is there any security?

What to Include in a Lease

Your lease is the legal agreement that makes it clear what each party will do (or won't do). Therefore it is vital that you get everything you expect regarding your store space written into the lease. For example, once you have located a space you really like there still may be a number of improvements that you want to have happen before you move in.

Regular Improvements

Regular improvements are the things that a landlord will do for any prospective tenant — no matter what their business. These are the things that need to be done to prepare the space. Some of the things you should expect (although you should check just to be sure) include:

- Having the space prepared and cleaned by a professional janitorial service

- Painting the interior or exterior of the building as part of normal wear and tear

- Replacing worn bathroom fixtures, mini blinds, or broken fixtures

- Replacing worn or damaged carpet or flooring

Specific Improvements Requests

Specific improvements are the things you want to see done to your space to make it the way you dream it should be.

This might include:

- Adding partitions

- Installing a door or a window

- Creating storage or office space

- A break room for employees

In short, these improvements are the things you might hire a contractor to do.

Based on the term of your lease (a longer-term lease makes a landlord more willing to help fund improvements), your landlord will need to agree to the specific improvements that you want to make to the space and all of this will need to be included in the lease agreement. You must determine what the landlord will let you do, what the landlord will fund, what you will need to fund, and who will do the work.

> **TIP:** If the space you are considering needs too many improvements, maybe you haven't found the right space. Consider looking for a space that fits more of your needs before you commit to a long or complicated improvement plan.

Types of Leases

First you will need to consider the type of lease that will work best for your store. Your lease will most likely fall into one of these categories:

Month-to-Month Lease

A month-to-month lease is the most flexible kind of lease agreement you can have. If you think you might want to get out of your lease quickly, all that is necessary to do so is 30 days notice. Naturally, there is a downside to this sort of a lease. With a month-to-month lease, you aren't locked into a price for a reasonable length of time, plus the landlord can ask you to leave with 30 days notice.

Short-Term Fixed Rate Lease

While a short-term fixed rate lease has all the benefits of a shorter month-to-month lease, it also locks you into a fixed price for the length of the lease. This sort of commitment might be wise if you are truly concerned about giving up your current job to open your store and want a short amount of time to see if it will really work. With a short-term lease, you can add verbiage in the lease to determine what happens after the lease ends. What happens next is up to you and the landlord to negotiate.

Long-Term Lease

A long-term lease is a lease with a term of a year or more. Long-term leases that are for several years or even longer are called "multi-year leases." The best thing about a long-term lease is that once you find a great space, you can stay there for as long as you want.

Negotiating Leases

Be very careful when negotiating a lease. If you commit to paying $1,200 a month for two years, that is nearly $30,000. Try to get the shortest term lease available, especially as you start out. There is a possibility this could backfire and you could lose your space, but finding a new space is a better alternative than owing thousands of dollars on a store that is not thriving.

Some store owners don't realize that a lease document prepared and presented by a potential landlord is a negotiating tool. You certainly don't have to accept the terms of a lease that you are uncomfortable with, and you can negotiate for the things you would like to see either added to or removed from the lease.

The lease written by a landlord is written in the landlord's best interests, not yours, so look for what you feel needs to be changed or amended to make the lease fit your requirements. Remember, the process of signing a lease is a negotiating experience. Both you and your landlord will probably need to bend a little to come up with a document that works well for both of you.

Don't feel pressured into signing a lease as soon as it is handed to you. Plan on taking the document away with you so you can read it carefully, and, if you wish, show it to a qualified attorney for advice. Good advice on leasing, including an article on "Negotiating the Best Commercial Lease Terms" can be found at **www.nolo.com/legal-encyclopedia/business-licenses/index.html** (scroll down to the "Your Business Space and Commercial Lease" section).

Sample Lease with Comments

In the sample lease below, we will point out potential problem areas. Note that the comments are simply suggestions about some matters you may want to consider. These are opinions based on our research, and do not come from a lawyer or a commercial real estate agent. As your own situation is unique, make sure you have a lawyer who is familiar with business leases look over any lease before you sign it.

Opening Section

This lease is made between Big Commercial Landlord, herein after called the Lessor, and Ima Wineseller, hereinafter called the Lessee.

This is a pretty standard clause in any contract and simply states who are the parties to the lease agreement. If you are a corporation, then you may want to try to use your corporate name as the Lessee. Sometimes, this clause will include your home address.

Lessee herby offers to lease from Lessor the premises located in the city of Greenfield, in the County of Hancock, in the State of Indiana, described as 197 State Street, Suite C, based upon the terms and conditions as outlined below.

This clause outlines the specific space you are agreeing to lease. Things to watch for would be any mistakes in the address. If it is a building with several store spaces, double check that the suite number is correct. You could wind up leasing more square feet than you wanted or losing a prime location.

1. Term and Rent

Lessee agrees to rent the above premises for a term of two years, commencing July 1, 2008, and terminating on June 30, 2010, or sooner as provided herein at the annual rental of 7,200 dollars

($7,200.00), payable in equal monthly installments of 600 dollars ($600.00) in advance on the first day of each month for that month's rental, during the term of this lease. All payments should be made directly to the Lessor at the address specified in paragraph one.

Some of this information is a little hard to break down, but section 1 basically outlines how much rent you will be paying. Double check that the monthly rent matches the yearly sum. Be sure the day you have agreed to is the day that the rent is due and not sooner. Also, you might want to try to get a shorter term on the lease, if possible. Many landlords will negotiate on this point. Two years is standard.

2. Use

Lessee shall use and occupy the premises for a retail wine store operation called Wine Time. The location shall be used for no other purpose. Lessor represents that the premises may lawfully be used for the purpose stated above.

This simply states what your business will be. The thing to be most cautious of here is making sure that all things are listed. One thing that jumps right out in the above description is that it does not allow for retail sales of other items besides the main retail sector merchandise. You may want to add additional complementary lines of merchandise that aren't directly related to the main retail business you're in. You should ask to have this added before signing the lease.

3. Care and Maintenance of the Premises

Lessee recognizes that the premises are in good repair, unless otherwise indicated herein. Lessee shall, at the Lessee's own expense and at all times, maintain the premises in good and safe order, including plate glass, electrical wiring, plumbing and heating and any other equipment on the premises. Lessee shall return the same at termination of contract, in as good condition as received, normal wear and tear excepted. Lessee shall be responsible for all repairs required, excepting the roof, exterior walls, and structural foundations.

As you can probably see already, there are many potential problems with this clause. You may have a hard time getting a landlord to change some of these requirements. While it is acceptable for them to ask you to fix any problems you may have caused, such as damage to walls, the idea that you are responsible for heating and cooling systems is a bit troublesome. This could run into very costly repairs. In addition, the lease does not state what responsibility the land-lord has to fix such problems. Ask that this section be made much more specific, with phrases such as "normal wear and tear" defined explicitly.

In addition, you might want to double check with your insurance company to be sure that if the roof leaks you would be covered under their policy. If not, will you be covered for any loss under the landlord's policy and what is the system for recourse?

4. Alterations

Lessee shall not, without first obtaining written consent of Lessor, make any additions, alterations, or improvements to the premises.

Again, this is way too vague. What is their definition of an addition or altera-tion? If you put in slat walls to display your merchandise, is that considered a violation of the contract? Ask for some more specifics here. The inability to add display fixtures could really hinder your business. Do not wait until after you have signed the contract to find out you can't create the store you have envisioned because of a clause in the lease agreement.

5. Ordinances and Statutes

Lessee shall comply with all ordinances, statues and require-ments of state, federal and local authorities.

This is pretty much a given and you really have no choice but to do this any-way.

6. Subletting

Lessee shall not assign or sublet any portion of this lease or prem-ises without prior written consent of the Lessor, which shall not be unreasonably withheld. Any such assignment or subletting without consent shall be void and may terminate this lease.

This is pretty straightforward and standard.

7. Utilities

All applications and connections for utility services on the stated premises shall be made in the name of the Lessee only, and Lessee shall be solely liable for utility charges as they become due, including charges for gas, water, sewer, electricity, and telephone.

This, too, is standard. It is your responsibility to cover your utilities with most landlords. There are a few who will cover some costs. It depends on the building and the landlord.

8. Entry and Inspections

Lessee will permit Lessor or agents of Lessor to enter the premises during reasonable times and with notice and will permit the Lessor to post "For Lease" signs within ninety (90) days prior to the expiration of this lease.

This is pretty standard, however, try to get a specific statement about what type of notice, how the Lessee will receive the notice and what constitutes reasonable times (i.e. regular business hours). It is also standard to allow them to place "For Lease" signs sixty days prior to the expiration of the contract. This is not a major point, but you may want to request it, if you feel the signs might hinder your business in any way.

9. Indemnification of Lessor

The Lessor will not be held liable for any damage or injury to Lessee, or any other person, or property occurring on the stated premises. Lessee agrees to not hold Lessor liable for any damages regardless of how they are caused.

This section is troubling. What if the Lessor knows there is a structural fault with the building, does not fix it and you or one of your customers are harmed? Get the landlord to strike this clause or have it changed.

10. Insurance

Lessee shall retain public liability and property damage insurance at the Lessee's own cost.

This is standard, and you will want this anyway. Some contracts may go on further and state the exact types of coverage you will need and/or amounts. Some will require proof of insurance.

11. Destruction of Property

Should the premises be destroyed in part or whole, Lessor shall repair the property within sixty (60) days. Lessee shall be entitled to a deduction in rent during the time the repairs are taking place. If there are repairs which cannot be made within sixty (60) days, this lease may be terminated at the request of either party.

You will want this standard clause, as well. If your space is compromised, you want the landlord to repair the defect as quickly as possible. Otherwise, you could lose business indefinitely. If they are not able to make the repairs in a timely manner, you have the option of terminating the lease and moving your store elsewhere.

12. Nonpayment of Rent

If Lessee defaults on regular payment of rent, or defaults on the other conditions herein, Lessor may give Lessee notice of the default and if the Lessee does not cure the default within thirty (30) days, after receiving written notice of the default, Lessor may terminate this lease.

This is pretty simple. If you do not pay your rent, then the landlord reserves the right to ask you to remove your store from the premises. You may want to try to get sixty days instead of thirty but there is not much wiggle room with this clause.

13. Security Deposit

Lessee shall pay a security deposit upon the signing of this lease to Lessor for the sum of 600 dollars ($600.00). Lessor shall keep the full amount of the security deposit available throughout the term of this lease.

Although a security deposit equaling the first month's rent is pretty standard, I would want to see a bit more detail here about how and under what conditions this money will be returned to the Lessee. This is pretty vague and you may wind up not getting your deposit back. Landlords have been known to make up phony repair or cleaning charges so they can keep your deposit.

14. Attorney's Fees

In the event of a suit being brought for recovery of the premises, or for any sum due under the conditions of this contract, the prevailing party shall be entitled to reimbursement of all costs, including but not limited to attorney's fee.

15. Notices

All notices to either party shall be provided in writing at the address listed on this contract.

Both clauses 14 and 15 are standard.

16. Option to Renew

As long as Lessee is not in default of this lease, Lessee shall have the option of renewing the lease for an additional term of twelve (12) months starting upon the expiration of the term of the original lease. All the terms and conditions herein outlined shall apply during the extension. This option can be implemented by giving written notice to the Lessor at least ninety (90) days prior to the expiration.

I would try for sixty days prior on the notice. You may be looking for another place and not quite sure if you are moving out in three months.

17. Entire Agreement

The preceding makes up the entire agreement between the parties and may only be modified by agreement of both parties in writing.

Signed this___ day of _____, 20__.

_____   _____
Ima Seller,   Big Commercial Landlord,
Lessee   Lessor

4.2 Store Design

Once you have chosen your space, you will need to decorate the inside and outside. To help you in this task, you may want to start by choosing a "theme" for your store. Once you have decided on a theme, you can choose your store layout, logo, background music, lighting, and even scents that will pull your store and its theme together.

Will your store be contemporary or old-fashioned? Will it be hip and young, relaxing, or upscale? It is important to choose an atmosphere that will draw customers into your store and reflect the type of merchandise you plan to offer.

Don't forget that displays will need to be updated to maintain your "look," so choose something low maintenance. Many customers prefer well-organized stores to trendy ones where they can't move without bumping into things.

4.2.1 Outside the Store

Remember the external appearance of your store is the first impression potential customers have of your business. It should be neat but eye-catching.

Does it need a fresh coat of paint? If the landlord is responsible for outside paint but does not seem in a hurry to finish the project, offer to paint it yourself for a discount on your rent that month. Let's say the paint costs you $30, and it takes you two hours to paint. You figure your time is worth $20 an hour. You would ask the landlord to grant you a seventy dollar credit on that month's rent (arrange this before you paint). Many landlords will work with you on this because it saves them money and the aggravation of hiring an outside contractor. Your bonus is a fresh coat of paint to hang your new, bright sign upon.

Signage

After your choice of name and location, your choice of signage is probably the most important aspect of creating interest in your location. You will want an eye-catching sign that customers can see from the street. A good sign can actually entice customers into your store. Your signage could mean the difference between bringing foot traffic right to your store or people walking right on by.

Your signs should reflect your style. To create more effective and professional-looking signs you might decide to have a local painter create a wonderful, vintage-looking sign for your storefront. Make sure you can see it from a distance and it shows clearly what your shop is selling.

Your sign should make a statement about your store, have a simple logo, and make the customer want to visit you. If your municipality allows it, you might also put up roadside signs to direct buyers to your store.

Logo

With some of today's inexpensive graphics software, it is possible to create your own simple logo and use it on your sign and other business materials. People will come to associate your store with that logo. There are companies, such as MyLogo.com or LogoYes.com, that you can pay to create a logo for you. MyLogo.com will create a custom designed logo for you for about $100 for a basic package. With LogoYes.com, you design your own logo using their online template that uses standard clip art. They charge about $50 for a logo design or $100 for a logo with 100 business cards.

You could also purchase software that lets you design your logo on your own. There are a number of different programs like Logo Design Studio (**www.summitsoftcorp.com**), for example, which sell for less than $50. If you decide you want to design your own logo with this type of software, be sure they offer a demo version that you can try out first, so that you know it meets your needs. Most local print shops also offer design services, since they already have the software for it. Keep in mind that, if you have already chosen a theme, your sign and logo can be a good place to tie into that theme again.

Lettering and Fonts

Make sure the letters on your sign are large enough that customers will be able to spot the words from a distance. If your sign will be more than 400 feet from the street front, then you will want to use seven- to ten-inch high letters. If you are located inside a mall, where you will not need to be visible from a street, then you may be able to use lettering between three and a half to seven inches.

Watch the fonts you use for your sign. A fancy script may look nice, but customers might have a difficult time reading the letters. Use both upper and lowercase letters for some variety and to make the sign easier to read. The colors of the sign should contrast with one another — dark and light colors work best (black and white, yellow and navy blue, white and royal blue).

You might find hiring an expert for this particular job worthwhile even though it will cost you a little extra money. Most small towns have stores that create signs for local businesses. Be sure that you get several quotes for your project, as prices can vary widely. Also, do not rule out buying the sign used. You may be able to locate a simple sign without a store name at a store that is going out of business

Be sure to check with your landlord or city zoning board to find out about any ordinances on signs. Some cities have very specific guidelines about height and other requirements, particularly if you're in a heritage area where local history is used as a tourism draw. It's better to check with your municipality before investing a lot of money in a sign you can't use.

Also, most malls have specific requirements for store signs, such as requiring a minimum/maximum letter height, lighted signs, etc. If your location comes with a place to install a sign, you will probably be able to order an appropriate sign with the help of the mall's management. Professional sign companies offer design and manufacturing — check in your local Yellow Pages under the "Signs — Commercial" category. Another option is to order a sign online.

Here are a few companies that specialize in signs for businesses:

- *Sandblasted Signs*
  www.sandblastedsigns.com

- *Spring Valley Signs*
  www.springvalleysigns.com

- *American Sign Carver*
  www.signcarving.com

- *Custom Hand-Carved Signs by Sally Claus Focht*
  www.customhandcarvedsigns.com

- *Lincoln Signs*
  www.lincolnsign.com

4.2.2   Wine Store Set-Up

It is important for the layout of any wine store to conform to a traditional layout like that of other retail or convenience stores. While you might like to experiment in the interior design of the store, if you play too much with the architectural design, then customers could have difficulty navigating through your store and locating products.

Remember these "10 Commandments" of professional layout design:

1. Place the sales counter carefully

A good layout is to place the sales counter away from the entrance (thirty feet so as to not block the entrance with a line of customers), and away from the center of store for the same reason. For best results try and situate the sales counter on a side wall, preferably to the left.

2. Lead your customers

Be sure to set up your aisles and displays so that your most popular items are to the rear or to one side of the store. By doing this, you will ensure that customers pass by other items for sale that might pique their interest. This is why milk and bread are usually located at the back of the supermarket. People coming into the store just for those staples have to pass through the rest of the store to get to them, possibly seeing other items they might need or want to purchase as well, even though they only came in for milk and bread.

3. Space aisles appropriately

A three foot wide aisle will barely accommodate one person. Space your aisles so that two people can comfortably pass through without bumping into each other. If customers keep bumping into each other, they will start to think of your store as a cramped, uncomfortable place to shop.

4. Maximize your floor space

Maximize your floor space by paying attention to common measurements. Avoid aisles that measure over 30 feet long and shelves over 60 inches high, as these can be overwhelming for a small store. (These are sometimes called bowling alleys.) Tall shelving is just as intimidating and worse yet, can limit the cashier's overall store view, which can encourage shoplifters.

5. Don't overburden your customers

Too much too soon, is how customers would subconsciously describe stores that start visually assaulting them upon entry. Store designers refer to a "decompression zone," the area around the entrance between 5-15 feet in length that customers use to adjust to the store's atmosphere. Therefore placing any packed aisles, large signs or anything too loud could be either a waste of time (they'll ignore it) or turn them off completely.

6. Assist shoppers with in-store signs

Keeping interior signs is important to help navigate the customer through the store. There are three types of signs you can use: large signs that can be viewed from a distance and define sections; aisle directories that are located above the merchandise and let the customer focus on a specific product line; and point of sale signs that highlight a specific wine product and its features.

7. Set up power zones

Why are so many small businesses afraid to act like large retail stores? Power zones, or focal areas, are an effective way to sell products. At least one power zone is recommended if not more. Never become complacent in your marketing efforts.

8. Create light (lots of it)

No one's going to want to stay in a dreary, dimly lit store. Make sure all of the light fixtures are in good working condition, particularly if you purchase an existing store, and ensure that a customer never has to squint to read a wine label.

9. Keep your wine store clean

A wine store should be free from dirt (meaning regular sweeping, mopping or vacuuming) as well as needless clutter. Unstocked merchandise is a very negative image to leave in the mind of your customer. Don't get out the boxes unless everything will be stocked relatively quickly. If you have windows at the entrance be sure to keep them clean.

10. Record these commandments and study them

Don't think just because you've set up your shop that you can lean back and take it easy for a while. Now it's up to you to continue to track the results of your layout by careful analysis of customer buying patterns. Do you notice customers have difficulty with some parts of the store? If you believe there's a problem make an adjustment and then study the results.

How to Organize Wine & Other Beverages

How you organize your merchandise is up to you but here are a few ideas to get you started thinking about how you will arrange your stock. If you sell beer, spirits and liquor besides wine, then you could organize an entire section with zone signs for each category.

If wine is your primary product then you could choose to organize wine according to:

- Name of wine or types of grapes; alphabetically sorted or by country

- Types of wine (natural, sparkling, fortified)

- Price (from least expensive to most expensive)

- Any combination of the above that works for you

Stocking and Facing

A customer should not notice a shortage of any product. As units are sold, product should be replaced from storage or leftover items pushed to the front. If an item is out of its correct place then return it to the right spot. This not only makes the inventory look organized and your shelves full, it prevents possible misunderstandings with customers in price.

4.2.3   Interior Design for a Wine Store

Creating the interior decor for a wine store is different than creating a social atmosphere, such as that found inside a wine bar. Your goal is not to keep customers inside your store and talking for hours. Rather, the goal is both to provide a pleasing, aesthetic design striking enough to bring them back to your store and to keep the line moving.

Finding a Balance

Obviously, nobody wants a store with just white walls and a black floor. There must be some elegance and some color to your wine store. However, you should also aim for good taste and professionalism in your design. The atmosphere cannot distract attention from the wine—it must complement it.

If you are opening a wine store for a general customer base, and also selling alcohol and liquors, then you are aiming at a more general demographic. With broader demographics comes more conservative interior design. A color pallet and any graphical images must be suitable for all shoppers. This setting would also call for large lettering and more contrast in the signs.

However, you might also want to experiment with the interior design if you have a specific marketing plan. In general, the artsy look as opposed to the traditional is a risk; you're not trying to please a colony of artists, just the local neighborhood. Genuine wine buffs are often upscale customers and might appreciate an artistic slant, but avoid anything too cutting edge. Remember, it's just enough decoration to get them to come back.

Construction Elements

If you are building a new property, then you will have to decide on the type of materials you want to use. The cheapest type of wall is drywall, and it may be the only type you can afford. However, pricier materials like mirror, brick, stone, wood, fabric, paper, glass, have been used in construction before—usually in big tourism locations and for a lot of money.

With wallpaper you could opt for a simple color combination or for a graphical theme. That route is attractive and will impress customers, but can be more expensive. Ceilings are usually more basic than walls, though the higher the ceiling the more outstanding and costly it will be.

The flooring should match the rest of the design, whether you choose carpeting, wood or tile. Remember, if everything goes well your flooring will suffer constant trampling; so it should be durable, comfortable and easy to clean. You might aim for wooden floors instead of vinyl if you're marketing to a more upscale clientele; just keep an eye on your budget.

Some studies in retail suggest that shoppers are more attracted to carpeted areas of the store. While many wine store owners might opt for a tile and carpeting combination to increase sales, you will also note the more locations you visit, that many owners prefer full carpeting. It creates a homier atmosphere and does reduce the threat of a lawsuit in case of accidental slipping. Even if you prefer to use tile, use non-slip flooring material for your own protection.

Other Customizable Elements

There's nothing wrong with adding personality to your store provided you don't assault your customers' senses. Here are some other design elements you can work with:

Lighting

Choose between:

- Fluorescent lighting: a sterile atmosphere but total readability (like grocery stores)

- Partial fluorescent lighting with pendants and light bulbs

- Track and recessed lighting

Here is a template that will assist you in visualizing your customer floor. Cut out the shapes and arrange them according to how you see your store. (If you are reading the print version of this guide, a printable template is included on the accompanying CD-ROM.)

Sample Store Design Sheet

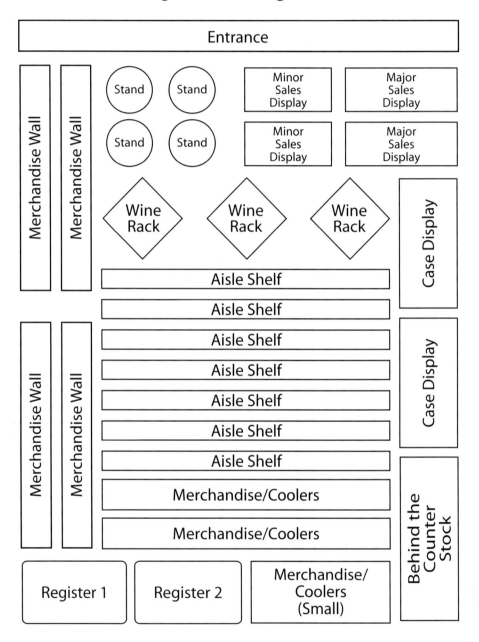

Recessed lighting, while certainly creating atmosphere, might backfire if customers cannot easily read wine labels. If possible, invest in a dimmer switch for your lights, which allows you adjust the intensity at will. This way you can match the bright, daytime sunlight with your own interior lights, rather than letting the sun darken your store.

Sound

Some wine store owners like to utilize music and background noise in their stores. This may sound more like a marketing technique for a wine bar but there's nothing wrong with increasing the energy level in a wine store in the same manner.

Temperature

Temperature inside the store will always fluctuate and will be influenced by the temperature outside. But your store should always be inviting whether it's ice cold on a hot day outside or warm as an oven during the dead of winter. As the anxious and constantly moving store manager, you might not be a good judge of temperature. The best way to gauge the comfort level is to study the body language of your customers.

Stage Setting

"Stage setting" is a general term for creating an event and inducing feelings in your customers. Most successful independent retail stores, especially in big city areas, have a stage setting; that is, a lifestyle, a mood, an event they give their customer for free along with the product. Think about your targeted demographic and what type of lifestyle they want — associate your store with their preferred tastes.

Signs and Displays

Displays should complement the color palette of the store, promote specific products and be conveniently located. You can also make cosmetic changes to your store's exterior decor. Neon signs, outdoor awnings, window graphics, store front displays and courtesy signs in the parking lot can also add a lot to the exterior design of a wine store.

If you have never had any natural ability or experience in interior design then it may be best to consult a professional if you are building or remodeling a store. It is important to keep a blueprint of your chosen design that will provide specific measurements when it comes to setting up shop. In business, taking a guess costs too much money.

Novelty Items

Don't underestimate the effectiveness of novelty items in setting the stage for your wine store. Whether you stock your wine store with unique bottle holders, neon signs, LED lighting or other interesting toys for grown ups, it can endear the average customer to your not-so-average store. The only word of caution is to make sure the novelty items fit in with the overall marketing direction of the store and aren't totally out of place.

4.2.4   Crime Prevention

There's something about alcohol that seems to provoke theft, vandalism and even armed robbery. Crime prevention methods are something every wine store owner should seriously consider when starting a new business. While property insurance will cover these types of threats, there are further steps you can take to protect yourself, your store and all that precious wine.

Video Surveillance and Security Systems

The majority of criminals involved in theft and vandalism are not easy to identify, prosecute and convict. Therefore, what might help is to buy large, visible surveillance cameras to scare away anyone entertaining the thought of harming your wine store.

Surveillance cameras are very detailed and could record footage of a crime taking place, perhaps with enough detail to identify the offender. Unfortunately, this is not always going to be the case.

If you go this route make sure to buy durable cameras and place them out of reach, so the equipment itself cannot be damaged. Sometimes an exterior sign reminding your customers that they are being videotaped can send a strong message.

Security systems can also help reduce crime. As opposed to crime prevention, a good security system would silently or noisily notify the police of a break-in with the intent to catch the criminal red-handed. Security systems (along with a warning sign) are probably a more reliable security measure than just a surveillance system.

Deterring Shoplifters

Many merchants report that it's not so much vandalism or armed robbery you have to guard against but shoplifting. How can you protect your wine against shoplifters? Consider some important tips in loss prevention.

Minimize "blind spots"

If you or your staff will be situated by the cash register, then arrange your aisles so that you can easily see your customers at all times.

Keep small and expensive drinks behind the counter

Get inside the mind of a shoplifter. The easier the job the better; they will look for small items on the back aisle away from the cash register. Keep small drinks out of the reach of shoplifters.

Closed-circuit television cameras

CCTV systems have proven to discourage shoplifting activity. Younger and smarter criminals are now ever-aware of hidden cameras, as various incidents have been notoriously caught on tape. Some cameras are large and obvious (or appear as domes), others can be hidden.

Post some creative signs

Reminding your shoplifting customers that they are being watched is another effective deterrent along with a CCTV system to back you up. The more creative you are with your signs (you can also remind them that they will be prosecuted) the more you can scare them into respecting your store.

Prosecute shoplifters

When you've just caught a shoplifter in the act it's not the time to be lenient. As soon as you catch someone shoplifting, call the police and then prosecute the offender. If you start feeling compassionate for shoplifters and let them get away with an attempted crime, then you've shown yourself vulnerable.

Practice good customer service

The most effective way to handle shoplifting, especially if you have a small to medium sized store, is by simply paying close attention and waiting patiently on your customers. You know how annoying some department store people can be with their assistance? That's because they know you're either a customer of a shoplifter. Keep an eye on all your customers and make sure your employees are alert.

What does a shoplifter look like?

Shoplifters can come in all ages, sizes and wardrobes. They are sometimes identifiable by their suspicious activity; for example, casing the entire area, needlessly picking up bottles and not buying anything. Experienced shoplifters are more frequently very methodical and may seem like the perfect customer: focused, ready to pay and out the door... with a few more items than you know.

What to Do In a Hold Up

There is a great scene in director David Cronenberg's film *A History of Violence* in which an ordinary guy in a coffee shop takes a big risk and goes postal on a pair of murderous thugs, saving the day. Do you remember that scene? No? Good, because that's not a good idea.

If you are ever held up at gunpoint don't try and be a hero. It doesn't matter how much dignity or finances you might lose, it's nothing compared to the medical bills you'll have to pay if you receive a gunshot wound to the head or, worse, you could be killed. Instead, take these cautionary steps whenever faced with a life-threatening situation.

- Remain calm and make no sudden movements

- Do not volunteer any extra information

- Do not speak unless asked a question

- Do as the robber says and give him the money in the register

- Try not to make direct eye contact with the robber

- After he leaves activate an your alarm system if you have one

- Call the police immediately even after alarm activation

- Close the store and lock every door

- If there are any witnesses to the event such as employees or customers, ask if they will stay and verify what happened with the police

- Do not discuss any details of the event with witnesses or employees

- Do not touch anything the robber may have touched and advise others to stay away from the scene of the crime

- Try and recall as much information as you can about the robber's appearance, voice and mannerisms so you will be ready when police arrive

- Step outside the store when police arrive so they will know the robbery is not still in progress

Holdups are scary situations that sometimes cannot be prevented. It is best to try and keep the store staffed with as many employees as possible, since this slightly reduces the threat of a holdup. In the worst case scenario, try and remain calm and do whatever it takes to escape with your life. You will live to fight (and drink) another day.

4.3   Wine Store Equipment and Supplies

4.3.1   Equipment and Supplies You'll Need

In addition to the fixtures you'll need to display merchandise, there are a variety of other items you will need to equip your store. This section begins with suggestions for various areas of the store, followed by information about suppliers. Check what your store already has, or what your landlord provides, and make your shopping list.

For information about how to find manufacturers and wholesalers who can supply you with inventory for your store, see section 4.4.

After constructing and designing the interior of the store it's time to install and set up the store equipment. You would not need as comprehensive a list for a wine store as you would for a wine bar or winery. Your main concerns will be with how to store wine and with the equipment you will need to complete retail transactions. Here is a list of items you will need.

General

- ❏ Cash Register or POS System/Software
- ❏ Color Receipt Printer
- ❏ Calculators
- ❏ Safe
- ❏ Computer
- ❏ Coin Sorter
- ❏ Financial Software
- ❏ Bar Code Labels
- ❏ Bottle Tags
- ❏ Price/Sale Labels
- ❏ Pricing Guns
- ❏ Tagging Guns
- ❏ Counterfeit Money Analyzer

Retail

- ❏ Counter
- ❏ Wine Racks (wood or metal with a capacity of 24-64; rack types: cubed, deluxe, scalloped, table-top, or display)
- ❏ Refrigerated Wine Racks
- ❏ Shelves (glass/wood/plastic/wire; shelf types: brackets/rests/ units/ molded/gondola)
- ❏ Swing Door Glass Merchandiser

- ❑ Display Stands/Platforms
- ❑ Display Counter Show Case
- ❑ Tables
- ❑ Wall Accessories (banners, art, decoration)

Storage

- ❑ Small Refrigerator/Freezer
- ❑ Coolers
- ❑ Cart
- ❑ Dolly
- ❑ Hand Truck
- ❑ Cooling System

Miscellaneous

- ❑ Liquor Bags
- ❑ Market Bags
- ❑ Colored Wine Bags
- ❑ Bulk Shipping Cartons
- ❑ Baskets
- ❑ Shopping Cart
- ❑ Trash Cans
- ❑ Custom Signs

Cleaning Supplies

- ❑ Mat
- ❑ Sweeper

- ❑ Mops
- ❑ Brooms
- ❑ Store Broom
- ❑ Vacuum
- ❑ Anti-Slip Floor Solution
- ❑ Mop Bucket & Ringer
- ❑ Air Freshener
- ❑ Rags
- ❑ Toilet Paper
- ❑ Duster
- ❑ Soap & Hand Sanitizer
- ❑ Paper Towels
- ❑ Insecticide

Wine-Related Merchandise (for resale)

- ❑ Stemware Holder
- ❑ Thermal Wine Cooler
- ❑ Wine Glasses
- ❑ Wine Decanters
- ❑ Corkscrews
- ❑ Bottle Openers
- ❑ Gift Bags
- ❑ Gift Wrap
- ❑ Wine Chillers
- ❑ Bottle Stopper

- ❑ Bottle Tags

- ❑ Insulated Tote Bag

- ❑ Wine Totes

- ❑ Wine Books & Magazines

- ❑ Coasters

Security

- ❑ Security Monitor

- ❑ Security Camera

- ❑ Security Mirrors

- ❑ Cables

- ❑ Camera Mounts

- ❑ Security Signage

- ❑ Connectors

- ❑ TV Mounts

- ❑ Lens

4.3.2   Special Equipment You'll Need

Wine Racks

Wine racks are not meant to store wine by themselves; wine racks usually make up an entire "wine cellar," which is an assemblage of different shape wine racks. These racks might come in various sizes and are classified according to type, such as commercial or decorative wine racks as well as counter top and corner racks.

You might not actually have a cellar on your property, but some type of large storage room will be necessary, along with a cooling system for your extra wine. Most high clientele wine stores sell wines from racks because racks keep the bottles sideways, which preserves flavor.

Wine Cellar/Storage

You will also need a commercial cooling unit for you store or bar. These units are essentially large air-conditioners that are able to cool a large volume of airspace, usually determined by the cubic foot. For example, if your wine cellar or storage room is 1500 cubic feet in volume you will need a fairly large cooling unit to keep it at the required temperature. A unit this size will probably cost around $5,000.

Your cellar or storage room will need to be insulated and vented and you'll need an exterior grade door with weather stripping to keep outside air from getting into your cellar. You can read more about basic building requirements and cooling units for your wine cellar or storage room at Rosehill Wine Cellars (**www.rosehillwinecellars.com**), a company specializing in wine cellar construction.

If you're opening a wine bar you will also need chilling units for back bar storage. These are smaller refrigeration units where you will keep your wine and beer or other beverages requiring chilling for ready accessibility by bar staff. To find out more about back bar storage systems visit the websites listed below.

4.3.3   Wine Store Equipment Suppliers

In this section you will find a sampling of suppliers of equipment to the wine retail sector.

Liquor Retailing Supplies

- *Store Supply Warehouse*
  Variety of retail supplies from bags to shelving
  http://store.storesupply.com

- *Wine Stuff*
  Stemware, decanters, etc. (click on "Wholesale Accounts" at the bottom of the page)
  http://winestuff.com

Specialty Store Services

- *Liquor retailer supplies*
  **www.specialtystoreservices.com/LandingPages/
  LiquorStore.aspx**

- *WineRacks.com*
  Retail wine rack supplier
  www.wineracks.com/Commercial/retailstore.htm

Wine Cellars and Cooling Units

- *Rosehill Winecellars*
  **www.rosehillwinecellars.com/3rsV2/
  manufacturer.php?category=wine_cooling**

- *Wine Enthusiast*
  Click on "Cooling Units".
  http://wineenthusiast.com

- *Glastender Inc.*
  Under bar and back bar coolers.
  www.glastender.com/vertdoorcooler.htm

- *ABestKitchen.com*
  www.abestkitchen.com/store/bar-refrigerators.html

4.4 Purchasing Your Inventory

4.4.1 Buying Wine and Other Beverages

After setting up your wine store it's time to fill your store with inventory. Make sure before you order any stock for your new store that your security systems are installed and you have left plenty of time for delivery and stocking the shelves before you're scheduled to open the doors for business. To order your inventory you'll need to contact a wholesale distributor. Be sure to have your retail liquor license handy because you'll need to prove to your supplier that you have one.

Wine or liquor stores will deal with a wholesale distributor to stock their store. The process is typically a three-tiered system:

- Winery sells their products to a wholesaler.

- The wholesaler sells to various retail accounts.

- Stores sell their line-up to individual wine drinkers.

An Overview of Wine Distribution

Here is list of duties that wine wholesalers perform.

- Travel to taste new wines from wineries, possibly all over the world

- Meet with qualified judges to determine quality, analysis and pricing of wine

- Attend wine tastings, fund raisers and other social events for promotion

- Visit retail store owners or managers and offer wine tasting

- Sell the background of the wine

- Create catalogs with wine descriptions and price quotes

- Negotiate prices with retailers and offer marketing help

- Organize wait staff seminars and table rents for restaurants

- Know and apply the state law regarding the three-tier system

- Visit retail accounts weekly and arrange for delivery according to need

- Evaluate their product's placement on the shelves

- Optimize space and stocking methods according to marketing research

- Reorder merchandise or order new products that complement the set up

In some cases, you may want to work with a number of different distributors. For example, in certain states, you can only buy from distributors (rather than from, say, a winery). You may want to work with several different distributors in order to get the broadest selection possible. However, there are some drawbacks to doing this.

Donnie Austin, owner of House Wine, says that working with multiple distributors is "a little more difficult on the operating end and we get a lot of sales calls throughout the week." Still, for Austin it's worth it because "it gives us access to more wine and we can provide the special order service to our customers." And, he notes, you should be aware that "every region has its own set of distributors who are responsible for that given region. You'll begin to find these distributors when you contact wineries to ask how you can get their wine locally."

Vern Foster of Alice Mae's Shoppers Cache in Chugiak, Alaska, explains how the staff works with distributors. "We choose from a list offered by the distributors, detailing the more popular sells. We also consider customer suggestions and requests." While some stores may have enough products with one distributor, Foster deals with three different companies, though he also sells other convenience store items in addition to liquor and wine products.

Alcohol Distribution in the Control States System

The eighteen states (and one county) collectively known as the "Control States" employ a stricter distribution system than in most states. In fourteen of the states, retail stores are controlled by the state and the only other stores allowed are designated agency stores. In the remaining states, private stores selling alcohol must purchase it directly from the state-run distributor. To find out which states fall under the "Control State Systems" in the U.S., visit **www.nabca.org/States/States.aspx**.

One state that is part of the Control State Systems, is Ohio. Surprisingly, there are certain advantages for wine owners in these states. Donnie Austin told us this about his experience in his home state:

> "Ohio was the home of Prohibition and still falls under the archaic three-tier system from when it was repealed. I can only buy from distributors. Ohio also utilizes state minimum pricing so a floor is set for pricing. The benefit for a small wine shop is that we don't compete

against the big box chains like Costco. Some stores can raise their pricing for higher margin, which they do, but we're competitive with the other local small shops or big box stores."

Here is Kimberly Eakin's impression of the system in Virginia, when she first opened her wine store, Wine Gourmet, as well as some advice for new wine store owners in these states:

"I knew wine was highly regulated by the government. I understood that, in Virginia, we have a three-tier system in place for wine distribution. What I did not know well was the very legislation that addressed the three-tier system and how it would affect the business of my wine shop everyday. Check your state code and read it thoroughly. Better yet, have your attorney read it too!"

Stocking Other Beverages

Should you stock beverages other than wine? That's a hard question to answer. The answer may depend on a variety of factors such as whether you're purchasing an existing store that previously included beverages other than wine, how quickly your wine store becomes known to wine lovers, and whether the extra revenue streams might help to keep your store going during the start-up phase. Vern Foster of Alice Mae's Shoppers Cache in the small town of Chugiak, Alaska, states that in some areas "on its own, a wine business would be difficult. It's better to include other spirits until you've been established."

You might choose to stock hard spirits, mixed drinks, beer and possibly even nonalcoholic beverages like soda if you are really interested in quickly increasing revenues. The more revenue streams you have, the higher your sales could potentially be. Even if a certified wine connoisseur would be turned off by a cheap vodka selection in the corner, they will ignore it if you stock wines that appeal to their tastes as well. Keep in mind, though, that there may be significant differences in cost between wine and liquor retailing licenses.

If you decide to carry liquor and beer in your wine store, you'll need to allow specifically for these in your business plan and your interior design. If you carry spirits then you will have to separate them from the wines and allow for a large selection, grouped by category: Vodka, Tequila, Whiskey, etc. You'll need to allow for some of your display space in the store to be dedicated to your liquor and beer areas, including having refrigerated storage for beer. You'll also need to divert some of your start-up budget to purchase liquor and beer inventory, which lowers the amount of wine inventory you'll be able to buy initially.

The good news, however, is that liquor and beer sell. According to the latest U.S. Census Bureau Economic Census, liquor stores accounted for $28.2 billion in sales revenues (stores that retailed packaged ale, beer, wine and liquor) across the U.S.

Wine and Liquor Retailing in Canada

The process is a little different in Canada where there is stricter government control. This tight regulatory system arose in the 1920s, primarily as a response to Prohibition when "rum running" and other illegal practices were rampant. As a result of the huge black market trade in illicit liquor, the Canadian government created laws to put liquor, beer and wine distribution solely in the hands of provincial government agencies specially created to the purpose after Prohibition ended. In most provinces, only the provincial government itself is licensed to distribute and sell wine and liquor at the retail level. If you're planning to become a wine merchant in Canada you should first check your province's liquor laws and distribution system very carefully.

In Ontario, for example, the industry operates under a government monopoly called the Liquor Control Board of Ontario (LCBO), which allows agency licenses in areas where residents do not have access to regular liquor stores owned and operated by the provincial government. However, these agent stores are strictly regulated and must charge the same prices as LCBO retail outlets.

The province relaxed its policies somewhat in the 1970s to allow independent wine retailing, although only manufacturers of wine are allowed to sell retail wines this way and they are only allowed to sell their own product. Under the current system there is little hope of opening a private retail wine or liquor store in Ontario, but a 2005 study commissioned by the Ontario government recommended that the LCBO concentrate on regulating the industry and leave retailing and wholesaling operations to the private sector, so this market may open up in the future.

B.C. now allows independent retailers, although in 2005 these accounted for only 25 percent of provincial retailers and there were only 12 independent wine stores in the entire province. Unfortunately, the private sector retail market is still fairly limited in that province, and there is a moratorium on new retail licenses.

Alberta is by far the freest market for retailing wine, beer and liquor in Canada. The Alberta government privatized the industry in the early 1990s and established Connect Logistics Inc. (**www. connect-logistics.com**) as the wholesale liquor distributor for the province's retailers. To find out more about wine and liquor retailing in Alberta and purchasing from Connect Logistics, visit the Connect Logistics website.

Most of the other provinces in Canada have distribution and retail systems similar to that of Ontario and B.C. You can find a list of liquor jurisdictions across Canada and links to their individual websites on the LCBO website at **www.lcbo.com/lcbo-ear/jsp/ RelatedSites.jsp**.

4.4.2   Choosing a Distributor

How do you get in touch with a distributor? You could ask local retail vendors what distribution companies they use and any advantages. There is plenty of information to help you get set up over the phone and or online, since wine distributors are listed in the business pages of your local directory.

According to Kyle McHugh, "Most states have a few large distributors (Southern Wine & Spirits and Wirtz Beverage Group operate in many states) that carry most of the well-known brands, but it's the little distributors, especially those that do their own importing, where a small store can find the great wines that the big stores are literally too big or too busy to find." Utilizing the smaller distributers to find wines that nobody else in your area carries, says McHugh, can be a great selling point for your store and differentiate you from the competition.

You can also get information from national or even worldwide organizations. Try Wine and Spirits Wholesalers of America (**www.wswa.org**) who will provide you with contact names and pertinent legal information, or the International Beverage Network, **www.international beveragenetwork.com/default_kainew.asp**, which operates on a worldwide basis, bringing wineries, distributors and retailers together.

It makes sense financially to only do business with one or just a few distributors, since you will save on additional distribution fees. Christina Martin of Martin Ulisse Imports comments that overhead, distribution costs and TABC tax are often added to each bottle, though some companies may also charge a flat fee.

For distributors of wine-related products, such as corkscrews, decanters, glass tags, etc., to sell in your store, check with your wine distributor to see if they stock such products. There are also distributors who sell only those products. Here are a few examples.

- *Oenophilia*
  www.oenophilia.com

- *Epic Products, Inc.*
  www.epicproductsinc.com

- *Wine Enthusiast Wholesale*
  www.wineenthusiastwholesale.com

- *The Wine Appreciation Guild*
  For books about wine, and other products.
  www.wineappreciation.com

Take into consideration your business plan and calculate the total cost of your merchandise, along with the distribution fees and the company discounts. Are you marketing more alcoholic beverages than just wine, and can you benefit from an all around catalog of wines, liquors and beer? Or are you primarily interested in building a large wine selection, with exotic wines from all over the world? If this is the case, it would make sense to choose a wine distributor with the most varied of products.

Christina Martin concludes with this advice to retailers:

"There are a lot of 'big dogs' out there that seem to monopolize the market, but the reality is every account has its needs. Larger retailers need the larger more generic distributors while fancy restaurants, local bars, more personal places, seem to enjoy the boutique style distributor that is not everywhere and in every place. The key is to create a relationship with your distributor...they will learn what you need as a merchant and help work with you to sell their product."

Purchasing from a Wine Importer

The purchasing process might involve an importer if wines are being brought in from overseas. Christina Martin works as both a wholesale distributor and an importer. "We knew using a distributor would only increase the price. The price of wine itself is not all that expensive but as it is imported into the U.S. the prices just keep on growing."

According to Martin, the process breaks down into a variety of costs from the importing stage to the shipping and delivery. "All in all when you get to the actual retailer, the price of the wine has increased enormously and that is without any markups. This greatly affects the price at which the distributor buys and sells the wine."

Distributor's Fees

There are additional fees and permits that importers have to pay on a federal and state level. Martin says that up to eleven importing related fees have to be paid before the wine can leave customs. To begin with you have to get the product to the U.S. and through Customs.

"On the importation side you must first account for the actual wine, the bottle, which because there are so many different styles, sizes, glass weight, can actually range from normal to expensive, the cost of currency conversion when paying for the wine and the use of banks to do so.

"When the wine arrives by sea to the U.S. Harbor the major price contributors set in. It is necessary to hire a Customs Broker, which is expensive, to handle the shipping, freight forwarding, customs fees, and so on."

— Christina Martin,
Martin Ulisse Imports

Then there is the distribution side of things, which involves "Agents permits for all sales personnel who are selling the wine, sales employee salaries, delivery employees, etc." Finally, after obtaining a Private Carrier's Permit required by the state of Texas, Martin lists the final distributor expenses. "The cost of the delivery vehicles, insurance and tags, gas for deliveries, gas and expenses for sales reps, workman's compensation for all employees, salary taxes, then the usual stuff like office supplies and marketing."

As you can see, importing wine is a complex and expensive process and can add considerably to the retail price of wine sold in your store. However, the extra costs of purchasing from a wine importer like Christina Martin might be worthwhile if you find that you have a clientele interested in purchasing rarer wines perhaps not imported by the major importers and distributors.

4.4.3   Working with Wholesalers

There are 1,800 wholesalers in the U.S. according to the Wine and Spirits Wholesalers of America (WSWA) organization. You cannot take wholesalers for granted. While direct-to-consumer business is growing, the only way you will make substantial profit as a retailer is to affiliate yourself with a distribution company and get products at wholesale discounts so you can apply the standard 30%-50% profit markup. You'll also be able to buy wine-related merchandise from whatever wholesaler you choose.

Christina Martin explains her company's discount process, which varies from company to company. "Most companies offer a standard price and then some form of a discount. Martin Ulisse Imports offers to a liquor store a one-case price and a three-case price...Other companies have case discounts like we do."

Some wholesaler pet peeves include retail store owners that frequently complain about price or delivery issues and merchants that can't make up their mind about what they want to sell. Wholesalers will also not appreciate a retailer demanding an emergency delivery every other week. Treat the representatives kindly and attempt to work out any misunderstandings.

Wholesalers are also important to wineries of course. Their segment of the industry is the portal allowing producers access to the consumer market. You need to develop excellent relationships with wholesalers and introduce your business to as many of them as you can in order to have access to the broadest market possible. Wholesalers can also offer you valuable advice and knowledge about current industry trends and how to effectively market your products.

Importers, Winemakers and Other Contacts

Importers, winery owners, vineyard owners, will expect you as a wine store owner to be organized, professional and to know what you want. They won't mind recommending a certain variety of wine product, but they do expect you to have a general idea of what kind of wine you're looking for. Most professional contacts have websites set up that detail what they do—which eliminates the need for an extensive question and answer discussion about what they sell.

You may never have to do business with an importer or exporter. It's very possible you could open a business and retire 30 or so years from now using just one distributor—if you're happy with the results. The problem with using a single distributor is that you will have a limited selection to build your inventory on. A better choice might be to find several distributors, with at least one that has a relationship with one or more importers.

Many wholesalers deal with importers on a regular basis and bring foreign wines in at discount prices. As a retailer you would only do business directly with an importer if you knew of a specific type of wine overseas that you wanted and can't find a wholesaler who offers it. Importers might not have a website, but they still want to know what you're looking for and how much you're willing to pay. Do your research ahead of time; it saves their precious time and saves you long distance charges.

5. Running Your Wine Business

5.1 Store Operations

5.1.1 Developing a Procedures Manual

As you move through the process of opening your store, you will begin to notice that you are starting to develop routines around how you do various things. These routines will fall eventually under the more official business term — operations. One of the great things about owning your own store is that you are in charge of deciding the routines of your operations, and you can plan how things run in your store to satisfy your needs and desires.

Every time you do something new, keep a record of how you did it. As you go along, take accurate notes about what works, what doesn't work, and what will need to be done a different way. Over time you will begin to see an organized system emerge — this is the beginning of the development of your operational procedures.

Having written records and instructions of important store procedures and tasks makes it possible for your employees to complete tasks more efficiently by themselves. Also, store procedures aren't necessarily things that you can (or even want to) store in your head. It is hard to remember all the passwords and codes for things, the procedures for receiving merchandise, or the steps in taking a check from a customer. The best thing to do is to make a guide for employees (and for you) to keep this information organized and accessible.

Putting together an operations manual for your store will help you get all of your procedures and instructions for every little task organized and in one spot for you and your employees to refer to. Follow the simple directions below to make your own Store Operations Manual.

What You Need

Here are the things you'll need to create your manual:

- Checklists for each area of the store (see below for some sample checklists)
- Three-ring binder or folder with clear plastic insert space on cover and spine
- Three-hole punch
- Binder dividers with section labels
- Checklist forms
- Task forms
- Special reminder forms
- Emergency forms

What to Do

Once you have gathered your materials, follow these steps:

- Carefully consider each area of your operations. Make divider tags for the binder with the following labels: Opening Tasks, Closing Tasks, Daily Tasks, Weekly Tasks, Monthly Tasks, Quarterly Tasks, Annual Tasks. Place these labeled dividers in the binder.

- Make a checklist for each area. Use the checklist examples on the following pages to get started. List the tasks that you can think of for each area. Remember to write down important reminder information like where things are located, which lights to turn on, etc. Think about how you would instruct someone unfamiliar with the task to do it. Sequentially ordered steps work the best.

- Fill out a separate sequential form or reminder sheet for each specific area of operations in your store.

- Make a list of emergency number and other emergency information for the first page of the binder. You might want to place a copy of every employee's emergency information card inside the binder directly behind the emergency number and procedure page.

- Label the binder clearly and make a copy of all the contents to store in a safe place away from your store.

TIP: Remember that this operations manual will be fluid and will change over time. As you change your procedures, remember to change the corresponding task page.

5.1.2 Areas of Operations Checklists

Here are some examples of various areas of the store and some things in each area that you might want to include in your operations manual:

Opening/Closing

- ❏ Door locks

- ❏ Lights — both indoor and outdoor

- ❏ Security systems and codes

- ❏ What to do if the alarm goes off accidentally

- ❏ Turning on/off the air-conditioning and heating units

- ❏ Turning on/off computers/fax/postal machine/copier

- ❏ Mail sorting and opening

- ❏ Brewing coffee

- ❏ Email

- ❏ Answering machine

- ❏ Cleaning break room and staff kitchen area

Cash Wrap

- ❏ Operating the cash register

- ❏ Preparing money drawer for opening

- ❏ Processing credit and debit cards

- ❏ Processing checks

- ❏ Accepting and selling gift certificates

- ❏ Completing a transaction

- ❏ Keeping track of what is sold/inventory

- ❏ Phone procedures

- ❏ Directions to store

- ❏ Using computers/fax/postal machine/copier

- ❏ Mailing list

- ❏ Promotions and sales

- ❏ Cash deposits and bank deposits

- ❏ Wrapping gifts

Merchandise and Sales

- ❏ Procedures for receiving inventory

- ❏ Pricing merchandise

- ❏ Putting tags on items

- ❏ Shelving merchandise

❑ Making displays

❑ Cleaning and organizing displays

❑ Answering customer questions

❑ When to discount prices on merchandise

❑ Handling refunds

Safety/Health/Emergency Procedures

❑ Emergency contact numbers—fire, police, hospitals, etc

❑ Staff and owner emergency contact numbers

❑ Procedures for emergency in-store illness—for both staff members and customers

❑ Evacuation procedures

❑ Emergency or natural disaster plan

❑ What to do in case of shoplifting

❑ What to do in case of robbery

5.2 Inventory Management

5.2.1 Choosing Which Wines to Sell

How do you know which labels will sell? A tricky question, because on the one hand you have the most popular wine labels worldwide and on the other you have the top selling wines in your local community. Major cities may report entirely different sales figures for wines than a large rural area with only one store for wine shopping.

According to statistics from the Wine Institute (**www.wineinstitute. org**), Chardonnay, Zinfandel, Merlot and Cabernet Sauvignon are among the top selling varietals in the U.S., accounting for 53 percent of all table wines sold in food stores; probably reason enough to stock these popular wines.

Common Wine Varieties

- *Alicante Bouschet:* Red wine from France, Spain, Portugal or California

- *Barbera:* White wine from France, Italy, Greece, Australia and California

- *Beaujolais:* Red wine from France

- *Bordeaux:* Red wine from France

- *Burgundy:* Red wine from France

- *Cabernet Franc:* Red wine from France or California

- *Cabernet Sauvignon:* red wine from California, Australia or France

- *Carignan:* Red wine from France, Italy, Mexico, South America and the US

- *Chablis:* White wine from France; Chablis from California is a different wine

- *Chardonnay:* White wine from California, Australia or France

- *Chenin Blanc:* White wine from South Africa, North and South America

- *Chianti:* Red wine from Italy

- *Frascati:* White wine from Italy

- *French Colombard:* White wine from France and South Africa

- *Gewurtztraminer:* White wine from France, California, Washington or Germany

- *Grenache:* Red wine from France, California or South America

- *Lambrusco:* Red wine from Italy

- *Liebfraumilch:* White wine from Germany

- *Malvasia:* White wine from Italy, Spain, France, Greece, Australia & the US

- *Merlot:* Red wine from California, France, Washington, New York or Oregon

- *Muscat of Alexandria:* White wine from France, Spain, Portugal, Chile or South Africa

- *Nebbiolo:* Red wine from Italy

- *Petite Sirah:* Red wine from California or South America

- *Pinot Blanc:* White wine from Italy, Germany or Austria

- *Pinot Grigio (Gris):* White wine from Italy, Oregon or France

- *Pinot Noir:* Red wine from France

- *Pouilly-Fuisse:* White wine from France

- *Riesling:* White wine from Germany, California, France or Washington

- *Roussanne:* White wine from France or California

- *Ruby Cabernet:* Red wine from California or South Africa

- *Sangiovese:* Red wine from Italy or California

- *Sauvignon Blanc:* White wine from California, France, New Zealand or South Africa

- *Semillon:* White wine from France, Australia, South America, California or Washington

- *Soave:* White wine from Italy

- *Syrah:* Red wine from France, South Africa, Australia or the US

- *Valpolicella:* Red wine from Italy

- *Viognier:* White wine from France, Australia and California

- *Zinfandel:* Red or white from California

Of course there are many other kinds of wines made from many different grapes from regions all over the world. You will also need to stock popular sparkling wines, which are made from the same types of grapes but are carbonated; wines created from hybrid grapes; and fortified wines which have more alcohol or sweetness added beyond the natural taste. The more you know about the many different types of wine bottled around the world, the better you will be able to answer your customers' questions and help them choose just the right wine they're looking for.

5.2.2 Inventory Control

There will be regular costs of sales to consider besides opening start up costs. The regular cost of sales involves more than just totaling your purchases. Tracking your cost of sales (which should be noted on the monthly profit and loss report) will mean taking inventory of your entire in-store stock. There are two popular methods of taking merchandise inventory: perpetual and periodic.

Perpetual Inventory System

With this system items are added and subtracted perpetually from the total inventory upon receipt. This lets the owner have a running count of all inventories at all times. This can be recorded by stock record card or a computer system. Data includes a description, receipts, quantity on hand, unit cost, vendors and a purchase document number. This will require a POS system and additional software, which is a notable expense.

Periodic Inventory System

This inventory system sees the company waiting until the end of an accounting period before taking a physical inventory count. Records maintained are not as detailed. It is mainly used just to compute a cost of goods sold. If you do not have a POS system or computer with software in the store, then this would be the only option.

In order to calculate the cost of sales you would use this formula:

Beginning Inventory + Purchases – Ending Inventory = Cost Of Sales

> **NOTE:** Beginning inventory + purchases – ending inventory = COS; COS ÷ number of sales for inventory period = average inventory cost per sale

Steps to Taking Inventory

Establish the beginning inventory. Start by listing all items by total quantity along with their unit price. (What you pay for it, not the price you sell it for.)

Create a sample sheet such as the following sample (a spreadsheet program is perfect for this):

Sample Inventory Count Form

ITEMS	COUNT	QTY (LB, OZ, GAL, EA.)	PRICE PER UNIT	TOTAL PRICE
			$	$
			$	$
			$	$
			$	$
			$	$
			$	$
			$	$
			Total Page _____	
			Total Sales For _____	

SUBTOTALS	
Total Wine	$
Total Spirits	$
Total Beer	$
Total Supplies	$
Total Food	$
Totals	$
Beginning Inventory	$
Purchases	$
Ending Inventory	$
Cost Of Goods Sold	$
Total Sales	$

- Multiply each item by the cost per unit and enter the total cost for each in the far right column.

- Now add up all the columns to find the total value of the beginning inventory by categories.

- Add the purchases for the new month to the total in the same way, multiplying all the items by the unit cost. This goes under "Purchases."

- At the end of the month you will take an "ending inventory" of all of your products, by quantity and total unit price.

- The beginning inventory plus new purchases minus ending inventory equals the cost of sales. You can also get the cost of sales as a percentage by dividing the cost of sales figure by the total sales figure.

- Enter the ending totals for each product category according to beginning inventory, purchases, ending inventory, cost of sales and total sales.

5.2.3   Inventory Software

Ask ten different store owners what inventory system they use to track sales and you will likely get ten different answers. There are a few owners still keeping track of items by hand; however, eventually most retail stores have to use some sort of software as sales volumes increase.

There are a wide variety of options available to store owners. Which software works best is often a personal choice and depends on the type of store, the size of store, and how many customers you have.

This is a big investment, so take your time. Fortunately, many of these software programs offer a free demo trial period, so you can try out several different versions before deciding which one you would like to purchase. Try the various demos. Find out which program works best for you before using up valuable hours punching in information on products, only to realize the software you purchased is not working to meet your needs.

Wine Store Software

Some wine stores are small and can get by with some simple financial software and a cash register. Quickbooks and Quicken are two popular financial programs that can help you organize your bookkeeping and prepare your taxes for an accountant's review. But if you have a POS system, then you can invest in special POS software specially designed for wine or liquor stores.

Plexis POS offers a professional system for as low as $299.95, with supports for liquor stores as well as other types of food stores. More expensive units that are made exclusively for liquor or wine stores include Windward Software's LiquorStorePOS for $2,195.00 (hardware is optional) and International Point of Sale for $2,799.00, which includes hardware. These systems incorporate additional features such as touch screen technology and easy inventory tracking.

When shopping around for wine or liquor store software, be sure to look for the specific term "POS" as opposed to wine cellar programs, which may provide access to wine information for auctions, but little assistance with direct sales.

Wine Bar Software

When shopping for wine bar software, look for restaurant and bar software as opposed to regular retail POS. Point of Success offers a system for $600.00 that allows for fingerprint log in, credit card processing and employee cards. Software programs like Liquor Monitor from Com-Cash can offer assistance on monitoring bar over-pours, if you or your staff serve a lot of mixed drinks.

Before deciding upon one system, you should shop around online and look for free trial programs of the actual interface so you can evaluate the products' usability.

Software and POS System Suppliers

- *Plexis POS*
  www.plexispos.com

- *LiquorStorePOS*
  www.liquorstorepos.wws5.com

- *International Point of Sale*
  www.internationalpointofsale.com/liquorstore.html

- *Point of Success*
  www.pointofsuccess.com

- *Liquor Monitor*
  www.liquormonitor.com/software-integrated.asp

- *Intelli-Scanner*
  Barcode scanners and a wine collection management system
  www.intelliscanner.com

- *Microsoft Retail Management System*
  Computerized inventory management system for wine retailers
  **www.microsoft.com/smallbusiness/products/retail-software/
  bundle.mspx#forbeer**

5.2.4   Inventory Stickers and Labels

To keep track of inventory some stores use simple tags they label by hand, while others use bar code tags that work with whatever type of software they are using. You should use whatever system makes the most sense for your store.

If your store is organized neatly and your prices are marked clearly, not only will shopping be easier and more comfortable for customers, you will find that keeping track of your inventory is easier. Using inventory systems to keep organized will help you avoid the frustration of not being able to find inventory or a special order.

Most retail stores use printed price stickers from a pricing gun or computer printer. You might consider self-adhesive labels, but be careful with them. Some labels leave glue residue on items and will sometimes cause a permanent mark when removed. Some retailers use bar code tags that work with whatever type of software and scanner they use. Although initially more expensive than stickers, if you get very busy the time you save keeping track of your inventory might easily pay for it. Your choice of which system to use will largely depend on the type of inventory you carry and your inventory turnover.

To find out more about labeling and bar code systems, you can visit Motorala POS Solutions at **www.motorola.com/staticfiles/Business/US-EN/AB/Retail_R.html** or **POSWorld.com**. Both of these companies offer labels, inventory management and bar code systems. Most office supply stores like Staples, Office Depot, and Office Max, sell price stickers and pricing guns.

5.3 Pricing Merchandise

5.3.1 Pricing Wine

How much should you sell your wine for? The answer depends on whether you sell wine by the bottle or by the glass. It also depends upon the wine's appellation (the geographic name by which wine producers identify and market their wine), how in-demand the label is, and the perception of the wine industry. That's right; it's less to do with overall quality than people realize. That's why it's possible to buy a good wine for a low price, and buy a wine you hate for well over $20.00 a glass.

For starters, wines from popular appellations, such as Napa Valley or Sonoma, can be pricey just because of reputation alone. Wines with well-known and preferred grape varieties like Pinot Noir and Cabernet also fetch premium prices. Some wines can qualify as a specific (and higher priced) appellation or variety by meeting the legal percentages, even though they're partially filled with cheaper blended wines. This is why it's important to pay close attention to state laws on winemaking—it can actually mean more money for you.

Two other factors that influence price are taste and vintage. Exotic-tasting wines, especially if they're from overseas, are predictably expensive. As for wines that have been matured for years, even decades, as long as they are high quality wines that age well, the general rule from wine store owners is that for every year a good wine matures, it earns an extra three dollars in price value. This general belief has many exceptions, however.

Tips for Wine Stores and Bars

On the local level, wine price is affected more by the label detail, and not so much the content of the product. Many wholesale distributors will provide suggested retail prices at request or by catalog. For additional price research, you can scout out your competition and see how much they are charging for variety wines, appellation wines and other popular brands.

For hard-to-find wines this might involve some Internet research, though if you communicate with an importer or wholesaler, they might be able to provide you with a suggested price. The important issue is to stay competitive. Experienced wine buyers will know when they are being overcharged.

Wine bar prices operate differently than wine store prices. You drastically overcharge for every ounce of wine, compared to buying it by the bottle. Christina Martin explains the wine bar price philosophy, "For most restaurants there is just the standard price and a glass price if that is possible. A restaurant tries to make at least 80% of the bottle cost on the first glass if it is a glass pour, so not all wine can be served by the glass." Therefore it makes sense from both your point of view and the customer's, to push whole bottle sales in a wine bar.

Selling wine by the bottle offers these advantages:

- Increases bartender and server interaction with patrons.

- Saves more time and earns more money than by the glass.

- Frees up bartenders and waiters to serve more bar patrons.

- Selling bottles makes more initial profit.

- Limits opened wine bottles, which quickly become stale after a few days.

When wine bar merchants encourage their staff to try and sell a bottle of wine at every table this seems to set the precedent for the entire room and actually stimulates other wine drinkers to order bottles instead of glasses. If new customers see everyone in the room with a bottle of wine and hear the servers suggesting a bottle of wine then they're more likely to purchase by the bottle themselves.

Selling Wine by the Glass

Selling wine by the glass is ideal for tentative drinkers—that is people who are just getting a sample of a wine, and who hopefully are going to taste something they like. Your ultimate goal is to sell them a bottle of wine based on the good sample. Consider wine by the glass an appetizer of a full "meal" to come later in the evening.

There are a few other advantages to wine by the glass. Many customers are touchy when it comes to paying high prices for a sample of wine. Penny pinching wine enthusiasts (and there is such a thing) usually will scoff at any bottle over $25.00 and any half-empty glass over $7.00. Some customers would pay for several inexpensive glasses of wine, but refuse to buy a whole bottle.

If you have a special collection of high-priced wines, then you could get away with selling expensive samples of it—as much as $15.00 a glass if the type of wine merits the price. (Remember some quality wines can sell for over $200.00 a bottle and still be competitively priced.) In this case, however, good salesmanship and wine knowledge is needed by the bartender or server to emphasize the uniqueness of the product.

Standard Markups

For Wine Stores

Depending on how friendly the distributor discount, (anywhere from 30% to 50%) retailers usually mark up their prices to 50% more than its wholesale cost.

> *The traditional mark-up for retail wine is 50% or 33% profit margin. Some wines are very popular and sell much better at a narrow margin (20-25%) so we also have wines that carry a heavier margin (40-50%) to make up the difference. Wines that are heavily marked-up should not be readily available to your local competition.*
>
> — Kimberly Eakin, Certified Wine Specialist,
> president of Wine Gourmet

For Wine Bars

Some restaurants and popular bars can easily mark up their retail wine samples by as much as 200-300%. After all, if you make 80% of the bottle on the first glass, then how much have you made after the bottle is gone?

The pricing is figured out by dividing the wine by the number of servings. One bottle of wine is traditionally equal to five servings of five ounces, though eight glasses has been suggested, for much smaller glasses or even "shots." Wine drinkers appreciate a little over half a glass; generous but not filled to the top. (Remember the nose may go in for inspection.)

In the next section, we'll look at some specific pricing formulas that you can use. These can be employed for wines and other beverages you sell, as well as for retail merchandise such as corkscrews, glassware, and other products.

5.3.2   Retail Pricing Formulas

There are different methods that wine retailers can use to arrive at their prices. Many manufacturers have a suggested retail price (MSRP) for retailers to follow. These are found along with their wholesale price to the retailer in their product catalogs. You can choose to follow a MSRP or not. The important questions to ask are whether the MSRP allows you sufficient profit and is it priced too high for your market. If the answer is no to the first and yes to the second, you might want to look for a different supplier.

A more efficient and profitable way to price is using a retail pricing formula. Generally, there are two concepts retailers should be aware of: percentage margin and price markup. Using these formulas will tell you what your percentage of profit is based on the percentage markup above your wholesale (i.e. purchase) price for that item. If the profit percentage is too low, then you'll want to use a different price markup percentage for that item.

As an example of how pricing affects your business, we'll use the break-even point for a fictional business. You may remember the formula for calculating the break-even point from section 3.4.2 as:

Break-even point = Total fixed costs ÷ (1 − total variable costs ÷ revenues)

In the example in section 3.4.2, the break-even point for the business was $69,000 in annual revenues. Also, for every dollar of sales, the company had 56 cents in variable expenses. Therefore, to break even, fixed costs can represent no more than 44 cents on every dollar. So if you had an item priced at $1.00, 56% of the selling price would be variable expenses and the rest would be fixed costs, leaving no room for profit. Obviously, nobody wants to run their store like that.

Based on these figures, the store owner might want to increase the profit margin. So for example, instead of selling a product for $1.00 as before, the owner might increase the retail price to $1.25. This would lower the percentage for each of fixed and variable costs as a percentage of revenue, resulting in an increased profit margin.

5.3.3   Profit Margin vs. Percentage Markup

Every retailer needs to understand the difference between profit margin and percentage markup. The profit margin is the amount of your retail price that represents profit for you over and above the cost of the merchandise. In a more sophisticated model, you would also include your total operating expenses as well. You would add in your fixed and variable costs and factor them into your pricing model, along with cost of goods.

The percentage markup is the percentage amount you increased the retail price over your cost for a given item. After you have been in business for a while, you will know what price markup generally works best for you. Pricing by percentage markup is less usual than pricing by profit margin.

Let's look at a specific example. Consider an item with a retail price of $1.00, that the owner paid 40 cents for.

The profit margin formula is:

$$\begin{aligned}
\text{Margin} &= (1 - (\text{cost} \div \text{selling price})) \times 100 \\
&= (1 - (40 \div 100)) \times 100 \\
&= (1 - .40) \times 100 \\
&= .60 \times 100 \\
&= 60
\end{aligned}$$

So in this example the profit margin is 60%.

If, however, you decided that you would set your prices by marking up everything by 60%, then the percentage markup formula is:

$$\text{Price} = \text{cost} + (\text{cost} \times 60 \div 100)$$
$$= 40 + (40 \times 0.60)$$
$$= 40 + 24$$
$$= 64$$

Using a fixed markup of 60%, the retail price on an item costing $0.40 would be $0.64.

Look carefully at these two formulas. Notice that markup pricing and profit margin pricing create two very different selling prices. In the first example, pricing based on a 60% profit margin required a selling price of $1.00. In the second example, using a percentage markup of 60% on cost resulted in a price of only 64 cents, a profit margin of only about 38%.

A quick way to calculate a profit margin price is to divide the cost price by the difference between 100 and the profit margin. For example, if you wanted to have a 5% profit margin you would divide your cost price by (100-5) or 95 percent. So if you paid 40 cents for a product and you wanted a 5% profit margin, to arrive at your selling price you would use the formula:

$$40 \div (100 - 5) = 40 \div .95 = 42 \text{ cents}$$

Here are some additional examples so you can see the trend:

$$10\%: \quad 40 \div (100 - 10) = 44 \text{ cents}$$
$$15\%: \quad 40 \div (100 - 15) = 47 \text{ cents}$$
$$25\%: \quad 40 \div (100 - 25) = 53 \text{ cents}$$
$$50\%: \quad 40 \div (100 - 50) = 80 \text{ cents}$$

Once you know your cost of doing business, you can easily arrive at a minimum profit percentage margin price that will meet your needs.

You'll also be able to look at a MSRP and determine if it meets your profit margin requirements.

Keep some of the other pricing concepts in mind as well. Your market may be able to support a higher profit margin in your pricing. Alternatively, you might be able to split margins by pricing higher ticket, lower volume items at a lower profit percentage, and use a higher profit margin on merchandise that sells for a lower price but at a higher volume. Another way to increase your profit margin is to reduce your variable expenses. If you find that your profit margin is too low, you can reduce costs like labor, store supplies, or even look for lower cost wholesale merchandise.

To read more about retail pricing concepts, try the following online resources:

- *Markup or Margin: Selling and Pricing*
  www.buildingtrade.org.uk/articles/markup_or_margin.html

- *Margin Markup/Profit Percentage Table*
  www.csgnetwork.com/marginmarkuptable.html

- *Pricing Your Products and Services Profitably*
  (Click on "Financial Management Series" and look for #7.)
  www.sba.gov/tools/resourcelibrary/publications/index.html

5.4 Getting Paid

As soon as you establish your business you will need to open a business checking account at a bank, trust company, or credit union. You can shop around to find a financial institution that is supportive of small business, or use the same one that you use for your personal banking.

In addition to your checking account, a financial institution may provide you with a corporate credit card used to make purchases for your business, a line of credit to purchase items for your store, and a merchant credit card account enabling you to accept credit card payments from customers.

You have a variety of options for getting paid by your customers.

5.4.1   Accepting Debit Cards

With a debit purchase, the funds come directly out of the customer's account at the bank and are deposited directly into your business bank account. There is no credit involved for customer or merchant. In order to set up debit payment, you will need to ask your bank for an application and you will need a debit machine. The equipment costs about $200 to $500, but some companies offer leases.

There may be a short delay or small charge to you, initially or ongoing, depending on the bank. And you will have to get the equipment to process the payments and print receipts. (Federal law mandates receipts be provided to customers for debit card purchases.) To find out more about debit card services in the U.S., visit the Electronic Transactions Association directory of member companies at **www.electran.org** (click on "Information Resources" then "Links"), or in Canada, visit the Interac Association at **www.interac.ca**.

5.4.2   Accepting Credit Cards

American Express and Discover cards set up merchant accounts nationally and internationally. MasterCard and Visa are local. To become a merchant accepting MasterCard and Visa, you will have to get accepted by a local acquirer (a financial institution like a bank licensed by the credit card company). Because yours is a new business, you may have to shop around to find one that gives you good rates (you may be charged between 1.5 and 3 percent per transaction for the service, and often an initial setup fee and perhaps ongoing fees for phone calls, postage, statements, and so on).

You might also have to provide evidence of a good personal financial record to set up an advantageous rate, at least until you've become established in your business and have a good track record for them to look at. Remember, the bank is granting you credit in this instance, "banking" on the fact that your customers will not want refunds or that you won't try to keep the money if they do.

These days, although the acquiring bank will be a local bank somewhere, it need not be in your hometown. Numerous services are available online to help you set up a merchant account. MasterCard and Visa accounts, as well as American Express and Discover, can all be set up through your local bank or by going to the websites of each of these companies.

- *MasterCard Merchant*
  www.mastercard.com/us/merchant
  www.mastercard.com/ca/merchant/en/index.html

- *Visa*
  http://usa.visa.com/merchants/merchant_resources/
  www.visa.ca/en/merchant/

- *American Express*
  https://home.americanexpress.com/homepage/
  merchant_ne.shtml?

- *Discover*
  www.discovernetwork.com/discovernetwork/howitworks/
  howitworks.html

5.4.3   Accepting Payment Online

If you have a website you can accept payments online through services such as PayPal (**www.paypal.com**). Typically, these services charge a greater "discount rate," which is what the 1.5 to 3 percent the banks and credit card companies hold from your payments is called. And the purchase must be made online. Still, there may be instances when you are doing business online with some of your clients, and it may be useful then. Also, it provides a safe route for conveying financial information over the Internet.

5.4.4   Accepting Checks

When you accept checks, especially to cover big-ticket items or major corporate purchases, you may want to have a back-up system for getting paid if the customer has insufficient funds in their checking account. It's important to get a credit card number, driver's license number, and full phone number and address (you might even want to check it online quickly to insure they are legitimate). If you have any doubts as to their honesty, it might be a good idea not to accept the check and let the sale go.

You can accept checks from customers with greater assurance by using a check payment service such as TeleCheck. TeleCheck compares checks you receive with a database of over 51 million bad check records, allowing you to decide whether to accept a check from a particular client. The company also provides electronic payment services, from telephone debit card processing to electronic checks. You can find out more about TeleCheck at **www.telecheck.com**.

5.5   Financial Management

Bookkeeping is not something you can learn over night. Accurate record keeping may be the single most important thing you learn about running your business. If you cannot stay on top of your bookkeeping, then your whole business could fall apart. It's not an exaggeration to say that your success as a wine store owner will be dependent upon good bookkeeping practice.

Keeping Good Records

This does necessarily mean that you personally have to become a certified public accountant just to open your own business. You always have the option of hiring a CPA to prepare your important tax records, an attorney to take care of your licensing fees, and another experienced worker to handle your day to day paperwork.

If you handle your own bookkeeping needs however, you can save a lot of money and a few headaches. When you give your records over to someone else to reconcile, you are not only giving them access to your private information, you also have to worry about their mistakes. You're the one who knows your finances the best and so you are qualified to handle the day-to-day activities if you put forth the effort to learn the basics.

5.5.1   Bookkeeping

Some people prefer to keep track of everything manually. Many business owners simply buy a few journals, write their accounts across the top and enter each month's expenses by hand. This method works well if you are organized, and love the feel of pen on paper. But if you have employees, several sources of income, and a steady flow of traffic through your store, you'll soon forget a few months, and it will become a monster lying in wait for you in your desk's bottom drawer.

Luckily for small business owners, there are several fairly inexpensive software systems that can easily guide you through the bookkeeping process. Intuit offers different types of financial software for different types of businesses. Intuit's Quickbooks, one of the most popular book-keeping systems, can run about $800 with point of sale functions, but will quickly pay for itself in the savings of not hiring a full-time book-keeper. Intuit also offers a basic program, Quicken Home & Business, which is a good option for new businesses and costs about $80.

Another maker of business management software is Acclivity (formerly MYOB). Their "Premier Accounting" suite allows you to track revenues and expenses, record bank deposits, generate reports, track customers and more. There are several other financial programs, including Simply Accounting which you can find at your local office supplies store.

- *Acclivity Premier Accounting*
  www.myob-us.com

- *Quicken*
  http://quicken.intuit.com

- *Quickbooks*
  http://quickbooks.intuit.com

- *Simply Accounting*
  www.simplyaccounting.com

Even though software can make most of the work easier for you, you might consider taking a beginning accounting or a bookkeeping class at a local community college. Accounting basics are vital information that all store owners need, but sometimes neglect to learn. Even if you hire someone to do your books, you'll need to know the basics so that you can understand what is going on in your accounts.

5.5.2   Types of Reports and Records

There are a number of reports, forms and other paperwork you need to be aware of as a wine store owner. In addition to keeping track of your own internal business paperwork, you'll need to meet some government requirements and file the relevant paperwork.

Daily Business Paperwork

Cash Register and POS System Reports

With the help of a high quality cash register, you can easily total the different amounts at the end of each business day: wine sales, spirits sales, food, wine supplies—as many categories as you need. You may also choose to buy a point-of-sale system instead of a cash register. The advantages of such a system are more inventory features, search options and detailed reports. POS systems are becoming increasingly more affordable, and if your business owns a computer you can easily purchase POS software for less than $500. (See section 5.2.3 for more about POS systems.)

Daily Sales Reports

A daily sales report (DSR) is recommended to help classify the different categories of revenues you receive every day, as well as the sales taxes due. (See the sample DSR on the next page.) In addition to the DSR, which should be filled out every business day, there are a few forms you will need to fill out on a regular and semi-regular basis.

Profit And Loss Statement (Monthly)

This is not an official document but should be created at the beginning of each month for the previous month's business. Included in this report are your sales, your expenses, and the cost of goods sold. Each category should be detailed and broken down by subcategories. This will help you better understand all the figures in auditing your own work and in the event of an IRS audit. (See the next section for a sample P&L Statement.)

Balance Sheet (Monthly or Quarterly)

Though this statement is usually required in the initial stage, it is a good idea to keep a regular balance sheet either monthly or quarterly to keep track of all your assets and liabilities. This form may also be required by your lending company.

Sample Daily Sales Report

Date: November 11, 20__

	Today	Month to Date
Total Sales	$1,315.73	$18,000.00
Cash	$529.49	$6,800.00
Checks	$485.31	$7,200.00
Master Card	$180.04	$2,400.00
Visa	$70.26	$1,200.00
Other	$50.63	$400.00
Store Credit	0	0
Subtotal	**$1,315.73**	**$18,000.00**
Starting Float (Subtract)	(-$300.00)	(-$300.00)
Deposit Total	**$1,015.73**	**$17,700.00**
Returns	0	$178.75
Voids	0	$43.92
Pay Outs	0	$250.00
Other	0	
Total Cash Paid Out	**0**	**$472.67**
Deposit Total Less Total Cash Paid Out	**$1,015.73**	**$17,227.33**
Sales Tax Collected	$229.04	$1,447.50
Cash Register Reading	$1,016.73	$17,227.65
Difference (+ or -)	(-$1.00)	$0.32

Bank Deposits (Daily)

Ring Out Your Register(s)

Register tills are pulled from the register after employee shifts, and kept for counting and deposit at the end of the day. A till of new currency is put into the cash register or POS system to start a new shift. Retail stores in busy season might see the arrangement of "cash drops" where a manager drops by a register (usually notified by the POS system) and pulls excess money from the till for security purposes.

Count Up Your Cash

A manager totals up all the money from the tills at the end of the day and compares them to the POS reports or cash register totals. At this point the cash is separated from the checks and credit card receipts. Count the largest denominations in bills down to every last penny. Do your cash counting with a fellow employee for verification and always have the door locked.

Subtract Tomorrow's Till

Before finalizing your deposit slip, subtract the amount for tomorrow's register. You need some money for change — try for $250.00 worth of small bills and coins. To make the deposit process easier you could keep a change bank on hand, made up $300.00-$400.00 worth of change money (and coin rolls) for emergencies. That way, you won't have to tamper with your daily takings and could deposit the entire amount in full.

$250.00 in your register breaks down this way:

- $100 in Twenties
- $50 in Tens
- $20 in Fives
- $50 in Ones (in Canada split between $1 and $2 coins)
- $20 in Quarters
- $5 in Dimes
- $4 in Nickels
- $1 in Pennies

Close Out the Credit/Debit Card Machine

This process is slightly different from printing out register totals. The credit company you choose will provide you with the machine and instructions. These sheets can be stapled to the DSR.

Total the DSR

Total up all the cash receipts, check receipts and credit card totals from the various categories. This is your Daily Sales Report.

Make the Deposit

The cash drawer remains at $250.00 for the next morning (or your chosen amount). All of your checks and cash on hand go towards the bank deposit. Fill out your bank deposit completely. Try and deposit it early the next morning so that you can get receipt from a living teller and avoid the risk of robbery.

You should track all of your monthly expenses on computer and on paper. You don't have to fill out a physical sheet, but you should print out a monthly report to have for your files. The monthly expense report should coincide with all of the expenses listed on your checkbook. The monthly statement you receive from the bank should be reconciled till the end of each month and compared with the expense report for any errors.

Tracking Errors

There may be times when you encounter an error in cash counting or in reconciling your checkbook. Reconciling a checkbook error is a matter of patience and diligent analysis. You must go over every listed transaction one by one until you find the discrepancy.

In the case of your money not matching the cash register receipts there's a chance you could be miscounting (which would simply mean you do a recount) or that an employee made a mistake in the actual sales transaction. (Wrong change returned or an item punched in incorrectly)

Two employees should verify the numbers which will minimize counting errors. Have both employees sign the DSR, as this can help for auditing purposes later on. If a mistake was made, correct the error in the books and notate it in as much detail as possible (with your initials). If there are frequent then overages or shortages it means that either your employees are not being trained properly or that someone could be stealing funds.

> **TIP:** To prevent checks being stolen, immediately after receiving a check a cashier should verify the payer's driver's license and then endorse the check with the company's signature.

Your Sales Pace

A good way to determine if your sales for the month are on track on any given day is to follow your sales pace. At any time during the month, this will tell you what you can expect to earn for the remainder of the month. Perhaps a big snow storm has caused a sales slump for several days during the week. How much will you need to earn for the rest of the month to meet your revenue target?

The basic formula for calculating sales pace is:

Sales Pace = (Total Sales ÷ Number of Business Days so far for the month) x the number of business days in the month

From the Daily Sales Report above, the store did $18,000 up to the 13th business day of the month. The sales pace is calculated using the preceding 10 days of sales as:

$$\$18,000 \div 10 \times 30 = \$1,800 \times 30 = \$54,000$$

So, for the entire month at the current sales pace, the store can expect around $54,000 in sales. If the store owner had projected $50,000 in sales for this month, then the sales pace is well on track. If the projection was $60,000, then sales are a bit behind.

Another point to consider is that sales on the 11th day of the month were above the average daily sales ($1,016 as compared to $1,800). The store owner can figure out now what the sales pace for the rest of the month will need to be to maintain the target pace.

Let's say the store owner had projected $60,000 in sales for the month. To calculate the sales pace that is needed for the remainder of the month, use the formula:

$$\text{Sales pace} = (\$80,000 - (\$1,800 \times 10)) \div 19 = \$2,211$$

The store will need to produce $2,211 in sales each day for the remaining 19 days of the month in order to reach the $60,000 sales target for the month. Based on the preceding 10 days of sales, the store is a bit behind in its daily and month-to-date target sales.

5.5.3   Financial Statements and Reports

When considering your expenses, divide them into two categories: expenses that cannot be controlled, and expenses that you can increase or decrease depending on your cash flow.

Non-controllable Expenses

Non-controllable expenses could include business loans, credit card company fees, rent, insurance, and attorney and accounting fees. These non-controllable amounts are not fixed, and can easily rise every year or even on a semi-annual basis. These bills cannot be withheld due to poor finances and negotiation is usually out of the question.

Utilities bill are sometimes considered a controllable expense, since you can conserve electricity. But of all your otherwise controllable expenses, this is the one that is most difficult to limit. In the summer, electricity bills soar and you will also keep a lot of electrical appliances, some that run constantly such as wine coolers, freezers or refrigerators. It's never a good idea to sacrifice the comfortable environment to save on monthly expenses.

Controllable Expenses

Expenses such as labor, repairs and maintenance, supplies, advertising, equipment rentals, replacements and entertainment can all easily be controlled on a month-to-month basis.

Labor can be controlled by limiting the number of employees you hire, along with their total hours per week. When you cut back on total employees and total hours you also save money on payroll tax, which can be as much as 18 percent of your total payroll costs.

TIP: Save money by lowering the hours of part-timers. If you keep cutting hours and eliminating benefits of full-time employees, you'll eventually find yourself without a staff!

Equipment rentals, replacements and supplies can also be cut back if you have a particularly bad month. Repairs and maintenance can also be cut back, as long as they don't involve serious health violations or put customers at risk.

Advertising, Telephones, Entertainment

Telephone expenses are controllable if you alter your service plan. If you plan on placing a lot of international or out-of-state phone calls, purchase a plan with unlimited or low long-distance charges. You may need a cell phone in addition to a regular line, not to mention Internet access. Shop around for the best deal; you may save some money by using your home Internet service rather than pay another ISP, or you can limit most of your local calls to the business line only.

Advertising is probably the first expense to be cut when there are budget problems. The store could theoretically survive on repeat customers as well as constant traffic if it is ideally located.

Entertainment costs you! And we're not just talking about live acts and subscription radio services. Even something as small as your personal CD playing softly in the background of your store will cost you in royalty payments. By law, you are required to pay the artist royalties for the right to play their music in your store.

A shrewd thing to do might be to capitalize on the legal loophole that says getting an artist's written permission to play their music eliminates the need for royalties. Search for local musical talent and work out an arrangement where you both can benefit, rather than pay expenses on old music.

For details on royalty payments for background music visit the American Society of Composers, Authors and Publishers (ASCAP) at **www.ascap.com/licensing/generallicensing.html**.

Deductable Business Expenses

You might be surprised at what purchases can be counted as a deductable business expense. Anything that's directly related to business like lunches and gasoline usually are countable as an expense. However, the one thing you need is documentation for all of these expenses. Keep all of your receipts for purchases related to the business. Visit the IRS website (**www.irs.gov/businesses/small/article/0,,id=109807,00.html**) for more information. In Canada, visit **www.cra-arc.gc.ca/tx/bsnss/tpcs/slprtnr/bsnssxpnss/menu-eng.html**.

Cash Flow Statement

The cash flow statement allows you to quickly see whether more cash is coming in than going out, or vice versa, at the end of each month. It also allows you to make projections for certain periods of the year (such as the summer months when you might have increased sales due to larger numbers of tourists in your area at that time), or project cash flow year-over-year, and budget accordingly. You can also use it to track monthly cash flow and make projections for the coming month. This is handy if you're planning to make a large equipment or inventory purchase and need to know if you can afford it.

Cash flow is an important element of your financial picture. Monitoring cash flow lets you see how well your business is doing from day to day. Are you paying expenses with the money you take in from your operating revenues, or are you paying for expenses with other business funds such as banked working capital? If you are doing so with the former, your business is self-sustaining.

To keep track of expenses, you will need to keep copies of all receipts. This can be a challenge for new business owners who might have a habit of tossing out receipts for small items or not asking for receipts in the first place. However, you are likely to have numerous small expenses related to your business, and these can add up over time. These expenses should be accounted for so you can minimize your taxes. And, of course, knowing exactly where your money is going will help you plan better and cut back on any unnecessary expenses. So make it a habit to ask for a receipt for every expense related to your business.

Here is a sample six-month cash flow worksheet for the first six months of operation.

Sample Six Month Cash Flow Worksheet

Month	1	2	3	4	5	6	Total
Starting Cash							
Cash Receipts							
Cash sales							
Layaways							
Credit card receipts							
Debit card receipts							
Total							
Cash Disbursements							
Start-up costs							
Advertising							
Bank charges							
Fees & dues							
Fixed assets							
Insurance							
Loans-Principal							
Loans-Interest							
Licenses & Taxes							
Purchases for resale							
Office supplies							
Professional fees							
Rent							
Repair & maintenance							
Telephone & internet							
Utilities							
Wages & benefits							
Owner's draw							
Monthly Surplus or Deficit (Cash less Disbursements)							
To Date Surplus or Deficit*							

[Monthly surplus/deficit to date is calculated by carrying through any deficit or surplus from month to month]

Accounts Payable/Receivable Reports

Accounts payable are those accounts that you must pay — the money or bills your store owes. Accounts receivable are any accounts that are owed your store — the money that others owe you. Accounts receivable reports can vary widely depending on how you do business. For instance, accepting credit cards or selling over the Internet will affect how this report looks. And you may sell more at certain times than at others. If you have a layaway plan, this will affect your accounts receivable as well.

Accounts payable reports will tell you what bills you owe and when they are due. It's important to know clearly what you owe before you make any additional purchases. You have to be able to pay all your incoming bills and still have enough money for the other things you need to purchase for your business. An accounts payable report will help you to schedule when you will pay your bills, and will help you make sure nothing is neglected or forgotten.

Income Statement (Profit and Loss)

Your income statement (also called a profit and loss or P&L statement) will tell you how much money you have in expenses and how much money you have in revenue for a given period. A number of things are necessary for an income statement.

You'll need to know:

- Your revenues for the period (gross sales minus returns and discounts)

- The cost of goods sold (what it cost you during the period to purchase merchandise for your store for the period)

- Your gross profit (revenues minus cost of goods sold)

- Your operating expenses (everything you must pay for to operate your store, including non-cash items like depreciation)

- Your net profit before and after taxes (revenues minus your operating expenses, and then subtract your tax liability)

The end result will tell you how much money your store is making — what is commonly referred to as "the bottom line."

You will want to decide which method of accounting you want to use, accrual method or cash method. In the accrual method, income is reported in the month it is earned and expenses reported in the month they are incurred (even if they have not yet been paid).

The cash method tracks actual money received and actual money spent. You do not consider any outstanding bills or invoices. The Business Owner's Toolkit website has an article entitled "Cash vs. Accrual Accounting" at **www.toolkit.cch.com/text/P06_1340.asp** that you can read as an introduction to this topic.

On the next page is an example of a typical income statement.

Balance Sheet

A good metaphor for a balance sheet is that it is a snapshot, like a photograph, of your business taken at one moment in time. A balance sheet is the quickest way to see how your store is doing at a glance. It shows you what you own and what you owe. In other words, it is a balance of your assets against your liabilities.

The balance sheet consists of:

- Assets (the items you own including your inventory)

- Liabilities (what you owe)

- Owner's Equity (what you've put into the business)

Types of assets are current assets and fixed assets (long-term and capital assets). A current asset is something that is acquired by your business over your business's fiscal year and will probably be used during that period to generate more revenue. Inventory, prepaid expenses such as rent already paid, and accounts receivable are examples of current assets. A fixed asset is an item that doesn't get used up quickly such as land, buildings, machinery, vehicles, long-term investments, etc., whose value is depreciated over time.

Sample Income Statement

Income Statement [Company Name]
for month ending July 31, 20___

REVENUE ($)

Cash sales	5,250
Credit card sales	1,600
Online sales	150
Total Sales	**$7,000**

COST OF GOODS SOLD

Inventory and material purchases	1,800
Shipping	50
Supplies	150
Total cost of goods sold	**$2,000**

GROSS PROFIT **$5,000**

EXPENSES

Lease	1,850
Insurance	75
Licenses & taxes	250
Office supplies & postage	100
Interest	95
Utilities	225
Wages	550
Telephone and Internet	115
Depreciation	55
Vehicle expenses	220
Repairs & maintenance	65
Total Expenses	**$3,040**

Net Income for the Month **$1,960**

There are two types of liabilities: current and long-term. A current liability includes all those bills waiting for you to send a check out, such as utilities, short-term loans, or anything else payable within twelve months. A long-term liability is something that will be paid over a period of time longer than twelve months, for instance, a mortgage, a long-term equipment lease, or a long-term loan.

Owner's equity is anything you've personally contributed to (invested in) the business or any profit that remains in the owner's account that you have not drawn out in wages for yourself. If you used money from your personal accounts, or put your own assets into the business's inventory, the business "owes" you and it is recorded in this section of the balance sheet.

On the next page is an example of what a typical balance sheet will look like. Note that assets balances exactly against liabilities + owner's equity. Also note that owner's equity equals assets minus liabilities.

5.5.4   Building Wealth

The following excellent advice on building wealth is adapted from the *FabJob Guide to Become a Coffee House Owner*, by Tom Hennessy.

Sometimes we get lost in the adventure of building a business and forget that on top of the perks of being our own boss, we can also make money in our venture However, like all things, success doesn't just happen—you have to create it.

Even when you are making a good net profit each month, if you don't have a system for managing that profit, it can leak out during the course of a year. Then you will have nothing to show for your labor come New Year's Eve. In order to build wealth, you need to know how to squeeze all the value out of each and every dollar through budgeting, saving and investing.

Through these practices, you can build up a substantial amount of money without having a huge business. That is because time goes by very quickly. Five or ten years can slip away fast, and if you have a plan to carry you through those years, you will be amply rewarded. The two magic ingredients of time and compound interest are very valuable allies indeed.

Sample Balance Sheet

Balance Sheet [Company Name]
As at June 30, 20___

ASSETS
Current Assets

Cash	12,200
Accounts Receivable	1,000
Inventory	80,000

Total current assets 93,200

Fixed Assets

Furniture	3,500
Vehicle	20,000

Total fixed assets 23,500

TOTAL ASSETS   **$116,700**

LIABILITIES
Current Liabilities

Accounts Payable	5,000
Taxes Payable	2,225
Loan (short-term)	12,500
Current Portion of long-term loan	667

Total Current Liabilities 20,392

Long-term liabilities

Loan	35,000

TOTAL LIABILITIES   **55,392**

OWNER'S EQUITY

Capital – Owner's Deposits	90,000
Less Owner's withdrawals	(32,500)
Net Income/Loss	3,808

Total Owner's Equity 61,308

TOTAL LIABILITIES AND OWNER'S EQUITY   **$116,700**

Compound Interest and Debt

Think of compound interest as a steep hill. People are either on one side of this hill or the other. On one side of the hill, you have compound interest that you pay. On the other side is compound interest that is paid to you.

When you first start out in business, you generate a lot of debt. Your $200,000 loan may seem like a deal at 9 percent over 7 years, but is it really? By the time you pay off the loan, you will have paid an additional $70,295 in interest. That's over 35% of your loan.

When you are paying off your loan, you are looking up from the bottom of a steep slope towards the debt-free top. Most of the monthly payment is interest—hence the steepness. During the first year of the note, you have paid $21,486 in principal and $17,128 in interest. That is a lot of interest compared to principal.

By the end of the note, this ratio will level off. In the final year, you will pay $36,795 in principal and only $1,818 in interest. At the top of the hill, you are debt free. You owe no interest and you receive no interest.

A business can't really move to the other side of the hill and receive interest because the government punishes businesses that retain profits by taxing them. You need to spend money on capital improvements or pay it out in wages or other forms of compensation, again triggering taxes. A good accountant will help you to minimize paying taxes while maximizing compensation.

Paying Off Debt

Accountants don't like businesses to pay off debt too fast because it creates phantom income. This is because you can only expense interest, not principal since you never really owned the principal in the first place. It wasn't your money; you borrowed it.

When you wrote that loan payment check every month, the principal you paid back wasn't yours in the first place so it is not considered a legitimate expense. Only the interest that you pay on that loan payment is considered yours and therefore you are allowed to expense that portion of the payment.

In the example earlier, you paid $21,486 in principal and $17,128 in interest during your first year. You expense the interest on your income statement, but where does the principal go? You'll find it in the bottom line as profit. Only you gave that profit back to the lender and you get taxed on it, even though you don't actually have the cash anymore. That is why it is called phantom income. A good accountant can help you deal with this issue and at the same time help you to pay down your loan quicker and minimize taxes on phantom income.

If you can pay off your loan in 5 years instead of 7 years, you can save $21,197 in interest payments. That is significant. To generate the cash to do this, though, you need to learn the value of money.

Here is a good math lesson for you and your employees. Let's assume that you are netting 8% profit before taxes. Every time you spend money on expense items, that is money that normally would go straight to the bottom line in the form of net profit (except you spent it).

Suppose you bought a box of mechanical pencils for $9.95 at the office supply store. How much in the way of sales do you need in order to produce enough profit to pay for them? The easiest way to figure it out is to divide $9.95 by your net profit percentage, which is 8%.

$$\$9.95 \div .08 = \$124.37$$

Looking at it another way, on $124.37 you would generate net profit of $9.95, which is 8% ($124.37 x .08).

You need to sell an additional $124.37 in merchandise to produce enough profit to cover your pencil purchase. Every time you spend a dollar, a corresponding sale is needed to pay for it. That's over an above your regular sales. You'll need to generate an additional $124.37 above your usual sales in order to pay for your pencils.

Thinking about the value of a dollar in these terms can have a drastic effect on your bottom line. When you think about the amount of related sales needed to offset expenses, you'll consider your purchases more carefully.

Forced Savings Account

In a forced savings account, you automatically transfer a specific amount of money from your checking account into an interest-bearing account on a certain day of each month. It follows the old rule "Pay yourself first." If you don't do this, the year will slip by and you will have nothing to show at the end of it for all your efforts.

Even $100 a month is easy to do for most businesses. At the end of the year you will have $1,200 plus interest to do whatever you like with. Use it to pay for a vacation, employee bonus, or a new piece of equipment (that you didn't have to borrow the money for, saving even more money in paid interest).

Your bank can set this up for you. Your interest is better if your money is invested in treasury securities. Talk to a stockbroker or investment advisor about different options. For example, $2,000 per month invested in an index fund averaging 10% per year will grow to $412,227 in 10 years. At the same time, you want your money invested in something safe, but you want it to be accessible in case you need to write a check for some emergency.

There is nothing wrong with creating wealth. It is only through profit that you provide capital to grow your business and pay wages. You're taking responsibility for your own financial well being. As you save and invest, you start to live on the other side of the interest hill and you start earning money without actually having to work for it. It's a beautiful thing to watch.

5.6 Employees

5.6.1 When to Hire Help

Even if you plan to start on a shoestring budget, chances are you will need at least one other employee to help during busy times (weekends, especially), or to give you a day off here and there.

Many business owners prefer to work all the hours their store is open, closing shop a couple of days a week, during holidays and for vacations. This system can work very well, especially if you notify your customers in advance of vacation time so they aren't disappointed with a wasted trip. You can even use the reminder as a selling tool by including a coupon for them to use when you return from vacation.

However, most shop owners reach a point in their careers where they want to make more profit by staying open more days or hours, or the store is so busy on a daily basis that they need the extra help at all times. In addition, malls and downtown business areas may have strict rules or bylaws about operating hours, and they'll fine you if you don't comply. You may not want to be in the store all the hours that it is required to be open, so you'll need to hire someone to be there when you're not.

Many retailers these days have a rule that if there are ever more than three people in line at the checkout, then they will open another line. You might want to adopt this "three's a crowd" policy, too. If you consistently have more than three people waiting for help, or to make a purchase, then you may need to hire.

Take a look at your finances and make sure you can afford another employee. Are you making enough profit to hire extra help on the weekends and holidays? Will it increase your profits even more? If customers are getting frustrated at the wait time and leaving, then it most definitely will. Perhaps your business has even grown to the point where you need a full-time employee.

There are several types of staff members you can hire, and each has its advantages and disadvantages. All employees should be considered as investments, since you will spend time and money hiring and training them. You will see a return on that investment in increased sales, higher productivity in your store, more free time for you, and even new ideas for running your store based on employee input.

Full-time staff members work 30 or more hours a week. Most people work only one full-time job at a time, so, since they spend so much of their week working with you, they will naturally develop a sense of loyalty to you. In addition, full-time employees become so familiar with your store's routines and procedures that they can assist in training new staff members and run things if you need to take a day off here and there. A particularly competent and loyal full-timer might even become your second-in-command as manager when you take a vacation or open your second location. Keep in mind that full-time employees also come with the extra burdens for you of increased paperwork, health and other benefits, employment insurance, and so on.

Part-time staff members generally work less than 30 hours a week. Many people work more than one part-time job, often because of the unavailability in certain industries for full-time opportunities. (As discussed above, full-time employees cost more to employ.) As a result, loyalty will be less assured from your part-time staff and they are more likely to leave you if they receive a higher-paying or full-time job offer from another employer. However, the advantage to you is that you will save money, time and paperwork by hiring part-timers.

Students, retirees, stay-at-home parents, or people who otherwise have flexible or irregular schedules make good candidates for part-time work. All of these potential staffers typically welcome the chance to earn some income without the demand on their time that a full-time job would have. However, you may find that they require more training, since they may not have worked in the retail industry before.

Temporary, casual or on-call help can also play an important role as staffers in your business. For example, you might offer a particular service in your store that needs only occasional attention, so you hire someone who specializes in that type of service to come in once a week or twice a month to perform it. Another source of temporary help is your own family members, who might occasionally assist with sales or other tasks, particularly during peak busy periods like holidays.

No matter which type of employees you decide to hire, start small. Hire a part-timer to get a feel for being an employer. If you like the person you hired and they're working out well, you might want to offer them increased hours or even a full-time position. If you hire someone on a full-time basis in the beginning and find that you can't afford to keep them on full-time, you will likely loose that employee and generate hard feelings. Hiring someone part-time also gives you the flexibility to hire someone else if the person you originally hired doesn't work out.

5.6.2 Recruiting Staff

Hiring employees can be one of the most challenging aspects of owning a business. It can be difficult to find an employee who learns easily, is friendly with your customers, is honest, and comes to work on time.

Qualities of Great Employees

Have you ever gone into a store and been treated rudely or without concern by an employee? Everyone has run into a rude salesperson at some time or another. Sometimes store salespeople are so rude and so unconcerned that potential customers leave the store without buying something they fully intended to purchase. A rude employee can hurt your sales and cost you customers.

But if you pick the right employees, you will have other people who care about your store and the customers who come there, and who will work to make your store a success. So it is vital that you choose carefully.

As you think about the demands of your new store, the niche you are hoping to fill in your community and the customers you hope to have, make a list of the qualities you want in your employees. Think about the type of people who will be easy for you to work with, who will be warm and helpful to the customers, and who will be an asset to your store.

Consider some of the following qualities of great retail employees:

- Honest

- Hardworking

- Responsible

- Reliable

- Friendly

- Knowledgeable

- Polite

- Good sales ability

- Good customer service ability

- Niche experience (e.g. if you sell used clothing it is helpful to have employees with experience selling clothing)

Now that you know the kind of people you want, you have to find them. If you talk about your store — and you should, because it's a good way to generate excitement — you can ask everyone you come into contact with if they know someone who would be a good employee for your store. Your regular customers are a good source for referrals, and more than one store owner has hired a customer to work as an employee in their store. Almost everyone knows someone who is looking for a job — it never hurts to ask around.

Advertising

The first place to advertise your job openings is in your own store. You can put a "Help Wanted" sign in the front window, and another by the cash register.

Also consider placing an ad in your local paper's employment classifieds. Depending on the job market in your community, this can be an excellent way to find good local employees. Make sure your ad is eye-catching and uses just a few words to get the right kind of people through your door. Consider the following ad:

> PASSIONATE ABOUT WINE? LOVE MEETING PEOPLE?
>
> Wine Time in Anytown Mall is looking for a bright, part-time sales associate to join our team. Are you knowledgeable about wine? Do you love helping people? Liquor store or other retail experience a plus. Great working environment. Fax resume to 555-1234 or come in for an application.

Make sure the ad gets the point across quickly. Classified advertising is expensive and is priced by the word. Therefore, it is important to get your point across as quickly as you can. The ad above is just over 50 words long.

Make sure all the vital information is included. Potential applicants need to know how to contact you or where to fax their resumes. Also, in order to save you lots of time with applicant questions, remember to include the basics about the job in your ad, including any benefits. One important thing to mention is whether the opportunity is full-time or part-time.

Make sure your ad is correct before it runs in the paper. When you work with an ad rep from your local paper, always ask them to give you a copy of your classified ad as it will appear, so you can check for mistakes. When your ad appears, check it again and make sure it is correct — especially your contact information.

Make sure that you include words or phrases that quickly help potential applicants find themselves in your ad. In the example advertisement above, the title includes the important words "wine" and "meeting people." Potential applicants who don't really like meeting people and aren't wine enthusiasts will know immediately that the job isn't for them, and the people who do like meeting and are passionate about wine will know they should send you a resume.

When you run an ad, decide ahead of time if you are too busy for phone calls and would prefer the first round of submissions to be sent by fax or email. Taking prescreening phone calls from applicants is time consuming. Alternatively, you could use an employment application form like the one below, which can also work as a pre-screening tool. After reviewing the completed application forms, you can ask any applicants you're interested in to send a formal resume to you or bring it in to your store in person. Decide what works best for you and your hiring schedule.

Employment Application Forms

If you find that your staff turnover rate is high, especially in a wine bar, you may want to create a standard employment application form for screening potential new employees.

Be sure to ask only for information that you as an employer are allowed to ask for by law. Check with your local employment standards agency for more information about what you can and cannot ask on an employment application or in an interview.

A sample application form appears on the next few pages.

Sample Employment Application Form

Instructions

Print clearly in ink.

Personal

Today's Date: _____

First Name: _____

Middle Name: _____

Last Name: _____

Social Security Number: _____

Street Address: _____

_____

City, State, Zip Code: _____

Phone Number: _____

Are you eligible to work in the United States? ❑ Yes ❑ No

If you are under age 18, do you have an employment/age certificates? ❑ Yes ❑ No

Have you been convicted of or pleaded no contest to a felony within the last five years? ❑ Yes ❑ No

If yes, please explain:

Position

Position Applied For: _____

Schedule

Days/Hours Available:

Monday:	_____ to	_____
Tuesday:	_____ to	_____
Wednesday:	_____ to	_____
Thursday:	_____ to	_____
Friday:	_____ to	_____
Saturday:	_____ to	_____
Sunday:	_____ to	_____

What date are you available to start work? _____

Education

NAME AND ADDRESS OF SCHOOL	DEGREE/DIPLOMA	GRADUATION DATE

Skills and Qualifications

LICENSES, SKILLS, TRAINING, AWARDS

Wine

What wine knowledge or experience do you have?

What's your favorite wine and why?

Employment History

Present Or Last Position:	
Employer:	
Address:	
Supervisor:	
Phone:	
Position Title:	
From:	
To:	
Responsibilities:	
Salary/Hourly Wage:	
Reason for Leaving:	
May we contact this employer?	
If not, explain:	

Previous Position:	
Employer:	
Address:	
Supervisor:	
Phone:	
Position Title:	
From:	
To:	
Responsibilities:	
Salary/Hourly Wage:	
Reason for Leaving:	
May we contact this employer?	
If not, explain:	

References

NAME/TITLE	ADDRESS	PHONE

I certify that information contained in this application is true and complete.

I release to the potential employer the right to check my credit report or use other screening methods to verify information provided.

Signature: _____

Date: _____

5.6.3   The Hiring Process

The selection process starts with the prospective employee filling out an application. Here are some other things to look out for when prospective employees come in to fill out an application or drop off a resume:

- Are they dressed nicely? Well-groomed?

- Are they polite or do they say, "Gimme an application"?

- Are they alone? Chances are that if the potential employee can't come to fill out an application without their best friend, they can't work without their friends either.

- What does your gut instinct tell you?

The Interview Process

The purpose of an interview is to get to know potential applicants as much as you can in a short period of time. It is therefore important that most of that time be spent getting the applicants to talk about themselves. Most employers with limited interviewing experience spend too much time talking about the job or their store. And while that is certainly important, it won't help you figure out to whom you are talking and if that person is a good match for your store. A good rule of thumb to follow is that the applicant should do 80% of the talking.

To make the best use of your time, have a list of questions prepared in advance. This will keep the process consistent between applicants. You can always add questions that pop up based on their answers as you go along.

Possible questions to ask include:

- Why did you apply to work here?

- What is the ideal schedule you would like to work?

- When can you absolutely not work?

- What sort of experience do you have that you feel qualifies you for this job?

- Tell me about your last job and why you left.

- What was the best job you ever had-the one you had the most fun in?

- Who was your best boss and what made them so great?

- If I talked to someone who worked with you, what would they say about your work habits?

- Do you have any ambitions in this business? If not, what would be your perfect job?

To get a sense of how an employee will actually behave on the job, it is also a good idea to ask "behavioral questions." Behavioral questions ask applicants to give answers based on their past behavior. An example is "Tell me about a time you had to deal with a difficult customer. What was the situation and how did you handle it?" Instead of giving hypothetical answers of what someone would do in a particular situation, the applicant must give examples of what they actually have done. While people's behavior can change, past performance is a better indicator of someone's future behavior than hypothetical answers.

You can also ask questions that communicate your store policies to discover if the applicant will have any issues in these areas. Some examples are:

- When you are working, I expect your full attention to be on my customers. I do not allow private phone calls unless it is an emergency. Is that a problem?

- It is important that we open on time. I expect my workers to be punctual. Is there anything that could keep you from being on time for every shift?

By being clear on specifics and details in the interview, you can hash out any potential problems right then and there or agree to go your own ways because it is not going to work.

Discussing Pay

Another area to be clear about is what the pay is. Some employers will tell you not to talk money until you make the actual job offer, but that is really your choice. You do not want to go through the interview process, agonize over your decision, choose Johnny Good, offer the job and find out he does not want it because he thought it paid more and included health and dental benefits.

The government establishes a minimum wage that workers must be paid. Whether or not you want to pay over this amount is up to you. However, if you want the best candidates, then you'll need to offer them a competitive salary. Ask around — find out what other retail stores in your area are paying. To learn more about minimum wages in your area check out the U.S. Department of Labor website at **www.dol.gov/esa/minwage/america.htm**.

For wage information in a variety of occupations in Canada, visit the Services Canada website at **www.labourmarketinformation.ca** (click on "English", and then choose "Wages & Salaries" in the left frame menu). Visit **www.hrsdc.gc.ca/eng/labour/employment_standards** for Employment Standards in Canada, including information about minimum wage.

Ask your accountant to set up a payroll for your store and maintain it for you. That way, you can be assured that you are making the correct amount of deductions for taxes and other benefits.

Employees are paid either weekly, bi-weekly, or on the 15th and last day of each month. You should have sufficient funds in your business checking account to ensure payroll checks will be covered. You may offer employees direct deposit paychecks (in which their pay is deposited into their bank accounts) or regular checks (which they may take to the bank themselves).

References

Once you have found an applicant who appears to be a good fit, you can learn more by checking their references. The best references are former employers. (Former co-workers may be friends who will give glowing references no matter how well the employee performed.)

Many companies will not give you detailed information about a past employee. They are only required to give you employment dates and sometimes they will confirm salary. But many times you will be able to learn a lot about a potential applicant from a reference phone call. A good employee is often remembered fondly and even asked about by a former employer. An employer may not be able to tell you much about a bad employee for liability reasons, but they can answer the question "Is this employee eligible to be rehired?" Here are some other additional questions from Tom Hennessy, author of the *FabJob Guide to Become a Coffee House Owner*:

- How long did this person work for you (this establishes the accuracy of their applications)?

- How well did they get along with everyone (looking for team skills)?

- Did they take direction well (code words for "did they do their job")?

- Could they work independently (or did they sit around waiting to be told what to do next)?

- How did they handle stressful situations (this is important, especially if you are busy)?

If the references make you feel comfortable, call the employee to let them know they have a job and to come in and fill out the paperwork.

5.6.4   New Employees

After you shake hands and say, "The job is yours!", you have to know how to work with the new employee to make sure it is a positive experience for everyone.

New Employee Paperwork

When a new employee is hired there will be paperwork they must fill out. In the U.S. this will be a W-4 and an I-9 form. In Canada, the employee will give you their social insurance number; you must also have them fill out a TD1. The U.S. W-4 and Canadian TD1 are legal documents that will determine the amount of tax that is to be deducted from an employee's wages. The U.S. W-4 and Canadian T-4 forms are legal documents verifying how many tax deductions a new employee has. The amount of tax you will withhold as an employer varies based on the amount of deductions that an employee has. Have the employee fill out the forms, and then file them in a folder labeled with their name which you will keep on file.

Check with your state or province's labor office to make sure you are clear about all the forms employees must fill out to work. The sites below give more information on legal paperwork, including where to get blank copies of the forms your employees will need to fill out.

- *SmartLegalForms.com*
  Sells blank forms on CD
  www.hrlawinfo.com/index.asp

- *GovDocs Products - Employee Records and Personnel Forms*
  Sells blank forms by the pack
  www.hrdocs.com/Posters/hrproducts/

- *Canada Revenue Agency*
  Download and print any form you need
  www.cra-arc.gc.ca/forms/

You can also use a checklist like the one below to ensure that you cover all aspects of initiating your new employees.

Sample Checklist for New Employee Initiation

Part I: Create a New File

❑ Create a file for the new employee.

❑ Include in the file the job application and resume.

❑ Include the interview summary and notes.

❑ Reference any special information if applicable to the job. (Licenses)

❑ Complete all necessary paperwork. (Signatures, forms, etc)

Part II: Explain Company Policies

❑ Verify the weekly hours of work that you will assign to the employee.

❑ Explain the company's policy on missed days and tardiness.

❑ Explain payroll periods and what day checks are delivered.

❑ Verify the rate of pay, whether salary or hourly wage.

❑ Verify the overtime rules, and whether you ever assign overtime.

❑ Explain the training employment period (90 days, etc) if you have one.

Part III: Explain Benefits

❑ Explain medical insurance and when they are eligible.

❑ Explain sick leave policies.

❑ Explain vacation policies and vacation time.

❑ Explain policies regarding personal leave, holidays or disability.

❑ Explain any savings programs, stock options or pension plans you offer.

❑ Explain life, disability, accident and life insurance programs.

Part IV: Explain Company Etiquette

❑ Explain how to advance in the company and promotion opportunities.

❑ Verify parking arrangements.

❑ Provide a copy of the employee handbook.

❑ Play any video/audio features further preparing employees for the job.

❑ Provide the employee with some written form of wine education.

❑ Explain your company's mission and philosophy of doing business.

Stay Informed

The government has many laws that protect workers in the workplace. It is important to be aware of these laws and to make sure that your store abides by them.

The U.S. and Canadian governments have websites which provide information on almost any issue concerning employment law. Make sure to check how these laws affect your store and how you can abide by them. The U.S. Department of Labor website is located at **www.dol.gov**. In Canada, you'll find employment law information at the Human Resources and Social Development Canada website at **www.hrsdc.gc.ca**.

Employment Agreements

These forms are not required but are often kept by business owners who want to avoid any legal risks. Employment agreements could include salary terms, duties and positions, and other agreements of exclusivity, confidentiality, and benefits.

A sample employment agreement appears on the next page.

Sample Employment Agreement

1. The company, *[insert company name]*, agrees to employ *[insert employee name]* (SSN: *[insert Social Security Number]*) on the following terms and conditions.

2. Term of Employment. The terms and conditions set forth begin on the agreed upon date of the ___ day of the month of ____ in the year 20__.

3. Salary. The company shall pay the employee a salary of $_____ per year OR an hourly wage of $_____ for the services of the employee. A check will be paid at regular payroll periods. The employer reserves the right to increase the salary or hourly wage as he or she sees fit.

4. Job Description. The company has hired the employee in the job title of *[insert title]*. The employee's duties may be modified or extended from time to time, within reasonable limits, and always under fair working conditions. The duties may include but are not limited to:

[insert a description of duties and responsibilities]

5. Confidentiality. The employee agrees to not reveal confidential information (trade secrets, marketing strategies, nonpublic employer and company information, financial information, and other sensitive information) to any person, firm, corporation or any other entity. Should the employee reveal or threaten to reveal confidential information, the company has a right to order a restraining order legally forbidding the sharing of confidential information by breach of contract.

6. Employee Reimbursement. The employee may incur expenses related to advancing company business, which may include entertainment and travel costs. The company will reimburse these costs after the employee presents an itemized list of expenses, in accordance with company policy.

7. Vacation. The employee is entitled to an annual vacation of ___ weeks at regular pay. The employee reserves the right to increase the amount of weeks annually, if he or she sees fit.

8. Company Benefits. Benefits related to disability, death, and other insurance and liability issues are covered in attached copies of policy statements. The employee understands the disability, life and health insurance policies as listed and also understands that terms are not fixed and are often subject to the employer and the insurance company's discretion.

9. No Compete. The employee agrees that if employment ends, for a period of *[# of months/years]* after the last day of work, the employee shall not control, consult or be employed by a competing company, or any business very similar to the company's primary operation.

10. Legal Assistance. In the event of a lawsuit, the current employee or former employee shall make him or herself available for legal assistance (information, testimony or other assistance) to the company if given reasonable notice.

11. Contract Binding. This contract is binding and even in the event where one or more provision is held invalid or not applicable by the employee, all other provisions will still remain in effect.

12. Successors and Assignees. In the event of a change in ownership, the company's rights and obligations will be passed on to the company's successors and assignees and continue to be legal and binding.

13. Oral Agreements. Oral agreements between the company (owner or supervisor) and employee that change the terms of this written agreement are not binding. Any change in company policy and or employment agreements must be documented and signed by both parties. Oral agreements in contrary position to this signed form are not binding.

14. Termination of Employment. Without cause, the company may terminate the employment at any time upon *[number of days]* written notice to the employee. Upon request, the employee will perform his or her duties until the day of termination, earning all the regular wage that is entitled. The employee may also terminate employment upon *[number of days]* written notice to the company.

Both parties have accepted the terms of this agreement and it has been signed this _____ day of _____ of the year 20____.

Owner, on behalf of [company name]

_____
Signature

_____
Print Name

Employee

_____
Signature

_____
Print Name

Witness

_____
Signature

_____
Print Name

NOTE: This employment agreement form is based on standard business forms in various industries. Whenever you enter into an agreement with any employee, you should get all implied or stated agreements in writing and signed by both parties. However, there is no guarantee that any contract will hold up in court. It depends upon the laws of the state and county you reside in. Consult your attorney for legal questions that concern your business.

Employee Emergency Contact Card

If the unexpected happens, as it sometimes will, you want to be prepared. Having employees fill out an emergency card for their file will help you contact their doctor, spouse, or other friends or family members in case of an emergency. Besides being the most rational and human thing to do, being prepared in this way can safeguard you against liability.

Make sure every employee's emergency card contains the following:

- Their correct and updated address and phone number

- Their family doctor and choice of hospital

- Any medications taken

- Allergies or special medical conditions

- The name and phone number of a family member emergency contact

- The name and phone number of an alternate emergency contact

Make sure that the emergency cards for staff, including one for you, are filled out and placed in alphabetical order in a filing cabinet or another location, and that everyone who works with you knows where this information is kept. Ask employees to verify that their emergency information is correct and updated as soon as it changes.

New Employee Orientation

Showing up on the first day of a new job is stressful for any employee. The new employees you hire are full of hope and anxiety, and are trying their best to make a good impression and be successful in your eyes. You should do your best to make them feel welcome and appreciated. Here are some tips to help them succeed:

- Make definite orientation plans for your new employee. Develop a list of what you will show and tell your employee, and go through each point. (This is where it helps to have a procedures manual as described in section 5.1.)

- Plan for the employee to have lunch with you or a friendly co-worker on the first day.

- Don't expect your brand new employee to be able to do everything on the first day. Realize that the first few days in your store will be a time for your new employee to learn and become comfortable with procedures.

- Don't throw your new employee into the fire. Starting them out on the day of the biggest sale in your store's history is a bad idea. Choose a time that is relatively slow-paced to let your new employee learn in a calm environment.

- Once your employee has been working for a few days, schedule an informal meeting to check in. Ask them to voice questions, comments, and possible concerns. Offer some positive feedback about your new employee's performance.

Taking the time to make sure your new employee feels comfortable and positive working in your store will pay off in the long run. Happy employees who feel positive about what they are doing often become long-term assets for your business.

Training, Motivating, and Retaining

It costs less to retain the staff you have than to recruit and train new staff, so make sure you keep open lines of communication with your employees. Take the time to ask them how things are going. Listen intently to what they say. Perhaps they are spending more time in your shop than you are and can offer valuable insight to problems you might not have noticed.

Encourage, and if you can, pay for staff to take courses to help them be the best they can be at their jobs. This not only helps them feel good about themselves, but will solidify their attachment to you and your business.

Think of interesting ways to motivate your sales staff. Could you offer a discount on items? An incentive bonus for hitting a sales target? Find out what motivates them, and create a sales incentive program that suits them.

Commission-Only Personnel

If you decide that you're going to offer only a commission and not an hourly wage, bear in mind that this can lead to overbearing sales staff. However, a guaranteed wage might mean that as soon as you leave they whip out their favorite novel. Perhaps a mix of commission and guaranteed salary might work best for you.

Usually, commission-based sales staff receives between 15 to 20 percent of a sale, so you must factor that in to your selling prices. It's often best to pay bi-weekly, after the credit card charges and checks have cleared the bank. Commission is also subject to withholding taxes and vacation pay, so be sure to put it through your bookkeeping system correctly. If you have any questions, it's wise to call your accountant. Additionally, you might want to have a lawyer draw up a commissioned sales staff contract. It's always better to be clear at the outset before any miscommunications occur.

Don't forget that you will need to fill out all the required paperwork when you hire a new employee as discussed above.

Employee Benefits and Bonuses

Regular covered, nonexempt employees who work over 40 hours in one week are entitled to overtime pay with every additional hour over the clock. Overtime pay is one and one half times an employee's regular hourly rate. Not surprisingly, many businesses will send employees home after 40 hours of work, rather than pay overtime.

Very little in the way of employee benefits is federally mandated, except overtime pay and minimum wage. You are not required to give your employees breaks, lunches, flexible schedules, insurance, family or medical leave or vacation time. But it's highly recommended that you do so, otherwise your employees will hate you.

You may skimp on some pricier purchases like insurance and simply choose to award employee performances with bonuses from an employee bonus fund. When figuring out your bonuses, it's best to incorporate a system based on net profit or total sales. For example, this employee would earn 2% or 3% of the bonus fund. Always make it a big deal to personally reward your hardworking employees with kind words.

This table details what some of your employees might cost you by the hour, week, month and year. (Remember that vacation weeks and holidays are not factored in here.)

		8 Hrs	5 Days	4-5 Wks	52 Wks
	Hour	*Day*	*Week*	*Month*	*Year*
Minimum	$7.25	58.00	290.00	1,160.00	15,080.00
Novice	$8.50	68.00	340.00	1,360.00	17,680.00
Standard	$10.00	80.00	400.00	1,600.00	20,800.00
Bartender	$12.53	100.24	501.20	2,004.80	26,062.40
Experienced	$15.00	120.00	600.00	2,400.00	31,200.00
Manager	$20.00	160.00	800.00	3,200.00	41,600.00

Source: U.S. Department of Labor Bureau of Labor Statistics

Weekly Work Scheduling

A work schedule can be used both for your reference, and also, if the format is copied and enlarged to poster size, used as a wall schedule for your employees. The name of the employee and their position goes first, followed by their daily schedule.

Daily entries should include two blocks of four hours; one block, such as 10:00 am to 2:00 pm then a 30 minute or one-hour period of as a lunch break, followed by another four hour block. This would make the standard eight hour a day schedule, though you can also use this schedule for part-time employees. The boxes might also include duties and total daily hours.

A sample employee scheduling form appears on the next page.

Staff Meetings

Staff training does not end after the first orientation or even the first 90 days. Consider training an ongoing process. People always change, and so customer service must constantly improve. Organize a few staff meetings throughout the year and analyze your progress as a company.

Sample Weekly Employee Work Schedule Form

Staff Names	Mon	Tue	Wed	Thur	Fri	Sat	Sun	Total Hours

Staff meetings are not cheap. They take away valuable time from employee tasks. If they take place before or after business hours, you still need to pay your employees for being at the meeting. So it's best to plan ahead of time for all your meetings, and decide what you hope to accomplish well in advance. If the meeting is called in light of some recent problems, then focus on the solutions as your unofficial "theme."

Tips for Staff Meetings

Make sure everyone who should be there (like employees who could use the improvement and supervisors) is there. If half of your staff is missing, then rearrange the meeting for a more convenient time.

Involve your listeners. Ask questions, ask for feedback; whatever gets them motivated. If you don't involve your employees and simply deliver a dry, colorless reiteration of the rules, then it's wasted time.

Arrange for a convenient time. Yes, your employees will attend a meeting at night or even on their day off. If they must. But they'll secretly hate you for it. So take your employees' comfort into consideration. If you don't want to shut down during business hours, then have the meeting extra early or after closing time.

Leave out the negative clichés. Negative comments that are designed to embarrass the staff like "Does anyone here not like their job? *[dramatic pause]* You can leave now," accomplish little except to remind everyone that they're in one of "those" meetings. Include criticism and warnings where applicable but always finish on a positive note.

Handling Negative Thinking

There's no doubt that negative thinking can destroy an otherwise solid team effort. The cure for negative thinking is not to come up with more negative thinking, nor is it to ignore the murmurings. The best solution is to confront the source of dissatisfaction. If you sense there is a problem with one or more members of your staff, then talk to each member and find out what is bothering them.

Is it a lack of confidence in their abilities or in company policy? Is there dissension between employees or resentment over responsibilities or rewards given by management? Before you can find the solution you must first understand the problem. Use your own judgment in making the final call, but try to be a diplomat more than a dictator for the welfare of your team.

Additional Topics to Cover

- Sexual harassment issues

- How to progress in your career

- Safety rules (including fire, robbery and theft)

- Prohibited employee practices

- Performance reviews

5.6.5 Handling Employee Theft

Sometimes, no matter how much productivity you aim for, good employees can go bad. Even the most professional applicants can try to steal from you, or become lazy, or unethical, or just bring a negative energy to the workforce. How do you handle troublesome employees?

The tricky part about employees stealing from you is that you must have sufficient evidence to fire an employee for theft. You must catch them in the act, have them under surveillance (video or personal) or compile some sort of strong evidence in order to accuse them of such a crime.

Two of the most common scams in retail are under-ringing sales on a register and ticket tearing. Cashiers in wine stores or wine bars can under-charge for an item, keep track of the difference by a mark, and then take the excess money out when they close the register. In ticket tearing, the server delivers a ticket and completes a transaction, but then tears up the order and pockets the cash. No record of loss is a dishonest employee's gain.

Guarding Against Theft

The best way to cut down on employee theft is not to allow your workers the temptation to steal. To guard against ticket tearing, for example, try buying sequentially numbered order pads for servers and waiters to use. Each waiter should be responsible for a specific sequence of order numbers. This way you or a manager can verify there are no missing numbers at the end of the day. Tips should be kept separately from the cash register, preferably under lock and key.

For cashiering, it is advisable to have one employee close out another employee's register at the end of the shift. Retail companies usually have a policy against cashiers ringing up any items for themselves.

In bookkeeping either you or a supervisor should sign outgoing checks even if someone else writes in the amounts and payee information. This helps prevent theft from your bank account.

Catching Them in the Act

Catching an employee in the act requires surveillance, with the theft caught on camera or witnessed by another person. A camera set up in the private counting area of the store would be a strong deterrent against employee theft.

Private investigators (whom you can also hire for help) recommend that you keep an eye on suspicious employees and set up undercover surveillance within your own ranks. Dishonest employees often appear to be model workers (almost "too good") and yet also have a way of avoiding direct contact with you or your manager. Nervousness and lack of eye contact could be a sign that the employee has something to hide.

You have two options to consider. First, you can hire a private investigator who specializes in retail loss and prevention. He or she can show you techniques to minimize theft as well as ways of keeping surveillance on suspicious behavior. You can also hire an auditor for the specific purpose of a fraud audit if you think a bookkeeper or accountant may be dishonest.

The Aftermath of the Crime

Once you find the guilty party, fire the employee firmly and quickly. If you have sufficient evidence then there's no need to delay the firing or discuss the issue. You may choose to prosecute the thief or simply let him or her go.

If you are intending to give a bad reference then it's necessary to file a police report. Simply providing hearsay that your former employee is a thief could be grounds for a lawsuit against you. If you lack strong evidence of theft, or if a "gray" situation comes up involving employee misconduct, then use your best judgment and always consider what's best for the company.

Some bosses choose to fire employees for "incompetence" rather than theft, eliminating the need for evidence. Consistently being short on the register or not keeping track of tickets and receipts is grounds for termination, without officially calling the employee a thief. For your own peace of mind you could ask an attorney for advice before firing an employee.

6. Getting and Keeping Customers

6.1 Marketing Your Business

Assuming you have a good location, you will get some foot traffic off the street. People will walk into your store out of curiosity and some of them will buy from you. While this walk-in business can certainly contribute to your success, you can achieve even greater success by attracting customers to your store through effective marketing.

If your store is located in a shopping mall, the mall administration will have a calendar of promotional events that you can participate in. Likewise, if you have a store in a popular shopping district, there will likely be a local merchants association that you can join for cooperative advertising and events. In addition to any marketing you do through your mall or merchants association, you will likely need to do additional promotion on your own. This section outlines a variety of techniques you can try.

6.1.1 Advertising

There are many places you can advertise your store, including the Yellow Pages, newspapers, magazines, radio, television, and the Internet.

It is wise to combine two or more of these media, but you will want to consider several factors before you decide for sure which you choose. You'll want to know how much a particular advertisement costs, how long it will last, and most importantly, what consumers it will reach.

Cost

Your advertising dollars go towards supporting the media organization you're buying an ad from. The more expensive the media, the more expensive their ads are likely to be. A high-school yearbook will be able to offer much lower rates than a daily newspaper, and a college radio station (if it takes ads at all) will be cheaper than the area's hottest new music station. And television ads are the most expensive of all.

To find out how much various ad types cost in your area, call your local media outlets and ask them to send you a rate card. Rate cards list all the advertising options offered by the media outlet, and they often include other useful information such as demographic statistics (age, gender, income level, etc.) about the target audience — the type of viewers, listeners, or readers the outlet tends to reach.

Before you make any decisions, read the rate card and target audience information carefully. Is this the media outlet where most of your customers will hear your message? Sixty percent of your advertising budget should be aimed at existing customers, so keep that in mind when you're looking at the rate cards.

If advertising in a local magazine is really inexpensive, but you know most of your customers prefer to listen to the radio, you might want to try the magazine ad as an experiment to see what kind of new customers you might get from it. On the other hand, if you know your customers read the local daily newspaper, you should plan on doing most of your advertising there, and perhaps even forego the expensive television ad that targets people unlikely to shop at your store.

Yellow Pages

Yellow Pages ads can help you attract people from outside of your immediate area, particularly if you have a unique niche. Take a look at Yellow Pages ads for other retail stores like yours to get ideas (look under categories that match your type of business).

You can either design the ad yourself, have the Yellow Pages design it for you, or hire a designer. If you are interested in advertising, contact your local Yellow Pages to speak with a sales rep. Check the print version of your phone book for contact information. To find the Yellow Pages online, go to **www.yellowpages.com** (U.S.) or **www.yellowpages. ca** (Canada).

Newspapers and Magazines

Consider specialty magazines for your area that pertain to your store's niche. (Most communities have free newspapers or magazines directed at parents.) Read a magazine or newspaper carefully to see if an advertisement for your store would fit with the theme of the paper, the articles, and the other ads.

Also consider advertising in newspapers with classified ads for merchandise like yours. These might be known locally as a bargain, trader, or shopper newspaper. For example, one major advertising newspaper in the U.S. is **www.traderonline.com**, and a similar paper in Canada is **www.buysell.com**. You'll often see collectable wines, for example, being offered for sale on these types of papers.

Many publications will provide you with a free media kit with lots of information about their readership. This information will help you determine if their readers are the sort of customers you are looking for and if it is the right publication for your ad. Some publications will design your ad for free, while others will design it for an additional cost and give you a copy of the ad that you can then run in other publications if you wish.

Creating Effective Ads

Some people spend years learning how to create the most effective ads. Since we do not have years, we're going to focus on a couple of key points. For additional tips on creating effective ads read the article entitled "How to Run Effective Advertisements" at **www.usatoday.com/ small/ask/2001-07-30-ask-ad.htm**.

Most people need to see an advertisement several times before they buy, so running an ad only once may not give you as much business as you hope. A small ad that you run every week for a couple of months can generate more business than a single full page ad.

You can test a variety of ads, relatively inexpensively, by buying local ads on Google at **http://adwords.google.com**. Try different offers and wording to see which ones are most effective. You can set a maximum daily spending limit which keeps your costs down if lots of people click on your ad without buying. The offers that result in sales might also be effective in your other advertising as well.

One of the most effective ways to draw people into your store – and to test the effectiveness of each ad – is with some sort of incentive. An incentive can be anything from a discount coupon to a free gift.

To measure advertising effectiveness with coupons, it's a good idea to put a time limit or expiration date on it. Make sure this date is clearly printed on the coupon. It should allow customers enough time to get themselves to your store – maybe a week or two – but not so much time that they forget about the coupon, thinking they can use it well into the future. Tie the coupon to a date that's easy to remember, such as the end of the month.

The coupon offer should be simple, but with high perceived value — a buy one, get one free offer, or perhaps "This coupon good for 30 percent off your entire purchase," or "Redeem this coupon for a free corkscrew with every purchase." Above all, it should require that customers come into your shop to redeem their coupons. The idea is to get them to pay you a visit, see what other things you have for sale, and maybe buy something besides what they came for with the coupon.

Of course, giveaways should be cost-effective, so decide on a budget before you start looking into ordering any promotional items. There are numerous companies that can supply you with these. Check the Yellow Pages or do an online search for "advertising specialties" or "promotional products."

6.1.2   Free Publicity

One of the best ways to market — with potentially excellent results for minimal cost — is to get free media publicity. While you don't have the final say over what gets reported, the exposure can give a boost to your business.

Public Service Announcements

If you are working with a charity, you may be able to get a Public Service Announcement aired on local radio stations. Write a 15 second or 30 second announcement and send it to "Public Service Announcements" at local radio stations. It probably will not be prime time, during the drive home, but every bit of exposure helps. Also, contact your local cable company to find out how to submit Public Service Announcements to the community channel.

Press Releases

Another way to get free publicity in local newspapers or magazines is by using a press release. Press releases typically announce an event. They should be a page or less, encompass the main points, and be put together as though they were going to be printed verbatim in the newspaper (they sometimes are). A sample press release appears below. You can find additional tips at **www.publicityinsider.com/release.asp** and **www.xpresspress.com/PRnotes.html**.

While you can self-promote, you do need to tie it into the community somehow. Try to brainstorm ways your activity benefits the community. If you donate to charity, then this should be an easy tie-in for you.

A sample press release appears on the next page.

Donations

Donations are a good way to get your shop's name and products into the public eye. You'll probably be approached for donations by churches, community centers, non-profit or not-for-profit organizations, schools, sports teams, and more. They might ask for a cash donation but, more often, will want a product, such as a bottle of fine wine or a gift basket that they can use as a prize in a raffle or drawing.

Sample Press Release

Date: December 12, 2009

WINE TIME ANNOUNCES
FREE WINE APPRECIATION SEMINAR

Wine Time, Anytown, PA — Wine Time today announces that it will be hosting free wine appreciation seminars every Saturday afternoon at its store located at 123 Main Street. The seminar will be facilitated by Wanda Wineschnosse, resident sommelier at Wine Time.

"Many people are intimidated by fine wines," says Ms. Wineschnosse. "We want to help people to meet with other enthusiasts and casual wine drinkers to help them better understand and enjoy the great variety of wines available right down the street."

The seminar will consist of a brief overview of how wine is produced around the world, followed by a wine tasting to compare the different varietals available at Wine Time. The seminar will also include helpful advice about pairing various wines with foods.

Donations for the local food bank will be gratefully accepted.

For more information contact:

Ima Wineseller
Wine Time
123 Main Street
Anytown, PA 18610

Phone: (570) 555-1234
Email: iwineseller@winetime.com

You don't, by any means, need to donate to every organization that asks. But ones that offer charitable tax receipts are worth considering, as are causes you believe in. Ones that you know will reach a large number of people are always worth supporting, because you'll have your shop name recognized by a large group of people as a donor. Be sure to ask for acknowledgment in any programs or posters made for the event.

When donating, it is nice to donate a notable bottle of wine or champagne that will catch the eyes of those who will see it. But consider donating coupons instead, something that will bring people into your store to collect their free product and possibly encourage them to buy something else besides.

Online Publicity

Social media and my email newsletters have been very effective because there's little time, effort and money involved, but they connect me to my current customers and bring in new customers as well.

— Donnie Austin, owner,
House Wine

As Donnie Austin owner of House Wine suggests, there are a number of low-cost but effect ways to get online publicity. You could publish your own blog, using a site such as Blogger (**www.blogger.com**) or Word-Press.com (**www.wordpress.com**), for example. However, it can take a while to build up an audience for a blog, and ongoing work to make regular updates. If you don't have time to devote to maintaining your own blog while doing everything else required to build your business, you may be able to get articles you write into other people's blogs by distributing them through EzineArticles at **http://ezinearticles.com**.

If you do have a good chunk of time to devote to online marketing, you can also use social networking sites such as FaceBook (**www.facebook. com**) and LinkedIn (**www.linkedin.com**), do micro-blogging (brief updates) at Twitter (**www.twitter.com**), create videos to post at YouTube (**www.youtube.com**), and create pages for sites such as Squidoo (**www. squidoo.com**), among other online marketing activities. Many entrepreneurs find the number of online "social media" sites overwhelming. If you want to learn more about how to use them, consider subscribing to the free Publicity Hound newsletter at **www.publicityhound.com**.

Even if you decide not to use online social media, you can nevertheless market your business online using methods discussed elswhere in this chapter, such as building a website, doing online advertising, and publishing an email newsletter.

6.1.3   Promotional Tools

When you start a new business you will have to invest in some business promotional tools at the outset. These tools should be designed in a way that promotes both your business and the style of your business. Fonts on business cards, letterhead, ink colors, and even your advertising should all be designed to reinforce that style.

If you have a computer with a high quality laser or ink jet printer, you may be able to inexpensively print professional looking materials from your own computer. Free templates for all the print materials you are likely to need in your business can be found online.

HP offers templates for a variety of programs at **www.hp.com/sbso/ productivity/office**. For example, you can create a matching set of stationery (business cards, letterhead, envelopes) in Microsoft Word or a presentation in PowerPoint. The site includes free online classes and how-to guides to help you design your own marketing materials.

Another excellent resource is the Microsoft Office Online Templates Homepage at **http://office.microsoft.com/en-us/templates**. At this site you can search a database to find templates for:

- Business stationery (envelopes, faxes, labels, letters, memos, etc.)

- Marketing materials (brochures, flyers, newsletters, postcards, etc.)

- Other business documents (expense reports, invoices, receipts, time sheets, etc.)

Business Cards

Business cards are a definite must in any business. A business card gives customers the essential contact information for your store, and every time you hand one out you should think of it as a mini-advertisement.

The cost of business cards can vary depending on how much or how little of the work you do creating them. You can make your own business cards if you own or have access to a computer. Office supply stores sell sheets of cards that come with perforated edges to go through any type of printer.

You can also hire a graphic artist to design a logo, do the layout and even arrange for printing. Most print shops have a design specialist on staff to help with these facets as well. Whichever way you decide to go, make sure the style of your card is in sync with the style you are promoting in your business.

When ordering your cards from a printer, the more you order the less expensive they are. When you order 500 cards, for example, the cost is minimal, generally around $50 to $65 depending on how many colors you have on your card and the card stock you use. Shop around to see where you can get the best deal.

Another alternative when you're just starting out is to use free business cards from VistaPrint.com. You can order 250 cards from them, using a variety of contemporary designs, and you only pay for shipping. The only catch is that they print their company logo on the back. If you don't mind having their logo on the back of your business cards, this is very economical. If you prefer not to have another company's name printed on the back of your business cards you can order 250 cards for about $20 plus shipping from VistaPrint without their logo.

Brochures

Having an attractive, catchy brochure is a good marketing tool especially when you go out to local business or other events; and you can also send your brochure to the media. Brochures give people a snapshot of what your business is all about. When coming up with a brochure, a graphic artist can help you design and lay it out. They also work closely with printers and know who is good and can do it in a timely matter for a good price.

The cost for printing brochures can range from a few hundred dollars (for one color on simple cardstock) or a few thousand dollars if you opt for color and glossy paper. Spend time on the copy and layout designs of your brochure and enlist the help of a professional designer if necessary.

Many printers will have an in-house design department who can do the artwork for you, but make sure you have a hand in developing the text. You are the best-qualified person to describe what your business is all about. Also, check for any typos in your phone number, email address or other contact information or you will be paying the printer to fix 1,000 brochures or doing it by hand.

You can use software such as Microsoft Publisher to design and print your own brochures, or you could try an online brochure-making service where you create the design from a template, such as Vistaprint (**www.vistaprint.com/brochures/gallery.aspx**). For a truly professional look you should enlist a service such as VistaPrint or a printer in your area to do it for you. Look in the Yellow Pages under "Printers."

While the challenge of designing an effective brochure is one thing, how to effectively distribute them is another. Brochures have an advantage over business cards in that they can sit in an office or a waiting room and will be picked up and read by the people waiting. Try to find places to leave them where people reading them might appreciate knowing about your store. Brochures can also be distributed by mail or handed out in conjunction with or instead of a business card.

Flyers

Flyers, also known as one-sheets, are essentially a brochure without the fold. They can be colorful and contain graphics, but often do not, making them more cost effective. A run of 250 one-sheets will cost very little, and the option to create these at home with a decent printer is also there.

Many of the tips mentioned for creating an effective brochure apply to one-sheets. Again, pay special attention to your contact information and make sure that it is correct.

One-sheets can be handed out at conventions and association meetings. Attaching a business card to your one-sheet is also a good strategy. You can also hang them in local grocery stores; ask to leave some out at the library, post them in laundromats and anywhere else your target market hangs out.

Printers

Brochures and one-sheets can be easily designed, paid for and delivered without leaving the house, using one of several on-line graphics companies. Here are a few you might want to consider:

- *FedEx Office*
  www.fedex.com/us/office/

- *Acecomp Plus*
  www.acecomp.com/printing_brochures.asp

- *The Paper Mill Store*
  www.thepapermillstore.com

- *VistaPrint*
  www.vistaprint.com

6.1.4   Your Website

A website is an excellent tool for any retail store owner. It lets people know what you do, who you are, how to contact you, and where you are located. Your website can also complement your other marketing efforts. Let people who come into your store know you have a website, and mention your web address in every piece of advertising or written material you create about your store.

Ideas for Your Website

The basic structure of your website should include the following:

- Home page to navigate through your site

- Categories pages (types of merchandise you sell), possibly with photos

- "About Us" page: this is where you let your customers know who you are and what expertise you have.

- Contact information with your store hours, address, phone number, fax number, and perhaps directions or a map

Here are some features and additional information to consider including on your own store's website:

- A photograph of the front of your store

- Information about parking around your store

- Gift certificate information

- Your email contact information

- A section for notes about your wine or tasting tips

- A newsletter or blog

Developing a Website

If you are already experienced at creating web pages, or learn quickly, you can design your website yourself using a program such as Microsoft's Front Page or a free program like SeaMonkey (available at **www.seamonkey-project.org**). Otherwise, it's a good idea to hire a web designer through word of mouth or the Yellow Pages. Of course you should visit sample sites they have created before hiring them.

To present a professional image and make your web address easier for clients to remember, consider getting your own domain name, such as www.your storename.com. There are a number of sites where you can search for and register a domain name. One web host we have found that provides good service for a low cost is **www.godaddy.com**. Microsoft also offers a quick search for domain name availability using their sign-up feature at **http://smallbusiness.officelive.com**. (They'll also help you to set up a free website for your business.)

Once you register your domain, you will need to find a place to "host" it. You can host it with the same company where you've registered the name. Your Internet Service Provider may also provide this service. You can find a wide variety of other companies that provide hosting services by doing an online search.

TIP: Do not use a free web hosting service unless you don't mind having your customers see pop-up ads for products unrelated to your store!

Promoting Your Website

A great site is only as good as how many people it attracts. No matter how much you spend on making it beautiful, if people don't know you exist, it won't help you sell your store or its merchandise.

Make certain you list your site on all your business forms, cards, brochures, signs, and even your car, van or truck. When you list items for sale on any other website, like eBay for example, add your website address. If you spend time on blogs (web logs) or newsgroups, add your site's hyperlink to your signature.

Make sure people can find your website by getting it into the search engines and listing it with industry websites. While some sites and search engines charge a fee to guarantee that your website will be included in their directory, you can submit your website for free to Google at **www. google.com/intl/en/submit_content.html**. Once you're on Google, your site is likely to be found by other search engines as well.

Your web hosting company may offer a search engine submission service for an additional fee. You can find information about "optimizing" your website, to help it rank higher on search engines, at the Search Engine Watch website at **http://searchenginewatch.com** and at Google's Webmaster Help Center at **www.google.com/support/webmasters**.

Photography for Your Website

Digital cameras are now within the budgets of most people, and using them has taken the hassle out of developing film and then scanning them into a digital format in order to show your items to your online visitors.

Some points to consider for photographs on your website:

Make sure the subject is well lit but not washed out and not under-exposed. Often, taking the shot in the daylight is your best bet. You might find the need to buy a box for photographing small merchandise in order to make your pictures look their best.

You only need images of 72 dpi (dots per inch) for the web as opposed to the higher resolutions needed for printing of 260 to 300 dpi. It's important that, if you intend to use the same pictures for a brochure or any printed item, you shoot the picture at the highest resolution possible. Failing to do so will mean grainy printed pictures and an overloaded website.

6.1.5 Networking and Referrals

One of the best ways to spread the word about your business is through other people. When you open your store, make sure you get the word out to your family and friends. Consider sending a postcard, and inviting them to your store's opening. You can also build your clientele by getting to know members of local clubs and by attending as many functions as possible to network with others who might help your business grow.

Chamber of Commerce

Often the local Chamber of Commerce and tourism groups are instrumental in getting the work out that you've opened a new business in town. Joining a group like the Chamber usually costs money, but the benefits, which include networking opportunities, educational seminars, and much more, is worth the investment for many business owners.

To find out how to contact your local Chamber, visit the national websites. For the U.S. Chamber of Commerce visit **www.uschamber.com/ chambers/directory/default.htm**. For the Canadian Chamber of Commerce Directory visit **www.chamber.ca/index.php/en/links/C57**.

Word-of-Mouth

It's time to get your customers working for you. If you can get an emotional connection between you (that is, your business) and your customers they will be your best sales tools. What they say is worth more than hundreds of expensive ads.

One person telling another that your store is the best place to find wonderful merchandise is money in the bank. But how do you get to that point? By being everything your customers expect, honest, hardworking, fun to be around, knowledgeable, and—it's worth repeating—honest.

> **TIP:** Ask special customers to write brief reviews of your store and services. Add these "testimonials" to your newsletter, brochures, and ads.

Get Referrals

One of the best ways to get referrals is to work with other complementary businesses. Put your fliers in their store and theirs in yours. You might also do promotions with them such as offering discounts to customers they refer to you.

You can find also get referrals from your existing customers. To do this, get to know your customers by chatting with them when they're in your store. Don't be afraid to ask them if they know of anyone who could use your products and services, and ask them to refer that person to your store. You might also give a small gift or a discount coupon for bringing in a friend.

Of course, the best way to get your customers referring business to you from others is to offer them the best possible customer service. In section 6.2, we'll offer some customer service tips that will keep your customers happy and get them talking about your store to others.

6.1.6   Your Grand Opening

One of the best ways to get people excited about your store is to hold special events. Some ideas for types of events and what you can offer include:

Holding a grand opening can be a great way to introduce yourself and your new business to potential customers. If planned carefully, such an event can make your target market aware of your presence in a big way. The goal is to generate curiosity and interest in your business, as well as to make people aware of how you differ from the competition. If you're taking over an existing business you may want to let people know that the business is under new ownership and let them know how you plan to keep existing customers happy and serve the needs of new customers.

If you are opening a franchise operation (as explained in section 3.2.2), your franchisor actually may require you to hold a grand opening. Usually they will provide you with guidance as to how they would like it to be conducted. Also, your franchisor may require you to have a certain amount of available capital on hand in order to pay for the event. For information about holding a grand opening for a franchise, you should consult with your franchisor. In this section, we will look at how a non-franchise business owner can host a grand opening event.

Some of the elements to consider when planning your grand opening are:

- *Budget:* How much money can you put toward the event?

- *Timing:* When is the best time to reach the most people?

- *Publicity:* How do you make people interested in attending your grand opening?

- *Invited guests:* Who can help to attract people to your event (local celebrities, for example)?

- *Advertising:* What are the best ways to get the message out to your target market?

- *Promotions:* How will you reward people for attending?

Budget Considerations

There are a number of factors you should consider when planning your grand opening budget. First, you should put aside a certain amount of money in your start-up budget (see section 3.4.2 for more about start-up financial planning) for the event. Whether your start-up capital comes from your own cash resources or a loan, your plan for a grand opening should be clearly stated in your business planning documents.

Some grand opening budget items include extra staffing, advertising, printing invitations, brochure or flyers, buying promotional items, hiring a master of ceremonies, hiring a remote local radio broadcast from your store, hiring a guest speaker or celebrity look-alike, hiring a D.J. or band, hiring a caterer to supply refreshments, etc. You should find out the costs for all of these things well in advance and then figure out how much of your start-up cash you can devote to each.

Timing Considerations

When to hold your grand opening is also a major consideration. If you are in a downtown location, then the best time to hold your grand opening might be through the week when traffic is high in the area. If you are opening in a mall or strip mall, then the best time might be on the weekend when these are busiest.

Another consideration is the season. You shouldn't plan a grand opening close to any major holidays, since people are too busy to give much attention to a new store opening. Worse, many people travel during holiday times and this can have a negative impact, too.

Time of day is important, also. According to one Chamber of Commerce source, the best time of day for a grand opening is from Tuesday through Friday, from 10:00 a.m. to 12:00 p.m., because this is the best time to get media attention and maximize attendance. You can informally survey local businesses where you plan to open to determine the highest traffic periods in that area.

Publicity and Advertising Considerations

There are a number of ways to get publicity for your event. You might want to consider a press release; distributing brochures, flyers or menus; contacting your local radio or television station to ask them to do an interview with you; paying for a remote on-location broadcast and so on. Earlier sections in this chapter have great advice on how to generate publicity and tips for effective advertising.

Promotional Considerations

In promoting your grand opening, you'll want to give people a reason to attend. Put yourself in the place of your hoped-for clientele and answer for them the question: "What's in it for me if I attend?" The answer might be something like a 10-20% discount on products or services, a free sampling of your services, free refreshments (some businesses offer coffee and doughnuts or a barbecue), gift merchandise (giveaways) and so on. The chance to meet a highly regarded celebrity can also be an incentive.

A Sample Grand Opening Plan

Grand Opening Budget

Extra staff (4 hours)......................................$100.00

Master of Ceremonies.................................$500.00

Advertising Costs...$600.00

Printing Costs $450.00

Catering service..$500.00

Balloons $50.00

Ribbon...$30.00

Remote on-location radio broadcast $500.00

Giveaways (at cost) $200.00

Total Grand Opening Costs $2,930.00

Schedule

9:00 a.m.	Meet with staff and go over the plan
9:15 a.m.	Start setting up, local radio crew to arrive to set up for on-location broadcast
9:30 a.m.	Caterer to arrive with refreshments
9:45 a.m.	Master of Ceremonies and Mayor to arrive
10:00 a.m.	Invited guests to arrive; greet guests and the public in front of the store
10:15 a.m.	Mayor to cut ribbon; invite guests and public inside
10:20 a.m.	Refreshments to be served
10:20-11:30 a.m.	Meet and greet; interviews with local radio talent
11:30-11:50 a.m.	Hold draws for door prizes
11:50 a.m.	Thank everyone for coming. Final words from M.C.
12:00 a.m.	Start clean-up

Invited Guests

Who you invite to your grand opening can also have an impact on attendance. You might want to have the mayor or other high-profile citizen cut the ribbon to officially open your business. Perhaps you know someone famous who wouldn't mind helping out for the event.

Another consideration is to invite people who have a wide network of contacts. They can help to spread the word about your business. Other people to invite include:

- Local Chamber of Commerce members

- City or town council members

- Other government officials

- Local business owners

- Any contractors who worked on remodeling your store

- Business Improvement Area representatives and members

- Any other person or group who you know has a wide sphere of influence

6.1.7   Wine Tastings

Another great way to promote your wine store is by hosting wine tastings. Wine tastings are an opportunity to showcase your wines and exercise your salesmanship. If you're not comfortable with leading this type of event you might consider inviting a local knowledgeable wine enthusiast or sommelier to help you out. Your tasting event can be a free-for-all in which you offer a selection of a number of different wines, including different varietals and different vintages, or you might want to offer either horizontal and vertical tastings or both (see sidebar below).

The principal elements of a wine tasting event include:

- A selection of varietals and vintages you sell

- A selection of similar competitors' wines (if you're conducting a horizontal tasting)

- Blind tasting (wrapping the bottles in paper or foil so people won't be swayed by labels)

- Bread or crackers (to help in clearing the palate)

- Spit bucket and glasses for guests to spit the tasted wine into

- Table(s) and chairs

- Wine glasses

During the event, guests sample the wine, perhaps instructed how to do so by you or your sommelier, then spit it out, make notes about what they've just tasted, and move on to the next wine. Allow everyone enough time to accomplish all these steps, before the next tasting. After each wine is tasted, discuss with your guests the characteristics of each wine. You'll be surprised at how lively these discussions can be.

Horizontal vs. Vertical Tasting

During your wine tasting event, you may want to focus on either vertical tasting or horizontal tasting, or both. A horizontal tasting refers to sampling wines from the same grape variety. For example, you can place a Merlot you regularly feature in your store alongside other well-known wines of the same type from wineries around the world. To minimize the tasting variables, you should use wines of roughly the same age. The point is to compare all the different qualities of the wines and illustrate for your guests just how well they stack up alongside each other. You want them to see what is unique about each wine when compared to others produced in the same year but in different regions.

In a vertical tasting, you will provide your guests with multiple vintages of the same varietal. You can use vintages from a single producer or from several different producers. The purpose of a vertical tasting is to show your guests how the wine has improved or changed over time, how each year's growing season changes the character of the wine, and so on. This type of tasting is a good way to get people interested in buying multiple vintages of one or more of the varietals you sell.

Your wine tasting events can be hosted for different groups. Offering such an event to the general public is a great way to introduce your wine store to the local wine lovers' community. It can be incorporated into a grand opening, too.

You might also offer wine tasting parties. These are private events in which you provide the wines and food, all taking place around learning more about your store, about wines in general, and especially about the wines you sell.

Corporate wine tastings are another possibility. This is a great way for a company to reward its employees with an afternoon of learning more about wine. For a flat fee, you can provide companies with wine and food and perhaps a bottle of wine for each employee to take home with them. This helps to make even more people aware of your wine store.

Finally, you might consider offering your services to local charities or other fundraisers. If it's a charity you would normally support or a cause you believe in, you might offer a discount or a donation in kind. The event could be hosted at your store or you could help the charity at their preferred venue. A wine tasting event is perfect for getting people together for charity.

Advertising the Event

You'll also have to take into account how you will advertise the event. Generating interest and awareness is an important factor in how many people will decide to attend. If you haven't already read the section on advertising (section 6.1.1), you should read it to learn more about how and where to advertise. You can also put out a press release, particularly if you have a charity tie-in for the event.

6.1.8   Other Marketing Ideas

There are a lot of unique ways to get the word out about your store. While you can and should use traditional methods of advertising, keep your mind open to new and exciting ideas as well, because you never know when you might stumble upon one that will be a huge success. Here are some additional ideas you may want to try to market your business:

- Hold a contest. For example, you could have a prize drawing or give an award to the person who writes the most amusing description of one of your wines. (You might even get some media coverage out of it.)

- Print and wear T-shirts or baseball hats with your store's name and logo. Give them out to your best customers.

- Get your business card printed onto fridge magnets, or put your store information on pens, wine glasses, corkscrews or other items you can sell or give away. (Check online or your Yellow Pages to find companies that print promotional products.)

- Paint your shop logo on your car. If possible, include your web address, location, and a benefit of shopping at your store.

- Contact your local Department of Motor Vehicles to get vanity license plates containing your company's name.

- Post your business card on every bulletin board you see.

- Have a frequent shopper card or offer specials such as 10 percent off one day a month to customers on your mailing list.

TIP: Remember, it's usually easier and less expensive to keep a good customer than to find a new one.

6.2 Customer Service

One common problem that many customers cite with wine stores is poor customer service. When people purchase wine or beer at a supermarket they don't expect quality customer service. They forgive cashiers or grocery stockers for not knowing a thing about what they merely stock and ring up on a register.

Wine stores, however, are expected to have excellent customer service. What a shame it is then, when a customer makes the effort to travel all the way to a wine store or liquor store and is barely greeted, shrugged off after a question and rung up in record time. The staff of a store—especially a wine store which is expected to be a little higher caliber—should be very courteous and knowledgeable about their wine products.

If you've purchased an existing store, it's very possible that excellent customer service is what helped establish customer loyalty there in the first place. Maybe the previous store owner was very knowledgeable about wine and would chat with his customers frequently, always offering recommendations. If you don't know that much about wine, and simply point to what you have on your aisles when asked, you will not establish any understanding of the needs of your store's established customer base.

6.2.1   Meeting Your Customers' Needs

To give customers what they want, you need to know something about them. While the amount of customer information you keep in a customer database is entirely up to you, try to keep as much information as your software program allows.

Here are a few of the things you might want to keep track of:

- Customer preferences

- Buying patterns

- Special interests

You will probably at least want regular customers' mailing information and some of their preferences listed. Once you know your customers' interests and preferences, you can make suggestions.

Suggesting items that you think will suit the customer can show you're interested in the customer themselves — not just a sale. Take the time to work with your clients and find out what their needs and desires are. Ask your customers what they want, whether it's something you currently carry or not (you could even include a brief survey in your email newsletter). Then create a wish list in a note book and keep it up-to-date.

Once you have been in business for a while, you will have a few regular customers who shop from you year round. Pay attention to their likes and dislikes and track them. If you get something in that you know they would love, pick up the phone and give them a call. Again, this is excellent customer service. You will more than likely make additional sales as well, because they will likely buy several things while they're in picking up the new item that you have put aside for them.

These extra touches and consultations can keep customers coming back again and again.

And don't be afraid to advertise the fact that your store is under new management. Maybe the previous owner made a lot of mistakes that drove customers away. When they hear the business is being run by a customer-conscious new wine store owner like you, they may give it a second chance.

Dealing with Difficult Customers

One of the best ways to deal with difficult customers is to gather as much information as you can. Let's use an example. Perhaps you have a customer who consistently buys items and returns them. You suspect that they are using them and then bringing them back to get their money back, but you do not really have any proof of this.

The customer comes into your store once again with a return and you ask what was wrong with the item. Do not immediately close your ears because you think you know the answer. Really listen to what they have to say; practice those listening skills we just discussed.

Asking customers for feedback can help you determine what the real issue is (they may not be using the item at all) and this may help you further develop your store policies manual as discussed in section 5.1.

Customer Surveys

Feedback from customers can help you keep your good customers coming back. Each time a person buys an item, ask them to take the time to complete a survey, which will include the types of wines they prefer or would like to try in future. Keep survey sheets near your cash register and also have a survey on your website. Be careful, though, because privacy laws are very specific, and you need to ensure you customers that you won't be sharing the information you collect and how you will be using it.

TIP: By offering an incentive, such as a prize (perhaps a gift certificate or discount coupon), you will find people are more
inclined to fill out your survey. Let them know that this way,
if you get something in they may love, they will be the first
to know.

Sample Customer Survey

Name: _____

Address: _____

_____

Phone: _____

Email: _____

Any particular item(s) you are interested in acquiring? Please describe your wish list.

_____

_____

_____

Can [Store Name] send you newsletters about events and special
promotions?   ❑ Yes   ❑ No

*Please note: [Store Name] will only use your information to provide
better services to you; your information will not be shared.*

Sorting through the contacts you make this way might seem time-con-
suming, but setting up a database, either by a simple listing in a spreadsheet, which you can sort and search, or using a database program, is
the key to making sure you use the information you have taken the
time to collect.

Set up your system to be able to search categories that match your customers' wish lists against new items you get in; for example, a simple
category listing that then expands to the various types in that category
that they are interested in.

You might want to rate which customers to contact first, perhaps by how well they pay or by how often they have been in the store. Let them know they are preferred customers.

6.2.2   Customer Service Tips

Ben Wallace of CellaRaiders advises that you as the wine store owner should be "responsive to your clients." He stresses "reliability, honesty, integrity and efficiency" as the most important qualities in dealing with your customers. In addition you as a retailer must have "a willingness to stand behind what you sell and be able to make confident recommendations." So if you're serious about keeping your customers loyal, then you owe it to yourself to learn more about their needs so that you can prove yourself as reliable a retailer as the previous business owner.

Be ready to ask customers these pointed questions:

How much are you looking to spend?

Wines can be cheap, less than $7.00 a bottle, moderate $7.00-$20.00, pricey, $20.00-$100.00 or even outrageously expensive! (How about a 1978 Montrachet for over $20,000?) You can also ask the customer if the wine is for every day use or a special occasion.

What kind of wine do you like?

Customers may invent all sorts of words to describe something they vaguely know as wine. Normal descriptions of white wines are: "crisp and dry, buttery, full-bodied, oaky, fruity and ripe"; red wines might be associated with "big, rich, soft, tannic, medium-bodied." You may even suggest some popular wine names like Merlot, Pinot Noir, Chardonnay, Cabernet Sauvignon in hopes that the customer recognizes a name.

What type of food will you be eating with this wine?

Whether it's every day meals or a special occasion, the food you eat will affect the taste of the wine. Generally speaking, wines should be paired with foods that have similar taste characteristics. Think of the basic qualities of the meal (salty, sweet, fruity, sour) and try and choose a wine that matches the same taste.

If you're not sure which foods to match with which wines, try these resources to increase your knowledge:

- *Tom Cannavan's Wine Pages*
  www.wine-pages.com/foodwine.htm

- *CellarNotes Food & Wine Basics*
  www.cellarnotes.net/foodwine.html

- *Matching Wine with Food*
  www.cs.utexas.edu/users/walter/wine/wine-food.html

- *Fosters Food and Wine*
  www.fosters.com.au/enjoy/wine/food_and_wine.htm

- *Wine Spectator Matching Wine with Food*
  www.winespectator.com/foodwinematching/search

Keeping Customers Happy

You should always talk to an unsatisfied customer in a professional and reasonable manner, assuring him or her that you understand the dispute and that you're trying to help. Remember that a satisfied customer is your best form of advertising.

The advantages to resolving conflict instead of ending it are:

- You earn the customer's respect and keep their business

- Customers don't tell all their friends about the horrible experience they endured. In fact, they might even compliment your company's customer service.

- Other customers who might be witness to the dispute will appreciate your willingness to resolve the issue.

Even if a customer storms away in rage, always bid them a friendly goodbye. Later, they may realize they were acting unreasonable and may return. The only time you should ever be assertive is if you feel you are being physically or otherwise threatened. In that case, ask them to leave under threat of a police intervention if necessary.

- *Smile:* This doesn't mean that you have to smile like a phony used car salesman. Rather, smile sincerely. Think about how happy you are to be in business selling wine. You should always smile on first coming into eye contact with a customer.

- *Keep an eye on your customer:* Always ask your customers if they need help. Even if you're busy, even if you don't feel well, and yes, even if you think they are shoplifting. (That way you can keep an eye on them.) A customer who is not waited upon may not come back.

- *Answer customer questions:* A disinterested "I don't know" is the absolute worst response from you. Customers will ask silly questions, "Do you have any good fruity (or oaky) wine?" and complex questions, "What kind of storage has this wine received?" It is important to do your research and know the wine industry so that you can easily answer tough customer questions, or if you honestly don't know, let customers know you will try to find out the answer to the questions they've asked.

- *Bid everyone a cheerful goodbye:* This applies to your angry customers, your regular customers, and even non-buying customers who "waste" your time. Saying a friendly goodbye could impress them to come back sometime in the future.

Asking For More

Don't forget to politely ask your customers if there's anything else you can get for them. Add some suggestions, to sound a little original and not so much like a Kwiki Mart employee. Never hesitate to give free wine advice to customers. They will appreciate your company's level of customer service and remember your courtesy.

Whether you are dealing with wine drinkers on a one-to-one basis or with distribution company representatives, you will be communicating with customers on a daily basis. Even if you work with a staff of managers, you'll still be thinking on behalf of customers, putting their comforts first. You must come to understand the customer's point of view and their motivation in doing business with you.

6.2.3   Return/Exchange Policy

For the most part, you are free to choose your own return and exchange policy. You may decide returns are not right for you because they create havoc with your bookkeeping. Or you may decide that the customer is always right and since you want them to come back to your store, you will work with them on the items they do not want.

It's up to you what returns policy you create, but remember a lot of people judge a shop by its returns policy. Perhaps you feel hanging the sign "Exchanges Only" is a fair policy, or perhaps you want to keep people happy no matter what and offer a no-questions-asked, money-back guarantee.

Many retail stores do not offer returns or exchanges. This will depend upon the items you are selling and whether customers abuse the return policy. This is a personal decision, but try to be flexible. There may be exceptions to any rule you establish.

If you seem hard to deal with (your sign at the cash register screams, "All Sales Final!") you may end up with very unsatisfied customers. Sometimes you will need to give customers their money back even if you think they're wrong or have abused your returns policy. It's always best to have a customer leave your store satisfied because an unsatisfied customer can be a word-of-mouth disaster for you.

Something else to keep in mind is that certain jurisdictions, usually under specific circumstances, have a "buyer's remorse" rule. This means that a customer has the right to change their mind about a purchase or contract, and back out of the sale within a specified time period (usually 10 days). You have no choice but to comply. Check for rules like this in your locality and retail sector before you implement a "No returns or exchanges" policy.

Think carefully about what kind of policy you want to speak for you.

Following is an example of a return and exchange policy [adjust or rewrite as required]:

Sample Return/Exchange Policy

[Name of your store] will accept returns/exchanges with receipt only within 10 days of purchase. Unopened bottles of wine and merchandise in its original packaging will be accepted for full refund.

If you feel the quality of the wine you purchased is not adequate after opening it, you may return it, with the cork returned to the bottle, within 24 hours of purchase. A valid receipt must accompany all returns.

We want to work with you to make sure you are happy with your experience in our store. Come in during regular business hours to discuss returns/exchanges with our friendly staff.

6.3   Taking an Old Business in a New Direction

You may have purchased an established business that reported a downward trend in profit and cash flow. This in itself doesn't mean you made a bad investment. You could still turn things around with a smart business plan. But it will depend upon you taking the business in a new direction and correcting the mistakes of the past.

The previous owner's problems may have been a result of poor customer service by the owner himself or his staff. Bad customer service happens when workers either don't care or they simply are not knowledgeable about the product they are selling.

Questionable Products

You may observe that the real problem with the previous owner was not in customer service but in product. Perhaps the previous owner marketed his or her products to the wrong type of clientele. In any event, by the time you buy the existing business you should know exactly what the problem is and how to fix it.

If you know that the problem is in promoting product then that's the new direction to pursue. This may require a new advertising campaign informing your community in subtle terms that you've corrected the problem. Advertise beer, liquor and other spirits if the old store sold only wine or more unique wine varieties if the previous owner only sold general beverages. If you have a new direction in the products you carry then it's worth announcing to your customers.

Price

While price is not always an issue—serious wine drinkers are willing to pay a hundred dollars for a good bottle of wine— in general you must keep your prices competitive with other wine store owners. Chances are an experienced wine drinker will know he or she is being overcharged for a certain label.

Not every customer you get will be an expert though, and some might find even a $10.00 wine too pricey. So along with your finer selections, you must also include some good selections for $20.00 or less. You must strive to please many different demographics within your basic demographic. (See section 5.3 for more about pricing your products.)

According to the Wine Institute, 66 percent of California wine revenues, the highest of any state, come from sales of premium wines of $7.00 and above. Revenues from cheaper wines priced under $7.00 have declined, representing only 34 percent of total revenues even while claiming 65 percent of the volume of wine sold. Clearly, people are drinking smarter and looking for quality.

Distribution Problems

If you choose to stock a different type of inventory (spirits, cheap or expensive wines) than the previous owner, then you may possibly have to go through the process of finding a new wine wholesaler. You might have to choose a new distributor and terminate the previous relationship, or it may simply be a matter of updating your regular orders.

Check with the current distributor to make sure there is not a pre-existing contract with a particular distributor or franchise. Vern Foster dismisses any problems with distributor contracts, stating, "Our agreement is a weekly delivery in which they itemize and replace stock according to volume of sells. As we pay by check for each delivery, the only agreement is in the signing of the receipts."

Christina Martin likewise comments that, for the most part, retailers and distributors work freely together. "There are times when some retailers will guarantee a certain amount of sales to have somewhat of an exclusive on a certain area. But my experience is that usually it is a verbal contract that is based on sales and can change at any time."

Conclusion

You've reached the end of the *FabJob Guide to Become a Wine Store Owner*. We hope you take away with you a new appreciation of this industry and its many facets. Becoming a wine store owner will be challenging, arguably the most challenging merchant career you could attempt. But you don't start your own business because you want to play it safe! You start your own business because you have great ambition. You love wine. That's what you want to do for a living.

You already had the desire and maybe even an educated appreciation for wine before opening this book. Now that you've completed the *FabJob Guide to Become a Wine Store Owner* you have the business savvy and know-how to succeed. All you need to do is take a sip of Louis Roederer Cristal Champagne for added courage and go out and turn your dream into a money-making enterprise!

Save 50% on Your Next Purchase

Would you like to save money on your next FabJob guide purchase? Please contact us at **www.FabJob.com/feedback.asp** to tell us how this guide has helped prepare you for your dream career. If we publish your comments on our website or in our promotional materials, we will send you a gift certificate for 50% off your next purchase of a FabJob guide.

Get Free Career Advice

Get valuable career advice for free by subscribing to the FabJob newsletter. You'll receive insightful tips on: how to break into the job of your dreams or start the business of your dreams, how to avoid career mistakes, and how to increase your on-the-job success. You'll also receive discounts on FabJob guides, and be the first to know about upcoming titles. Subscribe to the FabJob newsletter at **www.FabJob.com/newsletter.asp**.

Does Someone You Love Deserve a Dream Career?

Giving a FabJob® guide is a fabulous way to show someone you believe in them and support their dreams. Help them break into the career of their dreams with more than 75 career guides to choose from.

Visit www.FabJob.com to order guides today!

How to Install the CD-ROM

This bonus CD-ROM contains helpful forms and checklists you can revise and use when planning events. It also includes an electronic version of this book, which you can use to quickly connect to the websites we've mentioned (as long as you have access to the Internet and the Acrobat Reader program on your computer).

To install the CD-ROM, these simple steps will work with most computers:

1. Insert the CD-ROM into your computer CD drive.

2. Double click on the "My Computer" icon on your desktop.

3. Double click on the icon for your CD-ROM drive.

4. Read the "Read Me" file on the CD-ROM for more information.

Adult Hardbacks

01/12/25

BLUE $ 2.92

BLUE $ 2.92

Goodwill

Thank you for supporting